HACKNEY COACHMAN.

DICKENS' LONDON

ESSAYS SELECTED AND INTRODUCED
BY ROSALIND VALLANCE
ENGRAVINGS BY GEORGE CRUIKSHANK

THE FOLIO SOCIETY
LONDON 1966

INTRODUCTION © THE FOLIO SOCIETY 1966
THE ENGRAVINGS BY CRUIKSHANK WERE
FIRST PUBLISHED IN THE GENTLEMAN'S
POCKET MAGAZINE IN 1827 AND 1829

TEXT SET IN MONOTYPE BELL 11 POINT
LEADED ONE POINT. PRINTED AND BOUND
BY W & J MACKAY & CO LTD, CHATHAM, KENT
ILLUSTRATIONS PRINTED BY
THE BAYNARD PRESS, LONDON

Contents

Illustrations

Introduction

'I remember how immensely broad the streets seemed, now I was alone, how high the houses, how grand and mysterious everything.'

'London is shabby by daylight and shabbier by gaslight.'

Dickens wrote both these passages in his later years, but the first begins, 'I remember', for he is recalling that unforgettable hour when as a child he had got himself lost in the Strand, and spent the rest of the day in the first of those lonely, fascinated explorings of London which were to prove so vital to his life's work: the second is the verdict of the citizen of the world returned from one of his many visits to the Continent. Even in Rome itself, he writes, 'there is nothing shabbier than Drury Lane'.

Worse, far worse than merely shabby were the revolting slums, about which, in despair at the inertia of Parliament, 'the great dust-heap of Westminster', Dickens never ceased to cry out in his letters, speeches, novels, essays and journalistic writings. Nevertheless it is clear that from childhood until the year of his death he never escaped—that in his secret heart he had no real wish to escape—from the fascination of London; even, or perhaps especially, of the slums themselves towards which he confessed he felt a strong 'attraction of repulsion'.

'What inexhaustible food for speculation do the streets of London afford!' exclaims Boz, aged twenty-four; and The Uncommercial Traveller, aged fifty-one, is still adding to his 'always-lengthening list of the wonders of the world' curious speculations about the inner lives of the people and animals in all sorts of odd corners of Westminster, the City or the suburbs.

It is mainly from the work of these two explorers, Boz and The

Uncommercial, as Dickens at different periods was pleased to call himself, that this book has been compiled.

Charles Dickens was born in Portsmouth in 1812, the son of a clerk in the Navy Pay Office, spent a very happy childhood in the riverside naval town of Chatham in Kent, with lovely country and Rochester Cathedral close by, but at ten years old came to live in Bayham Street, a shabby street in Camden Town in north-west London, bringing with him as chief treasure *The Bee*, the little book of essays by Oliver Goldsmith which his schoolmaster William Giles had given him as a parting present. Goldsmith and the other periodical writers of the eighteenth century and the novels of Fielding, Smollet and Defoe—his father's small library —were to give Charles most of his book-learning for the next two years, for his kind but hopelessly improvident father (Mr Micawber to us) could not afford to send him to school again, and two years later was arrested and imprisoned for debt in the Marshalsea prison in the Borough, while Charles was sent to work in a blacking factory at Hungerford Stairs, where Charing Cross station now stands. But in those two years, while in his own tiny attic he continued his old habit of 'reading as if for life', Charles was also quite literally beginning to walk 'as if for life', for when he mooned about the streets or ran the family errands or took things to the pawnshop he was building up that intimate knowledge of working-class London which was to be the background of so many of the sketches in his first book and of his later novels; his childish impressions, he afterwards declared, remained always the true ones.

Sometimes he would walk to the end of the road and stand outside a small group of almshouses (which are still there in Bayham Street) and gaze across the intervening flat wastes of nettles and dust-heaps at the distant cupola of St Paul's, a sight which 'gave him food for hours of vague reflection afterwards'. Sometimes his father took him to Limehouse, where his godfather, Christopher Huffam, sail-maker and ships' chandler, had a fine house in Church Row and a workshop in Narrow Street. The River Thames, crammed with ships, a forest of masts, flowed under the windows of this paradise, and, as in Captain Cuttle's haunts, there were

'anchor and chain-cable forges, where sledge-hammers were ding-
ing upon iron all day long . . . the air was perfumed with chips;
and all other trades were swallowed up in mast, oar and block-
making, and boat building'.

Charles could wander around exploring the narrow waterways
where the grimy tide lapped the walls of incredibly old and dirty
pubs and warehouses; he could lean on wharfside walls brooding
over the dark swirling water; decrepit rowing-boats nosed their
way between the great ships, or lay marooned on muddy banks.
Knowledge of 'waterside characters', their lawful and unlawful
occupations, and the very tone and tang of the riverside was seep-
ing into him, to be revealed from time to time throughout his
writing life.

Another great delight of his boyhood was to be taken to 'the
real town' by his step-cousin, James Lamert (most probably the
'Someone' of *Gone Astray*), and if they went to the notorious slum
district of Seven Dials, which lay between Long Acre and Broad
Street, into which it was not safe to go alone, he was, he told John
Forster afterwards, 'perfectly entranced with pleasure'. 'Good
heavens!' he exclaimed. 'What wild visions of prodigies of wickedness, want and beggary arose in my mind out of that place!'

The boy was fortunate in having an uncle who lived in Gerrard
Street, Soho, over a second-hand bookshop, which gave him the
chance of brooding over many odd and unusual volumes. One day
he came across George Colman the Younger's *Broad Grins*, a
little book of bawdy tales in verse (curious fare for a ten-year-old),
where he read:

> 'Centrick, in London noise, and London follies,
>   Proud Covent Garden blooms, in smoky glory;
> For chairmen, coffee-rooms, piazzas, dollies,
>   Cabbages, and comedians, fam'd in story!'

Covent Garden is very near to Gerrard Street, so he slipped
down there to see if the real place bore out the poet's description.
We know he found the cabbages, for he told Forster years afterwards that on that day he had 'snuffed up the flavour of the faded
cabbage leaves as if it were the very breath of comic fiction'.

[7]

'The smell of things past', says Hazlitt, another devotee of Covent Garden, 'remains in the memory long after their look has faded.'

All Dickens' senses were highly developed. His sense of smell was particularly acute, and a long and amusing catalogue might be compiled of the smells he enjoyed, endured or revolted from. First prize must go to a certain Swiss village which always smelt to him 'like mouldy cheese wrapped in a very hot blanket'.

Covent Garden Market, now, alas! soon to be removed from its three-hundred-year-old site in the middle of Westminster, still provides a particularly varied assortment of smells, but in 1822 they must have been even more pungent. Mingled with the scent of roses, hay and horses, fruit and vegetables, deliciously fresh and not-so, there must have been some that later on revolted Dickens so much that he became more and more insistent that sanitation was London's first necessity. Did he as a child catch sight of the destitute children he describes so movingly in *Night Walks*, and were Little Dorrit's ideas of Covent Garden a remembrance of his own childish ones?

'Courtly ideas of Covent Garden as a place with famous coffee houses, where gentlemen wearing gold-laced coats and swords had quarrelled and fought duels; costly ideas of Covent Garden as a place where there were flowers in winter at guineas apiece, pineapples at guineas a pound, and peas at guineas a pint; picturesque ideas of Covent Garden, as a place where there was a mighty theatre, showing wonderful and beautiful sights to richly dressed ladies and gentlemen . . . desolate ideas of Covent Garden as having all those arches in it, where the miserable children in rags . . . like young rats, slunk and hid, fed on offal, huddled together for warmth, and were hunted about . . . teeming ideas of Covent Garden, as a place of past and present mystery, romance, abundance, want, beauty, ugliness, fair country gardens, and foul street gutters, all confused together . . .'

'The Garden' became for Dickens the microcosm of life itself, feeding his senses, his love of the dramatic, his flair for the theatrical, his interest in the eccentric and the bizarre, his deep attraction towards the tragic, his passionate sympathy with the poor and unfortunate; and all these impulses were already within him on that day of his first visit which he never forgot. Thirty years later, a world-famous novelist, he had established himself as the editor of *Household Words* in an office in the heart of this magnetic quarter—short of a miracle, an inconceivable destiny for such a small waif. But the miracle—his genius—was there, welling up within him; its 'first sprightly runnings' (in Forster's delightful phrase) had already begun to flow, for even at this age he had written plays and little character sketches and 'made stories for [himself] out of the streets and out of the men and women', and it was the knowledge that he had been suddenly reft away from his true vocation which made his time in the blacking factory so agonizing. It was one thing to be a fascinated onlooker at London's low life and quite another to find himself an actor in it— a supernumerary at that, one of those unknown unnamed drudges whose life indeed it is very difficult for us to imagine, for they and the cultured classes lived in almost unbelievably different worlds, with no educational ladder between them. And this boy was no ordinary boy. He was Charles Dickens, and he knew it.

In the event, he was soon rescued and sent to school, but those few months had been an eternity to him, which he was never to forget . . . 'My old way home by the borough made me cry, after my eldest child could speak.'

After leaving school he spent four years in lawyers' offices and learning shorthand, and by the time he was twenty he had become a Parliamentary reporter. *Doctors' Commons* and *A Parliamentary Sketch* are both full of his reminiscences, and readers will not be surprised to learn that he had no ambition to make either the law or politics his life's work. He wanted to become a professional writer. One never-to-be-forgotten day in December 1833 he walked swiftly down Whitehall and slipped into the harbouring shadows of the great Westminster Hall, his eyes 'so dimmed with joy and pride that they could not bear the street and were not fit to be seen there'. He was carrying an opened copy of *The Monthly Magazine*, in which for the first time he saw a story of his own in print. It was published anonymously and without payment, but what did that matter? The reputation he had already earned as being the most swift and accurate reporter in the House was as nothing to his pride in being at last able to consider himself an author.

He soon had a number of stories and sketches published in papers and periodicals, at first anonymously and then under the pseudonym of 'Boz' and occasionally of 'Tibbs'. It is a happy thought that both these names originated from Goldsmith. 'Boz' was a nasal version of Moses, his nickname for his young brother, after the boy in *The Vicar of Wakefield*; 'Tibbs', of course, was after the famous Beau. Dickens went on earning his living as a reporter, and was afoot at all hours of the day and night on his journeys to and from Westminster. On these walks he built up that phenomenal acquaintance with the teeming life of the streets of London which was to provide the closely observed, everyday foundation upon which his fantasy-world was always so firmly based.

In February 1836, when Dickens was just twenty-four, a selection from the published sketches, with the addition of eight new ones, with sixteen etchings by George Cruikshank, was issued by Macrone under the title of *Sketches by Boz*. In a modest preface the author expressed, as well he might, his pleasure in having secured the collaboration of so distinguished an artist.

The combination of Boz and Cruikshank was so successful that soon another series of the *Sketches* was called for, and another and another, so that by the time he was twenty-five the fame of Boz was established. Upon the publication of the third edition in 1837 his identity was disclosed, and *The London and Westminster Review* pronounced that the new writer had achieved 'a popularity extraordinary on account of its sudden growth, its vast extent and the recognition it has received from persons of the most refined taste as well as from the great mass of the reading public'.

He was accused of plagiarizing Leigh Hunt and Washington Irving, to whose writings his own did bear some resemblance, but he was always that which William Giles named him, 'The Inimitable Boz'. What other writer of his years (or indeed of any years) ever poured forth 'such a much' of people, places and things, so closely and clearly observed, or so confidently invented?

Readers were at once struck with the novelty of his subjects, for often he dealt vividly with classes and indidivuals previous writers had ignored—small shopkeepers, brokers' men, city clerks, cab-drivers, seamstresses—making these 'little pictures of everyday life', as he called them, lively, amusing and sometimes deeply touching. But he is at his most vivid once he has entered the magic aura of the theatre or anything in the nature of a show or enter-tainment, and he has a special talent for highlighting some odd or arresting character in the midst of a teeming, good-natured mêlée of ordinary people—'that diminuative specimen of humanity in the three-cornered pink satin hat with black feathers' in the tea-garden; the dwarf in the dolls' house or the cockney trickster with the 'three thimbles and vun little pea' on the road to Greenwich Fair.

His evocation of miserable street scenes, gin-palaces, pawn-brokers, prisons and criminal courts looked back to Goldsmith and foreshadowed his own more famous later writings with their mixture of satire, compassion and pungent humour. And after his death his friend George Augustus Sala told how he often met him 'in the oddest places and most inclement weather, in Ratcliffe Highway, on Haverstock Hill, on Camberwell Green, in Gray's Inn Lane, in the Wandsworth Road, at Hammersmith Broadway, in Norton Folgate, and Kensal Town. A hansom whirled you by the Bell and Horns at Brompton, and there he was striding, as with seven-leagued boots, in the direction of North End, Fulham. The Metropolitan Railway set you forth at Lisson Grove and you met him plodding speedily towards the Yorkshire Stingo. He was to be met rapidly skirting the grim brick wall of the prison in Cold-bath fields, or trudging along the Seven-Sisters Road at Holloway, or bearing, under steady press of sail, underneath the Highgate Archway, or pursuing the even tenor of his way up the Vauxhall Bridge Road.' As time went on he became, as Sala records, 'equally at home in the intricate byways of narrow streets as in the lengthy thoroughfares. Wherever there was "matter to be heard or learned" in back streets behind Holborn, in Borough courts or passages, in City wharfs or alleys, about the poorer lodging-houses, in prisons, workhouses, ragged schools, police courts, rag shops, chandlers shops, and all sorts of markets for the poor, he carried his keen observation and untiring study.'

In 1844, tired out by ten years of writing, Dickens took his wife and family to Italy, where he lived for a time in great content. But as soon as he began to write again he found that he would make no real headway without the impetus formerly given to his imagination and will by losing himself in crowded streets. 'I can't express how much I want these,' he wrote to John Forster. 'It seems as if they supplied something to my brain that it cannot bear, when busy, to lose. For a week or a fortnight I can write in a retired place (as at Broadstairs) and a day in London sets me up again and starts me—but the toil and labour of writing without that magic lantern is IMMENSE . . . *My* figures seem disposed to stagnate without crowds about them . . .' And again, 'at night I want them [the streets] beyond description'.

So he walked alone almost like a man under hypnosis. In the country, too, which in those days was at London's door, 'in my own wild way to think', but in the streets not only to think but to experience at a deeper level than thought his oneness with the pulsing tide of humanity, often in places of the kind which the artist Maclise once found too literally sickening, slums which only the callous or the men of firm purpose like Henry Mayhew and the later General Booth could stomach. 'Heart of London, I seem to hear a voice within thee that sinks into my heart, bidding me, as I elbow my way among the crowd, have some thought for the meanest wretch that passes, and, being a man, to turn away with scorn and pride from none that wears the human shape'. So he walked for hours and hours, bringing into being the peculiar human species known as 'Dickens characters' in the half-historical, half-phantasmagorical world that we think of as 'Dickens' London', a place to which there is no guide but his own books; and it may be, for this is a vandalistic age, no other enduring reminder than just the names of London streets. There are some in the Borough which an enlightened L.C.C. named in his honour— Pickwick Street, Weller Street, Sawyer Street, Doyce Street, Clenham Street (they got that wrong), Little Dorrit Court, Copperfield Street, Peggotty Place, and even Dickens Square.

INTRODUCTION

And there are those others, going farther back (and forwards, too, let us hope), names like the Strand, Fleet Street, Ludgate Hill, Cheapside, the Old Kent Road, Holborn, Gray's Inn, and the roads to Hampstead, Highgate, Hammersmith, Richmond, Wapping and Greenwich, where Londoners were once familiar with the small, lithe, rapidly striding figure, the big white hat and the face which Leigh Hunt said 'had the life and soul in it of fifty human beings'.

It is the London of the novels that we remember most vividly, the Saffron Hill of *Oliver Twist*, the Adelphi of *David Copperfield*, the fogs of *Bleak House*, the muddy riverside of *Our Mutual Friend*, but Dickens' deep concern with the everyday problems and joys of the people must be expressed not only in fiction but in up-to-the-moment journalism. 'No man shall gag me, and those are my opinions'—and in 1850 he started *Household Words* to proclaim them. This most successful periodical which ran for eight years at twopence a week was published from a bow-fronted office at 16 Wellington Street North (now the back end of Lloyds Bank), just opposite the Lyceum Theatre. Besides Dickens' own contributions, which like all the others were published anonymously, *Household Words* included articles from many authors who afterwards became famous. In 1859, after separating from his wife and disagreeing with his publishers, Dickens removed his office to No 11, now No 26 Wellington Street North, at the junction with (then) York Street, and immediately began a new periodical, *All the Year Round*, which he edited with equal discrimination and success until 1870, the year of his death, when he installed his eldest son Charles in his place.

Since 1857 he had been living at Gadshill in Kent, and he now found it convenient to keep some rooms over his office as a London *pied-à-terre*. It was from these rooms, which miraculously are still in existence—over a nurseryman's shop, where no doubt you can buy Dickens' favourite flower, a red geranium—that he set out on the perambulations described in *Titbull's Almhouses*, *The City of the Absent*, *Shy Neighbourhoods* and *Night Walks*, which were originally published in *All the Year Round* and reprinted in *The Uncommercial Traveller*.

[13]

Dickens' tremendous fame as a novelist has unfairly eclipsed his reputation in the less spectacular genre of the essay. The *Sketches*, of course, are full of the crudities of youth and inexperience, but of his later work Sir Arthur Quiller Couch had this to say to his students at Cambridge: 'If you will learn how he (ever a learner) learned to consolidate his style, study that neglected work of his, *The Uncommercial Traveller*, study such essays as that on Wapping Workhouse or the city churchyards' (*The City of the Absent*). Then he went on to claim that both Dickens and Thackeray could match the Augustans, Steele and Addison and the rest, on their own ground. 'Few recognize it,' he concluded, 'this pair being otherwise so great—but it is so.'

In *Shy Neighbourhoods* Dickens reveals that he has two kinds of walking, 'one, straight on end to a definite goal at a round pace; one, objectless, wandering and purely vagabond'. Broadly speaking, his writing may be said to be of these two kinds, the second of which is the true temper of the essayist, the man of 'negative capability', as Keats called it, who 'lives in gusto, be it foul or fine', who is content to be 'with no irritable searching out after fact and reason'. So Dickens, with plenty of gusto but with no irritable searching out after plots and counter-plots, was sometimes able to write things like *Meditations in Monmouth Street, Scotland Yard, Titbull's Almhouses* and, of course, *Shy Neighbourhoods*, his imagination playing unconstrainedly with 'all things counter, original, spare, strange'—the quirks of old pensioners and caretakers, the vagaries of second-hand clothes, doorknockers, and water-pumps, and the remarkable reasonings of dogs, donkeys and fowls.

There is sometimes, too, in the later essays a new, strangely sad cadence. 'I knew well enough where to find Vice and Misfortune of all kinds, if I had chosen; but they were put out of sight, and my houselessness had many miles upon miles of streets in which it could, and did, have its own solitary way.' And sometimes the rare note of utter quietude, as when he writes of the City churches: 'I have sat, in the singular stillness which belongs to resting places usually astir, in scores of buildings at the heart of the world's metropolis, unknown to far greater numbers of people speaking the English tongue than the ancient edifices of the Eternal City, or the Pyramids of Egypt.'

Dickens lived as lodger, tenant or owner in a great many London houses, mostly in the north-western districts. The happiest and most interesting of his homes (described by The Uncommercial as 'a frightfully first-class family mansion, involving awful responsibilities'), 1 Devonshire Terrace, Marylebone, has been changed into a block of offices, but in consideration of *David Copperfield* the conscience-stricken demolishers have put a bas-relief of certain of his characters upon the wall.

The Dickens Fellowship has saved 48 Doughty Street, the house in which he lived during the early years of his marriage and wrote *Oliver Twist, Barnaby Rudge, Nicholas Nickleby* and part of *Pickwick Papers*. It now guards a valuable library of successive editions of his books and many intimate reminders of his life. Hanging on the wall in an upstairs room is a small dilapidated attic window, rescued from the Bayham Street house—the very window through which in the intervals of reading Goldsmith or Fielding Charles must often have looked out towards 'the real town'—towards that Great Hall of Westminster which today some of us go to visit not so much for its memories of Charles the First, Warren Hastings and the rest as to be for a few moments where the young author walked in such a transport of joy to re-read his first story in print—so near to the Abbey, where he now lies among the poets.

DICKENS'
LONDON

Gone Astray

When I was a very small boy indeed, both in years and stature, I got lost one day in the City of London. I was taken out by Some-body (shade of Somebody forgive me for remembering no more of thy identity!), as an immense treat, to be shown the outside of Saint Giles's Church. I had romantic ideas in connection with that religious edifice; firmly believing that all the beggars who pre-tended through the week to be blind, lame, one-armed, deaf and dumb, and otherwise physically afflicted, laid aside their pretences every Sunday, dressed themselves in holiday clothes, and at-tended divine service in the temple of their patron saint. I had a general idea that the reigning successor of Bamfylde Moore Carew acted as a sort of churchwarden on these occasions, and sat in a high pew with red curtains.

It was in the spring-time when these tender notions of mine, bursting forth into new shoots under the influence of the season, became sufficiently troublesome to my parents and guardians to occasion Somebody to volunteer to take me to see the outside of Saint Giles's Church, which was considered likely (I suppose) to quench my romantic fire, and bring me to a practical state. We set off after breakfast. I have an impression that Somebody was got up in a striking manner—in cord breeches of fine texture and milky hue, in long jean gaiters, in a green coat with bright buttons, in a blue neckerchief, and a monstrous shirt-collar. I think he must have newly come (as I had myself) out of the hop-grounds of Kent. I considered him the glass of fashion and the mould of form: a very Hamlet without the burden of his difficult family affairs.

We were conversational together, and saw the outside of Saint Giles's Church with sentiments of satisfaction, much enhanced by a flag flying from the steeple. I infer that we then went down to

Northumberland House in the Strand to view the celebrated lion over the gateway. At all events, I know that in the act of looking up with mingled awe and admiration at that famous animal I lost Somebody.

The child's unreasoning terror of being lost comes as freshly on me now as it did then. I verily believe that if I had found myself astray at the North Pole instead of in the narrow, crowded, inconvenient street over which the lion in those days presided, I could not have been more horrified. But this first fright expended itself in a little crying and tearing up and down; and then I walked, with a feeling of dismal dignity upon me, into a court, and sat down on a step to consider how to get through life.

To the best of my belief, the idea of asking my way home never came into my head. It is possible that I may, for the time, have preferred the dismal dignity of being lost; but I have a serious conviction that in the wide scope of my arrangements for the future I had no eyes for the nearest and most obvious course. I was but very juvenile; from eight to nine years old, I fancy.

I had one and fourpence in my pocket, and a pewter ring with a bit of red glass on it on my little finger. This jewel had been presented to me by the object of my affections, on my birthday, when we had sworn to marry, but had foreseen family obstacles to our union, in her being (she was six years old) of the Wesleyan persuasion, while I was devotedly attached to the Church of England. The one and fourpence were the remains of half a crown presented on the same anniversary by my godfather—a man who knew his duty and did it.

Armed with these amulets, I made up my little mind to seek my fortune. When I had found it, I thought I would drive home in a coach and six, and claim my bride. I cried a little more at the idea of such a triumph, but soon dried my eyes and came out of the court to pursue my plans. These were, first to go (as a species of investment) and see the Giants in Guildhall, out of whom I felt it not improbable that some prosperous adventure would arise; failing that contingency, to try about the City for any opening of a Whittington nature; baffled in that, too, to go into the army as a drummer.

BAKER.

So, I began to ask my way to Guildhall: which I thought meant, somehow, Gold or Golden Hall; I was too knowing to ask my way to the Giants, for I felt it would make people laugh. I remember how immensely broad the streets seemed now I was alone, how high the houses, how grand and mysterious everything. When I came to Temple Bar, it took me half an hour to stare at it, and I left it unfinished even then. I had read about heads being exposed on the top of Temple Bar, and it seemed a wicked old place, albeit a noble monument of architecture and a paragon of utility. When at last I got away from it, behold I came, the next minute, on the figures at Saint Dunstan's! Who could see those obliging monsters strike upon the bells and go? Between the quarters there was the toyshop to look at—still there, at this present writing, in a new form—and even when that enchanted spot was escaped from, after an hour and more, then Saint Paul's arose, and how was I to get beyond its dome, or to take my eyes from its cross of gold? I found it a long journey to the Giants, and a slow one.

I came into their presence at last, and gazed up at them with dread and veneration. They looked better-tempered, and were altogether more shiny-faced, than I had expected; but they were very big, and, as I judged their pedestals to be about forty feet high, I considered that they would be very big indeed if they were walking on the stone pavement. I was in a state of mind as to these and all such figures, which I suppose holds equally with most children. While I knew them to be images made of something that was not flesh and blood, I still invested them with attributes of life—with consciousness of my being there, for example, and the power of keeping a sly eye upon me. Being very tired, I got into the corner under Magog, to be out of the way of his eye, and fell asleep.

When I started up after a long nap, I thought the giants were roaring, but it was only the City. The place was just the same as when I fell asleep: no beanstalk, no fairy, no princess, no dragon, no opening in life of any kind. So, being hungry, I thought I would buy something to eat, and bring it in there and eat it, before going forth to seek my fortune on the Whittington plan.

I was not ashamed of buying a penny roll in a baker's shop, but I looked into a number of cooks' shops before I could muster courage to go into one. At last I saw a pile of cooked sausages in a window with the label, 'Small Germans, A Penny.' Emboldened by knowing what to ask for, I went in and said, 'If you please will you sell me a small German?' which they did, and I took it, wrapped in paper in my pocket, to Guildhall.

The giants were still lying by, in their sly way, pretending to take no notice, so I sat down in another corner, when what should I see before me but a dog with his ears cocked. He was a black dog, with a bit of white over one eye, and bits of white and tan in his paws, and he wanted to play—frisking about me, rubbing his nose against me, dodging at me sideways, shaking his head and pretending to run away backwards, and making himself good-naturedly ridiculous, as if he had no consideration for himself, but wanted to raise my spirits. Now, when I saw this dog I thought of Whittington, and felt that things were coming right; I encouraged him by saying, 'Hi, boy!' 'Poor fellow!' 'Good dog!' and was satisfied that he was to be my dog for ever afterwards, and that he would help me to seek my fortune.

Very much comforted by this (I had cried a little at odd times ever since I was lost), I took the small German out of my pocket, and began my dinner by biting off a bit and throwing it to the dog, who immediately swallowed it with a one-sided jerk, like a pill. While I took a bit myself, and he looked me in the face for a second piece, I considered by what name I should call him. I thought Merrychance would be an expressive name, under the circumstances; and I was elated, I recollect, by inventing such a good one, when Merrychance began to growl at me in a most ferocious manner.

I wondered he was not ashamed of himself, but he didn't care for that; on the contrary he growled a good deal more. With his mouth watering, and his eyes glistening, and his nose in a very damp state, and his head very much on one side, he sidled about on the pavement in a threatening manner and growled at me, until he suddenly made a snap at the small German, tore it out of my hand, and went off with it. He never came back to help me seek

my fortune. From that hour to the present, when I am forty years
of age, I have never seen my faithful Merrychance again.

I felt very lonely. Not so much for the loss of the small German,
though it was delicious (I knew nothing about highly peppered
horse at that time), as on account of Merrychance's disappointing
me so cruelly; for I had hoped he would do every friendly thing
but speak, and perhaps even come to that. I cried a little more,
and began to wish that the object of my affections had been lost
with me, for company's sake. But, then I remembered that *she*
could not go into the army as a drummer; and I dried my eyes
and ate my loaf. Coming out, I met a milkwoman of whom I
bought a pennyworth of milk; quite set up again by my repast, I
began to roam about the City, and to seek my fortune in the
Whittington direction.

When I go into the City, now, it makes me sorrowful to think
that I am quite an artful wretch. Strolling about it as a lost child,
I thought of the British Merchant and the Lord Mayor, and was
full of reverence. Strolling about it now, I laugh at the sacred
liveries of state, and get indignant with the corporation as one of
the strongest practical jokes of the present day. What did I know,
then, about the multitude who are always being disappointed in
the City; who are always expecting to meet a party there, and to
receive money there, and whose expectations are never fulfilled?
What did I know, then, about that wonderful person, the friend
in the City, who is to do so many things for so many people; who
is to get this one into a post at home, and that one into a post
abroad; who is to settle with this man's creditors, provide for that
man's son, and see that other man paid; who is to 'throw himself'
into this grand Joint-Stock certainty, and is to put his name down
on that Life Assurance Directory, and never does anything pre-
dicted of him? What did I know, then, about him as the friend of
gentlemen, Mosaic Arabs and others, usually to be seen at races,
and chiefly residing in the neighbourhood of Red Lion Square;
and as being unable to discount the whole amount of that paper in
money, but as happening to have by him a cask of remarkable fine
sherry, a dressing-case, and a Venus by Titian, with which he
would be willing to make up the balance? Had I ever heard of

him, in those innocent days, as confiding information (which never by any chance turned out to be in the remotest degree correct) to solemn bald men, who mysteriously imparted it to breathless dinner-tables? No. Had I ever learned to dread him as a shark, disregard him as a humbug, and know him for a myth? Not I. Had I ever heard of him as associated with tightness in the money market, gloom in consols, the exportation of gold, or that rock ahead in everybody's course, the bushel of wheat? Never. Had I the least idea what was meant by such terms as jobbery, rigging the market, cooking accounts, getting up a dividend, making things pleasant, and the like? Not the slightest. Should I have detected in Mr Hudson himself, a staring carcass of golden veal? By no manner of means. The City was to me a vast emporium of precious stones and metals, casks and bales, honour and generosity, foreign fruits and spices. Every merchant and banker was a compound of Mr Fitz-Warren and Sinbad the Sailor. Smith, Payne, and Smith, when the wind was fair for Barbary and the captain present, were in the habit of calling their servants together (the cross cook included) and asking them to produce their little shipments. Glyn and Halifax had personally undergone great hardships in the valley of diamonds. Baring Brothers had seen Rocs' eggs and travelled with caravans. Rothschild had sat in the Bazaar at Bagdad with rich stuffs for sale; and a veiled lady from the Sultan's harem, riding on a donkey, had fallen in love with him.

Thus I wandered about the City, like a child in a dream, staring at the British merchants, and inspired by a mighty faith in the marvellousness of everything. Up courts and down courts—in and out of yards and little squares—peeping into counting-house passages and running away—poorly feeding the echoes in the court of the South Sea House with my timid steps—roaming down into Austin Friars, and wondering how the Friars used to like it—ever staring at the British merchants, and never tired of the shops—I rambled on, all through the day. In such stories as I made, to account for the different places, I believed as devoutly as in the City itself. I particularly remember that when I found myself on 'Change, and saw the shabby people sitting under the placards about ships, I settled that they were misers, who had embarked all their wealth to go and buy gold-dust or something of that sort, and were waiting for their respective captains to come and tell them that they were ready to set sail. I observed that they all munched dry biscuits, and I thought it was to keep off sea-sickness.

This was very delightful; but it still produced no result according to the Whittington precedent. There was a dinner preparing at the Mansion House, and when I peeped in at a grated kitchen window, and saw the men cooks at work in their white caps, my heart began to beat with hope that the Lord Mayor, or the Lady Mayoress, or one of the young Princesses their daughters, would look out of an upper apartment and direct me to be taken in. But, nothing of the kind occurred. It was not until I had been peeping in some time that one of the cooks called to me (the window was open), 'Cut away, you sir!' which frightened me so, on account of his black whiskers, that I instantly obeyed.

After that, I came to the India House, and asked a boy what it was, who made faces and pulled my hair before he told me, and behaved altogether in an ungenteel and discourteous manner. Sir James Hogg himself might have been satisfied with the veneration in which I held the India House. I had no doubt of its being the most wonderful, the most magnanimous, the most incorruptible, the most practically disinterested, the most in all respects astonishing, establishment on the face of the earth. I understood the nature of an oath, and would have sworn it to be one entire and perfect chrysolite.

Thinking much about boys who went to India, and who immediately, without being sick, smoked pipes like curled-up bell-ropes, terminating in a large cut-glass sugar basin upside down, I got among the outfitting shops. There, I read the lists of things that were necessary for an India-going boy, and when I came to 'one brace of pistols', thought what happiness to be reserved for such a fate! Still no British merchant seemed at all disposed to take me into his house. The only exception was a chimney-sweep —he looked at me as if he thought me suitable to his business; but I ran away from him.

I suffered very much, all day, from boys; they chased me down turnings, brought me to bay in doorways, and treated me quite savagely though I am sure I gave them no offence. One boy, who had a stump of black-lead pencil in his pocket, wrote his mother's name and address (as he said) on my white hat, outside the crown. *Mrs Blores, Wooden Leg Walk, Tobacco-stopper Row, Wapping.* And I couldn't rub it out.

I recollect resting in a little churchyard after this persecution, disposed to think upon the whole, that if I and the object of my affections could be buried there together, at once, it would be comfortable. But, another nap, and a pump, and a bun, and above all a picture that I saw, brought me round again.

I must have strayed by that time, as I recall my course, into Goodman's Fields, or somewhere thereabouts. The picture represented a scene in a play then performing at a theatre in that neighbourhood which is no longer in existence. It stimulated me to go to that theatre and see that play. I resolved, as there seemed to be nothing doing in the Whittington way, that on the conclusion of the entertainments I would ask my way to the barracks, knock at the gate, and tell them that I understood they were in want of drummers, and there I was. I think I must have been told, but I know I believed, that a soldier was always on duty, day and night, behind every barrack-gate, with a shilling; and that a boy who could by any means be prevailed on to accept it, instantly became a drummer, unless his father paid four hundred pounds.

I found out the theatre—of its external appearance I only remember the loyal initials G.R., untidily painted in yellow ochre on the front—and waited, with a pretty large crowd, for the opening of the gallery doors. The greater part of the sailors and others composing the crowd, were of the lowest description, and their conversation was not improving; but I understood little or nothing of what was bad in it then, and it had no depraving influence on me. I have wondered since, how long it would take, by means of such association, to corrupt a child nurtured as I had been, and innocent as I was.

Whenever I saw that my appearance attracted attention, either outside the doors or afterwards within the theatre, I pretended to look out for somebody who was taking care of me, and from whom I was separated, and to exchange nods and smiles with that creature of my imagination. This answered very well. I had my sixpence clutched in my hand ready to pay; and when the doors opened, with a clattering of bolts, and some screaming from women in the crowd, I went on with the current like a straw. My sixpence was rapidly swallowed up in the money-taker's pigeon-hole, which looked to me like a sort of mouth, and I got into the freer staircase above and ran on (as everybody else did) to get a good place. When I came to the back of the gallery, there were very few people in it, and the seats looked so horribly steep, and so like a diving arrangement to send me, headforemost, into the pit, that I held by one of them in a terrible fright. However, there was a good-natured baker with a young woman, who gave me his hand, and we all three scrambled over the seats together down into the corner of the first row. The baker was very fond of the young woman, and kissed her a good deal in the course of the evening.

I was no sooner comfortably settled, than a weight fell upon my mind, which tormented it most dreadfully, and which I must explain. It was a benefit night—the benefit of the comic actor—a little fat man with a very large face and, as I thought then, the smallest and most diverting hat that ever was seen. This comedian, for the gratification of his friends and patrons, had undertaken to sing a comic song on a donkey's back, and afterwards to give away the donkey so distinguished, by lottery. In this lottery, every person admitted to the pit and gallery had a chance. On paying my sixpence, I had received the number, forty-seven; and I now thought, in a perspiration of terror, what should I ever do if that number was to come up the prize, and I was to win the donkey!

It made me tremble all over to think of the possibility of my good fortune. I knew I never could conceal the fact of my holding forty-seven, in case that number came up, because, not to speak of my confusion, which would immediately condemn me, I had shown my number to the baker. Then, I pictured to myself the being called upon to come down on the stage and receive the donkey. I thought how all the people would shriek when they saw it had fallen to a little fellow like me. How should I lead him out—for of course he wouldn't go? If he began to bray, what should I do? If he kicked, what would become of me? Suppose he backed into the stage-door, and stuck there, with me upon him? For I felt that if I won him, the comic actor would have me on his back, the moment he could touch me. Then if I got him out of the theatre, what was I to do with him? How was I to feed him? Where was I to stable him? It was bad enough to have gone astray by myself, but to go astray with a donkey, too, was a calamity more tremendous than I could bear to contemplate.

These apprehensions took away all my pleasure in the first piece. When the ship came on—a real man-of-war she was called in the bills—and rolled prodigiously in a very heavy sea, I couldn't, even in the terrors of the storm, forget the donkey. It was awful to see the sailors pitching about, with telescopes and speaking trumpets (they looked very tall indeed aboard the man-of-war), and it was awful to suspect the pilot of treachery, though impossible to avoid it, for when he cried—'We are lost! To the raft, to the raft! A thunderbolt has struck the mainmast!'—I myself saw him take the mainmast out of its socket and drop it overboard; but even these impressive circumstances paled before my dread of the donkey. Even, when the good sailor (and he was very good) came to good fortune, and the bad sailor (and he was very bad) threw himself into the ocean from the summit of a curious rock, presenting something of the appearance of a pair of steps, I saw the dreadful donkey through my tears.

At last the time came when the fiddlers struck up the comic song, and the dreaded animal, with new shoes on, as I inferred from the noise they made, came clattering in with the comic actor on his back. He was dressed out with ribbons (I mean the donkey was), and as he persisted in turning his tail to the audience, the comedian got off him, turned about, and sitting with his face that way, sang the song three times, amid thunders of applause. All this time, I was fearfully agitated; and when two pale people, a good deal splashed with the mud of the streets, were invited out of the pit to superintend the drawing of the lottery, and were received with a round of laughter from everybody else, I could have begged and prayed them to have mercy on me, and not draw number forty-seven.

But, I was soon put out of my pain now, for a gentleman behind me, in a flannel jacket and a yellow neckerchief, who had eaten two fried soles and all his pockets full of nuts before the storm began to rage, answered to the winning number, and went down to take possession of the prize. This gentleman had appeared to know the donkey, rather, from the moment of his entrance, and had taken a great interest in his proceedings; driving him to himself, if I use an intelligible phrase, and saying, almost in my ear, when he made any mistake, 'Kum up, you precious Moke. Kum up!' He was thrown by the donkey on first mounting him, to the great delight of the audience (including myself), but rode him off with great skill afterwards, and soon returned to his seat quite calm. Calmed myself by the immense relief I had sustained, I enjoyed the rest of the performance very much indeed. I remember there were a good many dances, some in fetters and some in roses, and one by a most divine little creature, who made the object of my affections look but commonplace. In the concluding drama, she reappeared as a boy (in arms, mostly), and was fought for, several times. I rather think a Baron wanted to drown her, and was on various occasions prevented by the comedian, a ghost, a Newfoundland dog, and a church bell. I only remember beyond this, that I wondered where the Baron expected to go to, and that he went there in a shower of sparks. The lights were turned out while the sparks died out, and it appeared to me as if the whole play—ship, donkey, men and women, divine little creature, and all—were a wonderful firework that had gone off, and left nothing but dust and darkness behind it.

It was late when I got out into the streets, and there was no moon, and there were no stars, and the rain fell heavily. When I emerged from the dispersing crowd, the ghost and the Baron had an ugly look in my remembrance; I felt unspeakably forlorn; and now, for the first time, my little bed and the dear familiar faces came before me, and touched my heart. By daylight, I had never thought of the grief at home. I had never thought of my mother.

I had never thought of anything but adapting myself to the circumstances in which I found myself, and going to seek my fortune.

For a boy who could do nothing but cry, and run about, saying, 'O I am lost!' to think of going into the army was, I felt sensible, out of the question. I abandoned the idea of asking my way to the barracks—or rather the idea abandoned me—and ran about, until I found a watchman in his box. It is amazing to me, now, that he should have been sober; but I am inclined to think he was too feeble to get drunk.

This venerable man took me to the nearest watch-house; I say he took me, but in fact I took him, for when I think of us in the rain, I recollect that we must have made a composition, like a vignette of Infancy leading Age. He had a dreadful cough, and was obliged to lean against a wall whenever it came on. We got at last to the watch-house, a warm and drowsy sort of place embellished with greatcoats and rattles hanging up. When a paralytic messenger had been sent to make inquiries about me, I fell asleep by the fire, and awoke no more until my eyes opened on my father's face. This is literally and exactly how I went astray. They used to say I was an odd child, and I suppose I was. I am an odd man perhaps.

Shade of Somebody, forgive me for the disquiet I must have caused thee! When I stand beneath the lion, even now, I see thee rushing up and down, refusing to be comforted. I have gone astray since, many times, and farther afield. May I therein have given less disquiet to others, than herein I gave to thee!

Household Words, August 13th, 1853

The Streets – Morning

The appearance presented by the streets of London an hour before
sunrise, on a summer's morning, is most striking even to the few
whose unfortunate pursuits of pleasure, or scarcely less unfortunate pursuits of business, cause them to be well acquainted with
the scene. There is an air of cold, solitary desolation about the
noiseless streets which we are accustomed to see thronged at
other times by a busy, eager crowd, and over the quiet, closely
shut buildings, which throughout the day are swarming with life
and bustle, that is very impressive.

The last drunken man, who shall find his way home before sunlight, has just staggered heavily along, roaring out the burden of
the drinking song of the previous night: the last houseless vagrant
whom penury and police have left in the streets, has coiled up his
chilly limbs in some paved corner, to dream of food and warmth.
The drunken, the dissipated, and the wretched have disappeared;
the more sober and orderly part of the population have not yet
awakened to the labours of the day, and the stillness of death is
over the streets; its very hue seems to be imparted to them, cold
and lifeless as they look in the grey, sombre light of daybreak. The
coach-stands in the larger thoroughfares are deserted; the night-
houses are closed; and the chosen promenades of profligate misery
are empty.

An occasional policeman may alone be seen at the street
corners, listlessly gazing on the deserted prospect before him;
and now and then a rakish-looking cat runs stealthily across the
road and descends his own area with as much caution and sly-
ness—bounding first on the water-butt, then on the dust-hole,
and then alighting on the flag-stones—as if he were conscious
that his character depended on his gallantry of the preceding night

escaping public observation. A partially opened bedroom window here and there, bespeaks the heat of the weather, and the uneasy slumbers of its occupant; and the dim scanty flicker of the rushlight, through the window-blind, denotes the chamber of watching or sickness. With these few exceptions, the streets present no signs of life, nor the houses of habitation.

An hour wears away; the spires of the churches and roofs of the principal buildings are faintly tinged with the light of the rising sun; and the streets, by almost imperceptible degrees, begin to resume their bustle and animation. Market carts roll slowly along: the sleepy wagoner impatiently urging on his tired horses, or vainly endeavouring to awaken the boy, who, luxuriously stretched on the top of the fruit-baskets, forgets, in happy oblivion, his long-cherished curiosity to behold the wonders of London.

Rough, sleepy-looking animals of strange appearance, something between ostlers and hackney-coachmen, begin to take down the shutters of early public houses; and little deal tables, with the ordinary preparations for a street breakfast, make their appearance at the customary stations. Numbers of men and women (principally the latter), carrying upon their heads heavy baskets of fruit, toil down the park side of Piccadilly, on their way to Covent Garden, and, following each other in rapid succession, form a long straggling line from thence to the turn of the road at Knightsbridge.

Here and there, a bricklayer's labourer, with the day's dinner tied up in a handkerchief, walks briskly to his work, and occasionally a little knot of three or four schoolboys on a stolen bathing expedition rattle merrily over the pavement, their boisterous mirth contrasting forcibly with the demeanour of the little sweep, who, having knocked and rung till his arm aches, and being interdicted by a merciful legislature from endangering his lungs by calling out, sits patiently down on the doorstep, until the housemaid may happen to awake.

Covent Garden market, and the avenues leading to it, are thronged with carts of all sorts, sizes, and descriptions, from the heavy lumbering wagon, with its four stout horses, to the jingling costermonger's cart, with its consumptive donkey. The pavement

BRICKLAYER'S LABOURER.

is already strewed with decayed cabbage-leaves, broken hay-bands, and all the indescribable litter of a vegetable market; men are shouting, carts backing, horses neighing, boys fighting, basket-women talking, piemen expatiating on the excellence of their pastry, and donkeys braying. These and a hundred other sounds form a compound discordant enough to a Londoner's ears, and remarkably disagreeable to those of country gentlemen who are sleeping at the Hummums for the first time.

Another hour passes away, and the day begins in good earnest. The servant-of-all-work, who, under the plea of sleeping very soundly, has utterly disregarded 'Missis's' ringing for half an hour previously, is warned by Master (whom Missis has sent up in his drapery to the landing-place for that purpose), that it's half past six, whereupon she awakes all of a sudden, with well-feigned astonishment, and goes downstairs very sulkily, wishing, while she strikes a light, that the principle of spontaneous combustion would extend itself to coals and kitchen range. When the fire is lighted, she opens the street door to take in the milk, when, by the most singular coincidence in the world, she discovers that the servant next door has just taken in her milk too, and that Mr Todd's young man over the way is, by an equally extraordinary chance, taking down his master's shutters. The inevitable consequence is that she just steps, milk-jug in hand, as far as next door, just to say 'good morning' to Betsy Clark, and that Mr Todd's young man just steps over the way to say 'good morning' to both of 'em; and as the aforesaid Mr Todd's young man is almost as good-looking and fascinating as the baker himself, the conversation quickly becomes very interesting, and probably would become more so, if Betsy Clark's Missis, who always will be a-followin' her about, didn't give an angry tap at her bedroom window, on which Mr Todd's young man tries to whistle coolly, as he goes back to his shop much faster than he came from it; and the two girls run back to their respective places, and shut their street doors with surprising softness, each of them poking their heads out of the front parlour window, a minute afterwards, however, ostensibly with the view of looking at the mail which just then passes by, but really for the purpose of catching another glimpse of Mr Todd's young man, who being fond of mails, but more of females, takes a short look at the mails, and a long look at the girls, much to the satisfaction of all parties concerned.

The mail itself goes on to the coach-office in due course, and the passengers who are going out by the early coach stare with astonishment at the passengers who are coming in by the early coach, who look blue and dismal, and are evidently under the influence of that odd feeling produced by travelling, which makes the events of yesterday morning seem as if they had happened at least six months ago, and induces people to wonder with considerable gravity whether the friends and relations they took leave of a fortnight before have altered much since they have left them. The coach-office is all alive, and the coaches which are just going out are surrounded by the usual crowd of Jews and nondescripts, who seem to consider, Heaven knows why, that it is quite impossible any man can mount a coach without requiring at least sixpennyworth of oranges, a penknife, a pocket-book, a last year's annual, a pencil-case, a piece of sponge, and a small series of caricatures.

Half an hour more, and the sun darts his bright rays cheerfully down the still half-empty streets, and shines with sufficient force to rouse the dismal laziness of the apprentice, who pauses every other minute from his task of sweeping out the shop and watering the pavement in front of it, to tell another apprentice similarly employed how hot it will be today, or to stand with his right hand shading his eyes, and his left resting on the broom, gazing at the 'Wonder', or the 'Tally-ho', or the 'Nimrod', or some other fast coach, till it is out of sight, when he re-enters the shop, envying the passengers on the outside of the fast coach, and thinking of the old red brick house 'down in the country' where he went to school: the miseries of the milk and water, and thick bread and scrapings, fading into nothing before the pleasant recollection of the green field the boys used to play in, and the green pond he was caned for presuming to fall into, and other schoolboy associations.

Cabs, with trunks and band-boxes between the drivers' legs and outside the apron, rattle briskly up and down the streets on their way to the coach-offices or steam-packet wharfs; and the cab-drivers and hackney-coachmen who are on the stand polish up the ornamental part of their dingy vehicles—the former wondering how people can prefer 'them wild beast cariwans of homnibuses, to a riglar cab with a fast trotter', and the latter admiring how people can trust their necks into one of 'them crazy cabs, when they can have a 'spectable 'ackney cotche with a pair of 'orses as von't run away with no vun'; a consolation unquestionably founded on fact, seeing that a hackney-coach horse never was known to run at all, 'except', as the smart cabman in front of the rank observes, 'except one, and *he* run back'ards'.

The shops are now completely opened, and apprentices and shopmen are busily engaged in cleaning and decking the windows for the day. The bakers' shops in town are filled with servants and children waiting for the drawing of the first batch of rolls—an operation which was performed a full hour ago in the suburbs: for the early clerk population of Somers and Camden Towns, Islington, and Pentonville, are fast pouring into the city, or directing their steps towards Chancery Lane and the Inns of Court. Middle-aged men, whose salaries have by no means increased in the same proportion as their families, plod steadily along, apparently with no object in view but the counting-house; knowing by sight almost everybody they meet or overtake, for they have seen them every morning (Sundays excepted) during the last twenty years, but speaking to no one. If they do happen to overtake a personal acquaintance, they just exchange a hurried salutation, and keep walking on, either by his side or in front of him, as his rate of walking may chance to be. As to stopping to shake hands, or to take the friend's arm, they seem to think that as it is not included in their salary, they have no right to do it. Small office lads in large hats, who are made men before they are boys, hurry along in pairs, with their first coat carefully brushed, and the white trousers of last Sunday plentifully besmeared with dust and ink. It evidently requires a considerable mental struggle to avoid investing part of the day's dinner-money in the purchase of the stale tarts so temptingly exposed in dusty tins at the pastrycooks' doors; but a consciousness of their own importance and the receipt of seven shillings a week, with the prospect of an early rise to eight, comes to their aid, and they accordingly put their hats a little more on one side, and look under the bonnets of all the milliners' and staymakers' apprentices they meet—poor girls!— the hardest-worked, the worst-paid, and too often the worst-used class of the community.

Eleven o'clock, and a new set of people fill the streets. The goods in the shop windows are invitingly arranged; the shopmen in their white neckerchiefs and spruce coats look as if they couldn't clean a window if their lives depended on it; the carts have disappeared from Covent Garden; the wagoners have returned, and the costermongers repaired to their ordinary 'beats' in the suburbs; clerks are at their offices, and gigs, cabs, omnibuses and saddle-horses are conveying their masters to the same destination. The streets are thronged with a vast concourse of people, gay and shabby, rich and poor, idle and industrious; and we come to the heat, bustle, and activity of NOON.

The Morning Chronicle, July 21st, 1835
Sketches by Boz, Second Series, 1837

Greenwich Fair

If the Parks be 'the lungs of London', we wonder what Greenwich Fair is—a periodical breaking out, we suppose, a sort of spring-rash: a three days' fever, which cools the blood for six months afterwards, and at the expiration of which London is restored to its old habits of plodding industry, as suddenly and completely as if nothing had ever happened to disturb them.

In our earlier days we were a constant frequenter of Greenwich Fair, for years. We have proceeded to, and returned from it, in almost every description of vehicle. We cannot conscientiously deny the charge of having once made the passage in a spring-van, accompanied by thirteen gentlemen, fourteen ladies, an unlimited number of children, and a barrel of beer; and we have a vague recollection of having, in later days, found ourself the eighth outside, on the top of a hackney-coach, at something past four o'clock in the morning, with a rather confused idea of our own name, or place of residence. We have grown older since then, and quiet, and steady: liking nothing better than to spend our Easter, and all our other holidays, in some quiet nook, with people of whom we shall never tire; but we think we still remember something of Greenwich Fair, and of those who resort to it. At all events we will try.

The road to Greenwich during the whole of Easter Monday is in a state of perpetual bustle and noise. Cabs, hackney-coaches, 'shay' carts, coal-wagons, stages, omnibuses, sociables, gigs, donkey-chaises—all crammed with people (for the question never is, what the horse can draw, but what the vehicle will hold), roll along at their utmost speed; the dust flies in clouds, ginger-beer corks go off in volleys, the balcony of every public house is crowded with people, smoking and drinking, half the private houses are turned into tea-shops, fiddles are in great request, every little fruit-shop displays its stall of gilt gingerbread and penny toys; turnpike men are in despair; horses won't go on, and wheels will come off; ladies in 'carawans' scream with fright at every fresh concussion, and their admirers find it necessary to sit remarkably close to them, by way of encouragement; servants-of-all-work, who are not allowed to have followers, and have got a holiday for the day, make the most of their time with the faithful admirer who waits for a stolen interview at the corner of the street every night, when they go to fetch the beer—apprentices grow sentimental, and straw-bonnet makers kind. Everybody is anxious to get on, and actuated by the common wish to be at the fair, or in the park, as soon as possible.

Pedestrians linger in groups at the roadside, unable to resist the allurements of the stout proprietress of the 'Jack-in-the-box, three shies a penny', or the more splendid offers of the man with three thimbles and a pea on a little round board, who astonishes the bewildered crowd with some such address as 'Here's the sort o' game to make you laugh seven years arter you're dead, and turn ev'ry 'air on your 'ed grey vith delight! Three thimbles and vun little pea—with a vun, two, three, and a two, three, vun: catch him who can, look on, keep your eyes open, and niver say die! niver mind the change, and the expense: all fair and above board: them as don't play can't vin, and luck attend the ryal sportsman! Bet any gen'lm'n any sum of money, from harf a crown up to a suverin, as he doesn't name the thimble as kivers the pea!' Here some greenhorn whispers his friend that he distinctly saw the pea roll under the middle thimble—an impression which is immediately confirmed by a gentleman in top-boots, who is standing by, and who, in a low tone, regrets his own inability to bet, in consequence of having unfortunately left his purse at home, but strongly urges the stranger not to neglect such a golden opportunity. The 'plant' is successful, the bet is made, the stranger of course loses: and the gentleman with the thimbles consoles him, as he pockets the money, with an assurance that it's 'all the fortin of war! this time I vin, next time you vin: niver mind the loss of two bob and a bender! Do it up in a small parcel, and break out in a fresh place. Here's the sort o' game', &c—and the eloquent harangue, with such variations as the speaker's exuberant fancy suggests, is again repeated to the gaping crowd, reinforced by the accession of several new-comers.

The chief place of resort in the day-time, after the public houses, is the park, in which the principal amusement is to drag young ladies up the steep hill which leads to the Observatory, and then drag them down again, at the very top of their speed, greatly to the derangement of their curls and bonnet-caps, and much to the edification of lookers-on from below. 'Kiss in the Ring' and 'Threading my Grandmother's Needle', too, are sports which receive their full share of patronage. Love-sick swains, under the influence of gin-and-water, and the tender passion, become violently affectionate: and the fair objects of their regard enhance the value of stolen kisses by a vast deal of struggling, and holding down of heads, and cries of 'Oh! Ha' done, then, George —Oh, do tickle him for me, Mary—Well, I never!' and similar Lucretian ejaculations. Little old men and women, with a small basket under one arm, and a wine-glass, without a foot, in the other hand, tender 'a drop o' the right sort' to the different groups; and young ladies, who are persuaded to indulge in a drop of the aforesaid right sort, display a pleasing degree of reluctance to taste it, and cough afterwards with great propriety.

The old pensioners, who, for the moderate charge of a penny, exhibit the mast-house, the Thames and shipping, the place where the men used to hang in chains, and other interesting sights, through a telescope, are asked questions about objects within the range of the glass, which it would puzzle a Solomon to answer; and requested to find out particular houses in particular streets, which it would have been a task of some difficulty for Mr Horner (not the young gentleman who ate mince-pies with his thumb, but the man of Colosseum notoriety) to discover. Here and there, where some three or four couple are sitting on the grass together, you will see a sun-burnt woman in a red cloak 'telling fortunes' and prophesying husbands, which it requires no extraordinary observation to describe, for the originals are before her. Thereupon, the lady concerned laughs and blushes, and ultimately buries her face in an imitation cambric handkerchief, and the gentleman described looks extremely foolish, and squeezes her hand, and fees the gipsy liberally; and the gipsy goes away, perfectly satisfied herself, and leaving those behind her perfectly satisfied also: and the prophecy, like many other prophecies of greater importance, fulfils itself in time.

But it grows dark: the crowd has gradually dispersed, and only a few stragglers are left behind. The light in the direction of the church shows that the fair is illuminated; and the distant noise proves it to be filling fast. The spot, which half an hour ago was ringing with the shouts of boisterous mirth, is as calm and quiet as if nothing could ever disturb its serenity; the fine old trees, the majestic building at their feet, with the noble river beyond, glistening in the moonlight, appear in all their beauty, and under their most favourable aspect; the voices of the boys, singing their evening hymn, are borne gently on the air; and the humblest mechanic who has been lingering on the grass so pleasant to the feet that beat the same dull round from week to week in the paved streets of London, feels proud to think as he surveys the scene before him, that he belongs to the country which has selected such a spot as a retreat for its oldest and best defenders in the decline of their lives.

Five minutes' walking brings you to the fair; a scene calculated to awaken very different feelings. The entrance is occupied on either side by the vendors of gingerbread and toys: the stalls are gaily lighted up, the most attractive goods profusely disposed, and unbonneted young ladies, in their zeal for the interest of their employers, seize you by the coat, and use all the blandishments of 'Do, dear'—'There's a love'—'Don't be cross, now', &c, to induce you to purchase half a pound of the real spice nuts, of which the majority of the regular fair-goers carry a pound or two as a present supply, tied up in a cotton pocket-handkerchief. Occasionally you pass a deal table, on which are exposed pen'orths of pickled salmon (fennel included), in little white saucers: oysters, with shells as large as cheese-plates, and divers specimens of a species of snail (*wilks*, we think they are called), floating in a somewhat bilious-looking green liquid. Cigars, too, are in great demand; gentlemen must smoke, of course, and here they are,

two a penny, in a regular authentic cigar-box, with a lighted
tallow candle in the centre.

Imagine yourself in an extremely dense crowd, which swings
you to and fro, and in and out, and every way but the right one;
add to this the screams of women, the shouts of boys, the clanging
of gongs, the firing of pistols, the ringing of bells, the bellowings
of speaking-trumpets, the squeaking of penny dittoes, the noise
of a dozen bands, with three drums in each, all playing different
tunes at the same time, the hallooing of showmen, and an occasional
roar from the wild-beast shows; and you are in the very centre and
heart of the fair.

This immense booth, with the large stage in front, so brightly
illuminated with variegated lamps, and pots of burning fat, is
'Richardson's', where you have a melodrama (with three murders
and a ghost), a pantomime, a comic song, an overture, and some
incidental music, all done in five-and-twenty minutes.

The company are now promenading outside in all the dignity
of wigs, spangles, red ochre, and whitening. See with what a
ferocious air the gentleman who personates the Mexican chief,
paces up and down, and with what an eye of calm dignity the
principal tragedian gazes on the crowd below, or converses con-
fidentially with the harlequin! The four clowns, who are engaged
in a mock broadsword combat, may be all very well for the low-
minded holiday-makers; but these are the people for the reflective
portion of the community. They look so noble in those Roman
dresses, with their yellow legs and arms, long black curly heads,
bushy eyebrows, and scowl expressive of assassination, and vengeance, and everything else that is grand and solemn. Then, the
ladies—were there ever such innocent and awful-looking beings;
as they walk up and down the platform in twos and threes, with
their arms round each other's waists, or leaning for support on
one of those majestic men! Their spangled muslin dresses and
blue satin shoes and sandals (a *leetle* the worse for wear) are the
admiration of all beholders; and the playful manner in which they
check the advances of the clown, is perfectly enchanting.

'Just a-going to begin! Pray come for'erd, come for'erd,' exclaims the man in the countryman's dress, for the seventieth time:

and people force their way up the steps in crowds. The band suddenly strikes up, the harlequin and columbine set the example,
reels are formed in less than no time, the Roman heroes place
their arms a-kimbo, and dance with considerable agility; and the
leading tragic actress, and the gentleman who enacts the 'swell'
in the pantomime, foot it to perfection. 'All in to begin,' shouts
the manager, when no more people can be induced to 'come
for'erd', and away rush the leading members of the company to do
the dreadful in the first piece.

A change of performance takes place every day during the fair,
but the story of the tragedy is always pretty much the same. There
is a rightful heir, who loves a young lady, and is beloved by her;
and a wrongful heir, who loves her, too, and isn't beloved by her;
and the wrongful heir gets hold of the rightful heir, and throws
him into a dungeon, just to kill him off when convenient, for
which purpose he hires a couple of assassins—a good one and a
bad one—who, the moment they are left alone, get up a little
murder on their own account, the good one killing the bad one,
and the bad one wounding the good one. Then the rightful heir is
discovered in prison, carefully holding a long chain in his hands,
and seated despondingly in a large arm-chair; and the young lady
comes in to two bars of soft music, and embraces the rightful heir;
and then the wrongful heir comes in to two bars of quick music
(technically called 'a hurry'), and goes on in the most shocking
manner, throwing the young lady about as if she was nobody, and
calling the rightful heir 'Ar-recreant—ar-wretch!' in a very loud
voice, which answers the double purpose of displaying his passion,
and preventing the sound being deadened by the sawdust. The
interest becomes intense; the wrongful heir draws his sword, and
rushes on the rightful heir; a blue smoke is seen, a gong is heard,
and a tall white figure (who has been all this time, behind the arm-
chair, covered over with a table-cloth), slowly rises to the tune of
'Oft in the stilly night'. This is no other than the ghost of the
rightful heir's father, who was killed by the wrongful heir's father,
at sight of which the wrongful heir becomes apoplectic, and is
literally 'struck all of a heap', the stage not being large enough to
admit of his falling down at full length. Then the good assassin

staggers in, and says he was hired in conjunction with the bad assassin, by the wrongful heir, to kill the rightful heir; and he's killed a good many people in his time, but he's very sorry for it, and won't do so any more—a promise which he immediately redeems, by dying off hand without any nonsense about it. Then the rightful heir throws down his chain; and then two men, a sailor, and a young woman (the tenantry of the rightful heir) come in, and the ghost makes dumb motions to them, which they, by supernatural interference, understand—for no one else can; and the ghost (who can't do anything without blue fire) blesses the rightful heir and the young lady, by half suffocating them with smoke: and then a muffin-bell rings, and the curtain drops.

The exhibitions next in popularity to these itinerant theatres are the travelling menageries, or, to speak more intelligibly, the 'Wild-beast shows', where a military band in beef-eater's costume, with leopard-skin caps, play incessantly; and where large highly coloured representations of tigers tearing men's heads open, and a lion being burnt with red-hot irons to induce him to drop his victim, are hung up outside, by way of attracting visitors.

The principal officer at these places is generally a very tall, hoarse man, in a scarlet coat, with a cane in his hand, with which he occasionally raps the pictures we have just noticed, by way of illustrating his description—something in this way. 'Here, here, here; the lion, the lion (tap), exactly as he is represented on the canvas outside (three taps): no waiting, remember; no deception. The fe-ro-cious lion (tap, tap) who bit off the gentleman's head last Cambervel vos a twelvemonth, and has killed on the awerage three keepers a year ever since he arrived at matoority. No extra charge on this account recollect; the price of admission is only sixpence.' This address never fails to produce a considerable sensation, and sixpences flow into the treasury with wonderful rapidity.

The dwarfs are also objects of great curiosity, and as a dwarf, a giantess, a living skeleton, a wild Indian, 'a young lady of singular beauty, with perfectly white hair and pink eyes', and two or three other natural curiosities, are usually exhibited together for the small charge of a penny, they attract very numerous audiences.

The best thing about a dwarf is that he has always a little box, about two feet six inches high, into which, by long practice, he can just manage to get, by doubling himself up like a boot-jack; this box is painted outside like a six-roomed house, and as the crowd see him ring a bell, or fire a pistol out of the first-floor window, they verily believe that it is his ordinary town residence, divided like other mansions into drawing-rooms, dining-parlour, and bedchambers. Shut up in this case, the unfortunate little object is brought out to delight the throng by holding a facetious dialogue with the proprietor: in the course of which, the dwarf (who is always particularly drunk) pledges himself to sing a comic song inside, and pays various compliments to the ladies, which induce them to 'come for'erd' with great alacrity. As a giant is not so easily moved, a pair of indescribables of most capacious dimensions, and a huge shoe, are usually brought out, into which two or three stout men get all at once, to the enthusiastic delight of the crowd, who are quite satisfied with the solemn assurance that these habiliments form part of the giant's everyday costume.

The grandest and most numerously frequented booth in the whole fair, however, is 'The Crown and Anchor'—a temporary ball-room—we forget how many hundred feet long, the price of admission to which is one shilling. Immediately on your right hand as you enter, after paying your money, is a refreshment place, at which cold beef, roast and boiled, French rolls, stout, wine, tongue, ham, even fowls, if we recollect right, are displayed in tempting array. There is a raised orchestra, and the place is boarded all the way down, in patches, just wide enough for a country dance.

There is no master of the ceremonies in this artificial Eden—all is primitive, unreserved, and unstudied. The dust is blinding, the heat insupportable, the company somewhat noisy, and in the highest spirits possible: the ladies, in the height of their innocent animation, dancing in the gentlemen's hats, and the gentlemen promenading 'the gay and festive scene' in the ladies' bonnets, or with the more expensive ornaments of false noses, and low-crowned, tinder-box-looking hats: playing children's drums, and accompanied by ladies on the penny trumpet.

The noise of these various instruments, the orchestra, the shouting, the 'scratchers', and the dancing, is perfectly bewildering. The dancing itself beggars description—every figure lasts about an hour, and the ladies bounce up and down the middle, with a degree of spirit which is quite indescribable. As to the gentlemen, they stamp their feet against the ground, every time 'hands four round' begins, go down the middle and up again, with cigars in their mouths, and silk handkerchiefs in their hands, and whirl their partners round, nothing loath, scrambling and falling, and embracing, and knocking up against the other couples, until they are fairly tired out, and can move no longer. The same scene is repeated again and again (slightly varied by an occasional 'row') until a late hour at night: and a great many clerks and 'prentices find themselves next morning with aching heads, empty pockets, damaged hats, and a very imperfect recollection of how it was they did *not* get home.

The Evening Chronicle, April 16th, 1835
Sketches by Boz, Volume 1, 1836

Early Coaches

We have often wondered how many months' incessant travelling in a post-chaise it would take to kill a man; and wondering by analogy, we should very much like to know how many months of constant travelling in a succession of early coaches an unfortunate mortal could endure. Breaking a man alive upon the wheel would be nothing to breaking his rest, his peace, his heart—everything but his fast—upon four; and the punishment of Ixion (the only practical person, by the by, who has discovered the secret of the perpetual motion) would sink into utter insignificance before the one we have suggested. If we had been a powerful churchman in those good times when blood was shed as freely as water, and men were mowed down like grass, in the sacred cause of religion, we would have lain by very quietly till we got hold of some especially obstinate miscreant, who positively refused to be converted to our faith, and then we would have booked him for an inside place in a small coach, which travelled day and night: and securing the remainder of the places for stout men with a slight tendency to coughing and spitting, we would have started him forth on his last travels; leaving him mercilessly to all the tortures which the waiters, landlords, coachmen, guards, boots, chambermaids, and other familiars on his line of road, might think proper to inflict.

Who has not experienced the miseries inevitably consequent upon a summons to undertake a hasty journey? You receive an intimation from your place of business—wherever that may be, or whatever you may be—that it will be necessary to leave town without delay. You and your family are forthwith thrown into a state of tremendous excitement; an express is immediately dispatched to the washerwoman's; everybody is in a bustle; and you, yourself, with a feeling of dignity which you cannot altogether conceal, sally forth to the booking-office to secure your place. Here a painful consciousness of your own unimportance first rushes on your mind—the people are as cool and collected as if nobody were going out of town, or as if a journey of a hundred-odd miles were a mere nothing. You enter a mouldy-looking room, ornamented with large posting-bills; the greater part of the place enclosed behind a huge lumbering rough counter, and fitted up with recesses that look like the dens of the smaller animals in a travelling menagerie, without the bars. Some half-dozen people are 'booking' brown-paper parcels, which one of the clerks flings into the aforesaid recesses with an air of recklessness which you, remembering the new carpet-bag you bought in the morning, feel considerably annoyed at; porters, looking like so many Atlases, keep rushing in and out, with large packages on their shoulders; and while you are waiting to make the necessary inquiries, you wonder what on earth the booking-office clerks can have been before they were booking-office clerks; one of them, with his pen behind his ear, and his hands behind him, is standing in front of the fire, like a full-length portrait of Napoleon; the other with his hat half off his head, enters the passengers' names in the books with a coolness which is inexpressibly provoking; and the villain whistles—actually whistles—while a man asks him what the fare is outside, all the way to Holyhead!—in frosty weather, too! They are clearly an isolated race, evidently possessing no sympathies or feelings in common with the rest of mankind. Your turn comes at last, and having paid the fare, you tremblingly in-quire—'What time will it be necessary for me to be here in the morning?'—'Six o'clock,' replies the whistler, carelessly pitch-ing the sovereign you have just parted with into a wooden bowl on the desk. 'Rather before than arter,' adds the man with the semi-roasted unmentionables, with just as much ease and com-placency as if the whole world got out of bed at five. You turn into the street, ruminating as you bend your steps homewards on the extent to which men become hardened in cruelty by custom.

If there be one thing in existence more miserable than another, it most unquestionably is the being compelled to rise by candle-light. If you ever doubted the fact, you are painfully convinced of your error on the morning of your departure. You left strict orders, overnight, to be called at half past four, and you have done nothing all night but doze for five minutes at a time, and start up suddenly from a terrific dream of a large church-clock with the small hand running round, with astonishing rapidity, to every figure on the dial-plate. At last, completely exhausted, you fall gradually into a refreshing sleep—your thoughts grow confused —the stage-coaches, which have been 'going off' before your eyes all night, become less and less distinct, until they go off altogether; one moment you are driving with all the skill and smartness of an experienced whip—the next you are exhibiting *à la* Ducrow, on the off-leader; anon you are closely muffled up, inside, and have just recognized in the person of the guard an old schoolfellow, whose funeral, even in your dream, you remember to have attended eighteen years ago. At last you fall into a state of complete oblivion, from which you are aroused, as if into a new state of existence, by a singular illusion. You are apprenticed to a trunk-maker; how, or why, or when, or wherefore, you don't take the trouble to inquire; but there you are, pasting the lining in the lid of a portmanteau. Confound that other apprentice in the back shop; how he is hammering!—rap, rap, rap—what an industrious fellow he must be! you have heard him at work for half an hour past, and he has been hammering incessantly the whole time. Rap, rap, rap, again—he's talking now—what's that he said? Five o'clock! You make a violent exertion, and start up in bed. The vision is at once dispelled; the trunk-maker's shop is your own bedroom, and the other apprentice your shivering servant, who has been vainly endeavouring to wake you for the last quarter of an hour, at the imminent risk of breaking either his own knuckles or the panels of the door.

You proceed to dress yourself, with all possible dispatch. The flaring flat candle with the long snuff gives light enough to show that the things you want are not where they ought to be, and you undergo a trifling delay in consequence of having carefully packed up one of your boots in your overanxiety of the preceding night. You soon complete your toilet, however, for you are not particular on such an occasion, and you shaved yesterday evening; so

STAGE COACHMAN.

mounting your Petersham greatcoat, and green travelling-shawl, and grasping your carpet-bag in your right hand, you walk lightly downstairs, lest you should awaken any of the family, and after pausing in the common sitting-room for one moment, just to have a cup of coffee (the said common sitting-room looking remarkably comfortable, with everything out of its place, and strewed with the crumbs of last night's supper), you undo the chain and bolts of the street door, and find yourself fairly in the street.

A thaw, by all that is miserable! The frost is completely broken up. You look down the long perspective of Oxford Street, the gaslights mournfully reflected on the wet pavement, and can discern no speck in the road to encourage the belief that there is a cab or a coach to be had—the very coachmen have gone home in despair. The cold sleet is drizzling down with that gentle regularity which betokens a duration of four-and-twenty hours at least; the damp hangs upon the house-tops and lamp-posts, and clings to you like an invisible cloak. The water is 'coming in' in every area, the pipes have burst, the water-butts are running over; the kennels seem to be doing matches against time, pump-handles descend of their own accord, horses in market carts fall down, and there's no one to help them up again, policemen look as if they had been carefully sprinkled with powdered glass; here and there a milk-woman trudges slowly along, with a bit of list round each foot to keep her from slipping; boys who 'don't sleep in the house', and are not allowed much sleep out of it, can't wake their masters by thundering at the shop door, and cry with the cold—the compound of ice, snow, and water on the pavement, is a couple of inches thick—nobody ventures to walk fast to keep himself warm, and nobody could succeed in keeping himself warm if he did.

It strikes a quarter past five as you trudge down Waterloo Place on your way to the Golden Cross, and you discover, for the first time, that you were called about an hour too early. You have not time to go back; there is no place open to go into, and you have, therefore, no resource but to go forward, which you do, feeling remarkably satisfied with yourself, and everything about you. You arrive at the office, and look wistfully up the yard for the Birmingham High-flier, which, for aught you can see, may have

flown away altogether, for no preparations appear to be on foot
for the departure of any vehicle in the shape of a coach. You
wander into the booking-office, which with the gas-lights and
blazing fire looks quite comfortable by contrast—that is to say,
if any place *can* look comfortable at half-past five on a winter's
morning. There stands the identical book-keeper in the same
position as if he had not moved since you saw him yesterday. As
he informs you that the coach is up the yard, and will be brought
round in about a quarter of an hour, you leave your bag, and re-
pair to 'The Tap'—not with any absurd idea of warming yourself,
because you feel such a result to be utterly hopeless, but for the
purpose of procuring some hot brandy-and-water, which you do—
when the kettle boils!—an event which occurs exactly two minutes
and a half before the time fixed for the starting of the coach.

The first stroke of six peals from St Martin's church steeple
just as you take the first sip of the boiling liquid. You find yourself
at the booking-office in two seconds, and the tap-waiter finds himself much comforted by your brandy-and-water, in about the same
period. The coach is out; the horses are in, and the guard and two
or three porters are stowing the luggage away, and running up
the steps of the booking-office, and down the steps of the booking-
office, with breathless rapidity. The place, which a few minutes
ago was so still and quiet, is now all bustle; the early vendors of
the morning papers have arrived, and you are assailed on all sides
with shouts of '*Times*, gen'lm'n, *Times*'. 'Here's *Chron—Chron—
Chron*', '*Herald*, ma'am', 'Hightly interesting murder, gen'lm'n',
'Curious case o' breach o' promise, ladies'. The inside passengers
are already in their dens, and the outsides, with the exception of
yourself, are pacing up and down the pavement to keep themselves
warm; they consist of two young men with very long hair, to
which the sleet has communicated the appearance of crystallized
rats' tails; one thin young woman cold and peevish, one old
gentleman ditto ditto, and something in a cloak and cap, intended
to represent a military officer; every member of the party, with a
large stiff shawl over his chin, looking exactly as if he were playing a set of Pan's pipes.

'Take off the cloths, Bob,' says the coachman, who now appears for the first time, in a rough blue greatcoat, of which the buttons behind are so far apart, that you can't see them both at the same time. 'Now, gen'lm'n,' cries the guard, with the waybill in his hand. 'Five minutes behind time already!' Up jump the passengers —the two young men smoking like lime-kilns, and the old gentleman grumbling audibly. The thin young woman is got upon the roof, by dint of a great deal of pulling, and pushing, and helping and trouble, and she repays it by expressing her solemn conviction that she will never be able to get down again.

'All right,' sings out the guard at last, jumping up as the coach starts, and blowing his horn directly afterwards, in proof of the soundness of his wind. 'Let 'em go, Harry, give 'em their heads,' cried the coachman—and off we start as briskly as if the morning were 'all right', as well as the coach: and looking forward as anxiously to the termination of our journey, as we fear our readers will have done, long since, to the conclusion of our paper.

The Evening Chronicle, February 19th, 1835
Sketches by Boz, Volume 2, 1836

Private Theatres

———⊃∘◉∘⊂———

RICHARD THE THIRD.—DUKE OF GLO'STER, 2l.; EARL
OF RICHMOND, 1l.; DUKE OF BUCKINGHAM, 15s.; CATES-
BY, 12s.; TRESSEL, 10s. 6d.; LORD STANLEY, 5s.; LORD
MAYOR OF LONDON, 2s. 6d.

Such are the written placards wafered up in the gentlemen's
dressing-room, or the green-room (where there is any), at a
private theatre; and such are the sums extracted from the
shop-till, or overcharged in the office expenditure, by the donkeys
who are prevailed upon to pay for permission to exhibit their
lamentable ignorance and boobyism on the stage of a private
theatre. This they do, in proportion to the scope afforded by the
character for the display of their imbecility. For instance, the Duke
of Glo'ster is well worth two pounds, because he has it all to himself; he must wear a real sword, and what is better still, he must
draw it several times in the course of the piece. The soliloquies
alone are well worth fifteen shillings; then there is the stabbing
King Henry—decidedly cheap at three-and-sixpence, that's eigh-
teen-and-sixpence; bullying the coffin-bearers—say eighteenpence, though it's worth much more—that's a pound. Then the
love scene with Lady Ann, and the bustle of the fourth act can't be
dear at ten shillings more—that's only one pound ten, including
the 'off with his head!'—which is sure to bring down the applause,
and it is very easy to do—'Orf with his 'ed' (very quick and loud;
then slow and sneeringly)—'So much for Bu-u-u-uckingham!'
Lay the emphasis on the 'uck'; get yourself gradually into a
corner, and work with your right hand, while you're saying it,
as if you were feeling your way, and it's sure to do. The tent scene
is confessedly worth half a sovereign, and so you have the fight in,

gratis, and everybody knows what an effect may be produced by a
good combat. One—two—three—four—over; then, one—two—
three—four—under; then thrust; then dodge and slide about;
then fall down on one knee; then fight upon it, and then get up
again and stagger. You may keep on doing this, as long as it
seems to take—say ten minutes—and then fall down (backwards, if you can manage it without hurting yourself), and die
game: nothing like it for producing an effect. They always do it
at Astley's and Sadler's Wells, and if they don't know how to do
this sort of thing, who in the world does? A small child, or a
female in white, increases the interest of a combat materially—
indeed, we are not aware that a regular legitimate terrific broadsword combat could be done without; but it would be rather
difficult, and somewhat unusual, to introduce this effect in the last
scene of Richard the Third, so the only thing to be done is, just to
make the best of a bad bargain, and be as long as possible fighting
it out.

The principal patrons of private theatres are dirty boys, low
copying-clerks in attorneys' offices, capacious-headed youths from
city counting-houses, Jews whose business, as lenders of fancy
dresses, is a sure passport to the amateur stage, shop-boys who
now and then mistake their masters' money for their own; and a
choice miscellany of idle vagabonds. The proprietor of a private
theatre may be an ex-scene-painter, a low coffee-house-keeper, a
disappointed eighth-rate actor, a retired smuggler, or uncertifi-
cated bankrupt. The theatre itself may be in Catherine Street,
Strand, the purlieus of the city, the neighbourhood of Gray's Inn
Lane, or the vicinity of Sadler's Wells; or it may, perhaps, form
the chief nuisance of some shabby street, on the Surrey side of
Waterloo Bridge.

The lady performers pay nothing for their characters, and, it is
needless to add, are usually selected from one class of society; the
audiences are necessarily of much the same character as the performers, who receive, in return for their contributions to the
management, tickets to the amount of the money they pay.

All the minor theatres in London, especially the lowest, constitute the centre of a little stage-struck neighbourhood. Each of

them has an audience exclusively its own; and at any you will see
dropping into the pit at half-price, or swaggering into the back of
a box, if the price of admission be a reduced one, divers boys of
from fifteen to twenty-one years of age, who throw back their
coat and turn up their wristbands, after the portraits of Count
D'Orsay, hum tunes and whistle when the curtain is down, by way
or persuading the people near them that they are not at all anxious
to have it up again, and speak familiarly of the inferior performers
as Bill Such-a-one, and Ned So-and-so, or tell each other how a
new piece called *The Unknown Bandit of the Invisible Cavern* is in
rehearsal; how Mister Palmer is to play *The Unknown Bandit*;
how Charley Scarton is take the part of an English sailor, and
fight a broadsword combat with six unknown bandits, at one and
the same time (one theatrical sailor is always equal to half a dozen
men at least); how Mister Palmer and Charley Scarton are to go
through a double hornpipe in fetters in the second act; how the
interior of the invisible cavern is to occupy the whole extent of the
stage; and other town-surprising theatrical announcements.
These gentlemen are the amateurs—the *Richards, Shylocks,
Beverleys,* and *Othellos*—the *Young Dorntons, Rovers, Captain
Absolutes,* and *Charles Surfaces*—of a private theatre.

See them at the neighbouring public house or the theatrical
coffee-shop! They are the kings of the place, supposing no real
performers to be present; and roll about, hats on one side, and
arms a-kimbo, as if they had actually come into possession of
eighteen shillings a week, and a share of a ticket night. If one of
them does but know an Astley's supernumerary he is a happy
fellow. The mingled air of envy and admiration with which his
companions will regard him, as he converses familiarly with some
mouldy-looking man in a fancy neckerchief, whose partially
corked eyebrows, and half-rouged face, testify to the fact of his
having just left the stage or the circle, sufficiently shows in what
high admiration these public characters are held.

With the double view of guarding against the discovery of
friends or employers, and enhancing the interest of an assumed
character, by attaching a high-sounding name to its representative, these geniuses assume fictitious names, which are not the

least amusing part of the play-bill of a private theatre. Belville, Melville, Treville, Berkeley, Randolph, Byron, St Clair, and so forth, are among the humblest; and the less imposing titles of Jenkins, Walker, Thompson, Barker, Solomons, &c, are completely laid aside. There is something imposing in this, and it is an excellent apology for shabbiness into the bargain. A shrunken, faded coat, a decayed hat, a patched and soiled pair of trousers— nay, even a very dirty shirt (and none of these appearances are very uncommon among the members of the *corps dramatique*) may be worn for the purpose of disguise, and to prevent the remotest chance of recognition. Then it prevents any troublesome inquiries or explanations about employment and pursuits; everybody is a gentleman at large, for the occasion, and there are none of those unpleasant and unnecessary distinctions to which even genius must occasionally succumb elsewhere. As to the ladies (God bless them), they are quite above any formal absurdities; the mere circumstance of your being behind the scenes is a sufficient introduction to their society—for of course they know that none but strictly respectable persons would be admitted into that close fellowship with them which acting engenders. They place implicit reliance on the manager, no doubt; and as to the manager, he is all affability when he knows you well—or, in other words, when he has pocketed your money once, and entertains confident hopes of doing so again.

A quarter before eight—there will be a full house tonight— six parties in the boxes, already; four little boys and a woman in the pit; and two fiddles and a flute in the orchestra, who have got through five overtures since seven o'clock (the hour fixed for the commencement of the performances), and have just begun the sixth. There will be plenty of it, though, when it does begin, for there is enough in the bill to last six hours at least.

That gentleman in the white hat and checked shirt, brown coat and brass buttons, lounging behind the stage-box on the O.P. side, is Mr Horatio St Julien, alias Jem Larkins. His line is genteel comedy—his father's, coal and potato. He *does* Alfred Highflier in the last piece, and very well he'll do it—at the price. The party of gentlemen in the opposite box, to whom he has just nodded, are friends and supporters of Mr Beverley (otherwise Loggins), the *Macbeth* of the night. You observe their attempts to appear easy and gentlemanly, each member of the party, with his feet cocked upon the cushion in front of the box! They let them do these things here, upon the same humane principle which permits poor people's children to knock double knocks at the door of an empty house— because they can't do it anywhere else. The two stout men in the centre box, with an opera-glass ostentatiously placed before them, are friends of the proprietor—opulent country managers, as he confidently informs every individual among the crew behind the curtain—opulent country managers looking out for recruits; a representation which Mr Nathan, the dresser, who is in the manager's interest, and has just arrived with the costumes, offers to confirm upon oath if required—corroborative evidence, how- ever, is quite unnecessary, for the gulls believe it at once.

The stout Jewess who has just entered is the mother of the pale bony little girl, with the necklace of blue glass beads, sitting by her; she is being brought up to 'the profession'. Pantomime is to be her line, and she is coming out tonight, in a hornpipe after the tragedy. The short thin man beside Mr St Julien, whose white face is so deeply seared with the smallpox, and whose dirty shirt- front is inlaid with open-work, and embossed with coral studs like ladybirds, is the low comedian and comic singer of the establish- ment. The remainder of the audience—a tolerably numerous one by this time—are a motley group of dupes and blackguards.

The footlights have just made their appearance: the wicks of the six little oil lamps round the only tier of boxes are being turned up, and the additional light thus afforded serves to show the presence of dirt, and absence of paint, which forms a prominent feature in the audience part of the house. As these preparations, however, announce the speedy commencement of the play, let us take a peep 'behind', previous to the ringing-up.

The little narrow passages beneath the stage are neither especially clean nor too brilliantly lighted; and the absence of any flooring, together with the damp mildewy smell which pervades the place, does not conduce in any great degree to their comfort- able appearance. Don't fall over this plate basket—it's one of the 'properties'—the caldron for the witches' cave; and the three un-couth-looking figures, with broken clothes-props in their hands, who are drinking gin-and-water out of a pint pot, are the weird sisters. This miserable room, lighted by candles in sconces placed at lengthened intervals round the wall, is the dressing-room common to the gentlemen performers, and the square hole in the ceiling is *the* trap-door of the stage above. You will observe that the ceiling is ornamented with the beams that support the boards, and tastefully hung with cobwebs.

The characters in the tragedy are all dressed, and their own clothes are scattered in hurried confusion over the wooden dresser which surrounds the room. That snuff-shop-looking figure, in front of the glass, is *Banquo*: and the young lady with the liberal display of legs, who is kindly painting his face with a hare's foot, is dressed for *Fleance*. The large woman, who is con-sulting the stage directions in Cumberland's edition of *Macbeth*, is the *Lady Macbeth* of the night; she is always selected to play the part, because she is tall and stout, and *looks* a little like Mrs Siddons—at a considerable distance. That stupid-looking milksop, with light hair and bow legs—a kind of man whom you can war-rant town-made—is fresh caught; he plays *Malcolm* tonight, just to accustom himself to an audience. He will get on better by degrees; he will play *Othello* in a month, and in a month more, will very probably be apprehended on a charge of embezzlement. The black-eyed female with whom he is talking so earnestly, is dressed for the 'gentlewoman'. It is *her* first appearance, too—in that character. The boy of fourteen who is having his eyebrows smeared with soap and whitening, is *Duncan*, King of Scotland; and the two dirty men with the corked countenances, in very old green tunics, and dirty drab boots, are the 'army'.

'Look sharp below there, gents,' exclaims the dresser, a red-headed and red-whiskered Jew, calling through the trap; 'they're a-going to ring up. The flute says he'll be blowed if he plays any more, and they're getting precious noisy in front.' A general rush immediately takes place to the half-dozen little steep steps leading to the stage, and the heterogeneous group are soon assembled at the side scenes, in breathless anxiety and motley confusion.

[57]

'Now,' cries the manager, consulting the written list which hangs behind the first P.S. wing, 'Scene 1, open country—lamps down—thunder and lightning—all ready, White?' [This is addressed to one of the army.] 'All ready.'—'Very well. Scene 2, front chamber. Is the front chamber down?'—'Yes.'—'Very well.'—'Jones' [to the other army who is up in the flies]. 'Hallo!'—'Wind up the open country when we ring up.'—'I'll take care.'—'Scene 3, back perspective with practical bridge. Bridge ready, White? Got the "tressels" there?'—'All right.

'Very well. Clear the stage,' cries the manager, hastily packing every member of the company into the little space there is between the wings and the wall, and one wing and another. 'Places, places. Now then, Witches — Duncan — Malcolm — bleeding officer — where's the bleeding officer?' — 'Here!' replies the officer, who has been rose-pinking for the character. 'Get ready, then; now, White, ring the second music-bell.' The actors who are to be discovered are hastily arranged, and the actors who are not to be discovered place themselves, in their anxiety to peep at the house, just where the audience can see them. The bell rings, and the orchestra, in acknowledgment of the call, play three distinct chords. The bell rings — the tragedy(!) opens — and our description closes.

The Evening Chronicle, August 11th, 1835
Sketches by Boz, Volume 2, 1836

A Parliamentary Sketch

We hope our readers will not be alarmed at this rather ominous title. We assure them that we are not about to become political, neither have we the slightest intention of being more prosy than usual—if we can help it. It has occurred to us that a slight sketch of the general aspect of 'the House', and the crowds that resort to it on the night of an important debate, would be productive of some amusement: and as we have made some few calls at the aforesaid house in our time—have visited it quite often enough for our purpose, and a great deal too often for our personal peace and comfort—we have determined to attempt the description. Dismissing from our minds, therefore, all that feeling of awe which vague ideas of breaches of privilege, Serjeant-at-Arms, heavy denunciations, and still heavier fees, are calculated to awaken, we enter at once into the building, and upon our subject.

Half past four o'clock—and at five the mover of the Address will be 'on his legs', as the newspapers announce sometimes by way of novelty, as if speakers were occasionally in the habit of standing on their heads. The members are pouring in, one after the other, in shoals. The few spectators who can obtain standing room in the passages scrutinize them as they pass, with the utmost interest, and the man who can identify a member occasionally becomes a person of great importance. Every now and then you hear earnest whispers of 'That's Sir John Thomson.' 'Which? Him with the gilt order round his neck?' 'No, no; that's one of the messengers—that other with the yellow gloves, is Sir John Thomson.' 'Here's Mr Smith.' 'Lor!' 'Yes, how d'ye do, sir?—(He is our new member)—How do you do, sir?' Mr Smith stops: turns round with an air of enchanting urbanity (for the rumour of an intended dissolution has been very extensively circulated this morning); seizes both the hands of his gratified constituent, and, after greeting him with the most enthusiastic warmth, darts into the lobby with an extraordinary display of ardour in the public cause, leaving an immense impression in his favour on the mind of his 'fellow townsman'.

The arrivals increase in number, and the heat and noise increase in very unpleasant proportion. The livery servants form a complete lane on either side of the passage, and you reduce yourself into the smallest possible space to avoid being turned out. You see that stout man with the hoarse voice, in the blue coat, queer-crowned, broad-brimmed hat, white corduroy breeches, and great boots, who has been talking incessantly for half an hour past, and whose importance has occasioned no small quantity of mirth among the strangers. That is the great conservator of the peace of Westminster. You cannot fail to have remarked the grace with which he saluted the noble Lord who passed just now, or the excessive dignity of his air as he expostulates with the crowd. He is rather out of temper now, in consequence of the very irreverent behaviour of those two young fellows behind him, who have done nothing but laugh all the time they have been here.

'Will they divide tonight, do you think, Mr ——?' timidly inquires a little thin man in the crowd, hoping to conciliate the man of office.

'How *can* you ask such questions, sir?' replies the functionary, in an incredibly loud key, and pettishly grasping the thick stick he carries in his right hand. 'Pray do not, sir. I beg of you; pray do not, sir.' The little man looks remarkably out of his element, and the uninitiated part of the throng are in positive convulsions of laughter.

Just at this moment some unfortunate individual appears, with a very smirking air, at the bottom of the long passage. He has managed to elude the vigilance of the special constable downstairs, and is evidently congratulating himself on having made his way so far.

'Go back, sir—you must *not* come here,' shouts the hoarse one, with tremendous emphasis of voice and gesture, the moment the offender catches his eye.

The stranger pauses.

'Do you hear, sir—will you go back?' continues the official dignitary, gently pushing the intruder some half-dozen yards.

'Come, don't push me,' replies the stranger, turning angrily round.

'I will, sir.'

'You won't, sir.'

'Go out, sir.'

'Take your hands off me, sir.'

'Go out of the passage, sir.'

'You're a Jack-in-office, sir.'

'A what?' ejaculates he of the boots.

'A Jack-in-office, sir, and a very insolent fellow,' reiterates the stranger, now completely in a passion.

'Pray do not force me to put you out, sir,' retorts the other—'pray do not—my instructions are to keep this passage clear—it's the Speaker's orders, sir.'

'D—n the Speaker, sir!' shouts the intruder.

'Here, Wilson!—Collins!' gasps the officer, actually paralysed at this insulting expression, which in his mind is all but high treason; 'take this man out—take him out, I say! How dare you, sir?' and down goes the unfortunate man five stairs at a time, turning round at every stoppage, to come back again, and denouncing bitter vengeance against the commander-in-chief and all his supernumeraries.

'Make way, gentlemen—pray make way for the Members, I beg of you!' shouts the zealous officer, turning back, and preceding a whole string of the liberal and independent.

You see this ferocious-looking gentleman, with a complexion almost as sallow as his linen, and whose large black moustache would give him the appearance of a figure in a hairdresser's window, if his countenance possessed the thought which is communicated to those waxen caricatures of the human face divine. He is a militia officer, and the most amusing person in the House. Can anything be more exquisitely absurd than the burlesque grandeur of his air, as he strides up to the lobby, his eyes rolling like those of a Turk's head in a cheap Dutch clock? He never appears without that bundle of dirty papers which he carries under his left arm, and which are generally supposed to be the miscellaneous estimates for 1804, or some equally important documents. He is very punctual in his attendance at the House, and his self-satisfied 'He-ar-He-ar', is not unfrequently the signal for a general titter.

This is the gentleman who once actually sent a messenger up to the Strangers' Gallery in the old House of Commons, to inquire the name of an individual who was using an eye-glass, in order that he might complain to the Speaker that the person in question was quizzing him! On another occasion, he is reported to have repaired to Bellamy's kitchen—a refreshment-room, where persons who are not Members are admitted on sufferance, as it were—and perceiving two or three gentlemen at supper, who he was aware were not Members, and could not, in that place, very well resent his behaviour, he indulged in the pleasantry of sitting with his booted leg on the table at which they were supping! He is generally harmless, though, and always amusing.

By dint of patience, and some little interest with our friend the constable, we have contrived to make our way to the Lobby, and you can just manage to catch an occasional glimpse of the House, as the door is opened for the admission of Members. It is tolerably full already, and little groups of Members are congregated together here, discussing the interesting topics of the day.

That smart-looking fellow in the black coat with velvet facings and cuffs, who wears his *D'Orsay* hat so rakishly, is 'Honest Tom', a metropolitan representative; and the large man in the cloak with the white lining—not the man by the pillar; the other with the light hair hanging over his coat collar behind—is his colleague. The quiet gentlemanly-looking man in the blue surtout, grey trousers, white neckerchief, and gloves, whose closely-buttoned coat displays his manly figure and broad chest to great advantage, is a very well-known character. He has fought a great many battles in his time, and conquered like the heroes of old, with no other arms than those the gods gave him. The old hard-featured man who is standing near him is really a good specimen of a class of men now nearly extinct. He is a county Member, and has been from time whereof the memory of man is not to the contrary. Look at his loose, wide, brown coat, with capacious pockets on each side; the knee-breeches and boots, the immensely long waistcoat, and silver watch-chain dangling below it, the wide-brimmed brown hat, and the white handkerchief tied in a great bow, with straggling ends sticking out beyond his shirt-frill. It is a costume one seldom sees nowadays, and when the few who wear it have died off, it will be quite extinct. He can tell you long stories of Fox, Pitt, Sheridan, and Canning, and how much better the House was managed in those times, when they used to get up at eight or nine o'clock, except on regular field-days, of which everybody was apprised beforehand. He has a great contempt for all young Members of Parliament, and thinks it quite impossible that a man can say anything worth hearing, unless he has sat in the House for fifteen years at least without saying anything at all. He is of opinion that 'that young Macaulay' was a regular impostor; he allows that Lord Stanley may do something one of these days, but 'he's too young, sir—too young'. He is an excellent authority on points of precedent, and when he grows talkative, after his wine, will tell you how Sir Somebody Something, when he was whipper-in for the Government, brought four men out of their beds to vote in the majority, three of whom died on their way home again; how the House once divided on the question, that fresh candles be now brought in; how the Speaker was once upon a time left in the chair by accident, at the conclusion of business, and was obliged to sit in the House by himself for three hours, till some Member could be knocked up and brought back again, to move the adjournment; and a great many other anecdotes of a similar description.

There he stands, leaning on his stick; looking at the throng of Exquisites around him with most profound contempt; and conjuring up, before his mind's eye, the scenes he beheld in the old House, in days gone by, when his own feelings were fresher and brighter, and when, as he imagines, wit, talent, and patriotism flourished more brightly, too.

You are curious to know who that young man in the rough greatcoat is, who has accosted every Member who has entered the House since we have been standing here. He is not a Member; he is only an 'hereditary bondsman', or, in other words, an Irish correspondent of an Irish newspaper, who has just procured his forty-second frank from a Member whom he never saw in his life before. There he goes again—another! Bless the man, he has his hat and pockets full already.

We will try our fortune at the Strangers' Gallery, though the nature of the debate encourages very little hope of success. What on earth are you about? Holding up your order as if it were a talisman at whose command the wicket would fly open? Nonsense. Just preserve the order for an autograph, if it be worth keeping at all, and make your appearance at the door with your thumb and forefinger expressively inserted in your waistcoat-pocket. This tall stout man in black is the doorkeeper. 'Any room?' 'Not an inch—two or three dozen gentlemen waiting downstairs on the chance of somebody's going out.' Pull out your purse—'Are you *quite* sure there's no room?'—'I'll go and look,' replies the doorkeeper, with a wistful glance at your purse, 'but I'm afraid there's not.' He returns, and with real feeling assures you that it is morally impossible to get near the gallery. It is of no use waiting. When you are refused admission into the Strangers' Gallery at the House of Commons, under such circumstances, you may return home thoroughly satisfied that the place must be remarkably full indeed.*

Retracing our steps through the long passage, descending the stairs, and crossing Palace Yard, we halt at a small temporary doorway adjoining the King's entrance to the House of Lords. The order of the Serjeant-at-Arms will admit you into the Reporters' Gallery, from whence you can obtain a tolerably good view of the House. Take care of the stairs, they are none of the best; through this little wicket—there. As soon as your eyes become a little used to the mist of the place, and the glare of the chandeliers below you, you will see that some unimportant personage on the Ministerial side of the House (to your right hand) is speaking, amidst a hum of voices and confusion which would

* This paper was written before the practice of exhibiting Members of Parliament, like other curiosities, for the small charge of half a crown, was abolished.

rival Babel, but for the circumstance of its being all in one language.

The 'hear, hear' which occasioned that laugh proceeded from our warlike friend with the moustache; he is sitting on the back seat against the wall, behind the Member who is speaking, looking as ferocious and intellectual as usual. Take one look around you, and retire! The body of the House and the side galleries are full of Members; some, with their legs on the back of the opposite seat; some, with theirs stretched out to their utmost length on the floor; some going out, others coming in; all talking, laughing, lounging, coughing, oh-ing, questioning, or groaning; presenting a conglomeration of noise and confusion, to be met with in no other place in existence, not even excepting Smithfield on a market-day, or a cock-pit in its glory.

But let us not omit to notice Bellamy's kitchen, or, in other words, the refreshment-room, common to both Houses of Parliament, where Ministerialists and Oppositionists, Whigs and Tories, Radicals, Peers, and Destructives, strangers from the gallery, and the more favoured strangers from below the bar, are alike at liberty to resort; where divers honourable Members prove their perfect independence by remaining during the whole of a heavy debate, solacing themselves with the creature comforts; and whence they are summoned by whippers-in, when the House is on the point of dividing; either to give their 'conscientious votes' on questions of which they are conscientiously innocent of knowing anything whatever, or to find a vent for the playful exuberance of their wine-inspired fancies, in boisterous shouts of 'Divide', occasionally varied with a little howling, barking, crowing, or other ebullitions of senatorial pleasantry.

When you have ascended the narrow staircase which, in the present temporary House of Commons, leads to the place we are describing, you will probably observe a couple of rooms on your right hand, with tables spread for dining. Neither of these is the kitchen, although they are both devoted to the same purpose; the kitchen is further on to our left, up these half-dozen stairs. Before we ascend the staircase, however, we must request you to pause in front of this little bar-place with the sash-windows; and beg

your particular attention to the steady honest-looking old fellow
in black, who is its sole occupant. Nicholas (we do not mind mentioning the old fellow's name, for if Nicholas be not a public man,
who is ?—and public men's names are public property)—Nicholas
is the butler of Bellamy's, and has held the same place, dressed
exactly in the same manner, and said precisely the same things,
ever since the oldest of its present visitors can remember. An excellent servant Nicholas is—an unrivalled compounder of salad-
dressing—an admirable preparer of soda-water and lemon—a
special mixer of cold grog and punch—and, above all, an un-
equalled judge of cheese. If the old man have such a thing as
vanity in his composition, this is certainly his pride; and if it be
possible to imagine that anything in this world could disturb his
impenetrable calmness, we should say it would be the doubting
his judgment on this important point.

We needn't tell you all this, however, for if you have an atom
of observation, one glance at his sleek, knowing-looking head and
face—his prim white neckerchief, with the wooden tie into which
it has been regularly folded for twenty years past, merging by
imperceptible degrees into a small-plaited shirt-frill—and his
comfortable-looking form encased in a well-brushed suit of black
—would give you a better idea of his real character than a column
of our poor description could convey.

Nicholas is rather out of his element now; he cannot see the
kitchen as he used to in the old House; there, one window of his
glass-case opened into the room, and then, for the edification and
behoof of more juvenile questioners, he would stand for an hour
together, answering deferential questions about Sheridan, and
Perceval, and Castlereagh, and Heaven knows who beside, with
manifest delight, always inserting a 'Mister' before every com-
moner's name.

Nicholas, like all men of his age and standing, has a great idea
of the degeneracy of the times. He seldom expresses any political
opinions, but we managed to ascertain, just before the passing of
the Reform Bill, that Nicholas was a thorough Reformer. What
was our astonishment to discover shortly after the meeting of the
first reformed Parliament, that he was a most inveterate and de-

cided Tory! It was very odd: some men change their opinions
from necessity, others from expediency, others from inspiration;
but that Nicholas should undergo any change in any respect was
an event we had never contemplated, and should have considered
impossible. His strong opinion against the clause which empowered the metropolitan districts to return Members to Parliament, too, was perfectly unaccountable.

We discovered the secret at last; the metropolitan Members
always dined at home. The rascals! As for giving additional
Members to Ireland, it was even worse—decidedly unconstitu-
tional. Why, sir, an Irish Member would go up there, and eat
more dinner than three English Members put together. He took
no wine; drank table-beer by the half-gallon; and went home to
Manchester Buildings, or Millbank Street, for his whiskey-and-
water. And what was the consequence? Why, the concern lost—
actually lost, sir—by his patronage. A queer old fellow is Nicholas,
and as completely a part of the building as the house itself. We
wonder he ever left the old place, and fully expected to see in the
papers, the morning after the fire, a pathetic account of an old
gentleman in black, of decent appearance, who was seen at one of
the upper windows when the flames were at their height, and
declared his resolute intention of falling with the floor. He must
have been got out by force. However, he was got out—here he is
again, looking as he always does, as if he had been in a band-box
ever since the last session. There he is, at his old post every night,
just as we have described him: and, as characters are scarce, and
faithful servants scarcer, long may he be there, say we!

Now, when you have taken your seat in the kitchen, and duly
noticed the large fire and roasting-jack at one end of the room—
the little table for washing glasses and draining jugs at the other
—the clock over the window opposite St Margaret's Church—the
deal tables and wax candles—the damask tablecloths and bare
floor—the plate and china on the tables, and the gridiron on the
fire; and a few other anomalies peculiar to the place—we will
point out to your notice two or three of the people present, whose
station or absurdities render them the most worthy of remark.

It is half past twelve o'clock, and as the division is not expected for an hour or two, a few Members are lounging away the time here in preference to standing at the bar of the House, or sleeping in one of the side galleries. That singularly awkward and un-gainly-looking man, in the brownish-white hat, with the strag-gling black trousers which reach about half-way down the legs of his boots, who is leaning against the meat-screen, apparently deluding himself into the belief that he is thinking about some-thing, is a splendid sample of a Member of the House of Commons concentrating in his own person the wisdom of a constituency. Observe the wig, of a dark hue but indescribable colour, for if it be naturally brown, it has acquired a black tint by long service, and if it be naturally black, the same cause has imparted to it a tinge of rusty brown; and remark how very materially the great blinker-like spectacles assist the expression of that most intelligent face. Seriously speaking, did you ever see a countenance so expres-sive of the most hopeless extreme of heavy dullness, or behold a form so strangely put together? He is no great speaker: but when he *does* address the House, the effect is absolutely irresistible.

The small gentleman with the sharp nose, who has just saluted him, is a Member of Parliament, an ex-Alderman, and a sort of amateur fireman. He, and the celebrated fireman's dog, were ob-served to be remarkably active at the conflagration of the two Houses of Parliament—they both ran up and down, and in and out, getting under people's feet, and into everybody's way, fully impressed with the belief that they were doing a great deal of good, and barking tremendously. The dog went quietly back to his kennel with the engine, but the gentleman kept up such an incessant noise for some weeks after the occurrence that he became a positive nuisance. As no more parliamentary fires have occurred, however, and as he has consequently had no more opportunities of writing to the newspapers to relate how by way of preserving pictures he cut them out of their frames, and performed other great national services, he has gradually relapsed into his old state of calmness.

That female in black—not the one whom the Lord's-Day-Bill Baronet has just chucked under the chin; the shorter of the two—is 'Jane': the Hebe of Bellamy's. Jane is as great a character as

Nicholas, in her way. Her leading features are a thorough contempt for the great majority of her visitors; her predominant quality, love of admiration, as you cannot fail to observe, if you mark the glee with which she listens to something the young Member near her mutters somewhat unintelligibly in her ear (for his speech is rather thick from some cause or other), and how playfully she digs the handle of a fork into the arm with which he detains her, by way of reply.

Jane is no bad hand at repartees, and showers them about, with a degree of liberality and total absence of reserve or constraint, which occasionally excites no small amazement in the minds of strangers. She cuts jokes with Nicholas, too, but looks up to him with a great deal of respect; the immovable stolidity with which Nicholas receives the aforesaid jokes, and looks on, at certain pastoral friskings and rompings (Jane's only recreations, and they are very innocent, too) which occasionally take place in the passage, is not the least amusing part of his character.

The two persons who are seated at the table in the corner, at the farther end of the room, have been constant guests here, for many years past; and one of them has feasted within these walls many a time, with the most brilliant characters of a brilliant period. He has gone up to the other House since then; the greater part of his boon companions have shared Yorick's fate, and his visits to Bellamy's are comparatively few.

If he really be eating his supper now, at what hour can he possibly have dined! A second solid mass of rump-steak has disappeared, and he ate the first in four minutes and three quarters, by the clock over the window. Was there ever such a personification of Falstaff! Mark the air with which he gloats over that Stilton, as he removes the napkin which has been placed beneath his chin to catch the superfluous gravy of the steak, and with what gusto he imbibes the porter which has been fetched, expressly for him, in the pewter pot. Listen to the hoarse sound of that voice, kept down as it is by layers of solids, and deep draughts of rich wine, and tell us if you ever saw such a perfect picture of a regular *gourmand*; and whether he is not exactly the man whom you would pitch upon as having been the partner of Sheridan's parliamentary carouses, the volunteer driver of the hackney-coach that took him home, and the involuntary upsetter of the whole party?

What an amusing contrast between his voice and appearance, and that of the spare, squeaking old man, who sits at the same table, and who, elevating a little cracked bantam sort of voice to its highest pitch, invokes damnation upon his own eyes or somebody else's at the commencement of every sentence he utters. 'The Captain', as they call him, is a very old frequenter of Bellamy's; much addicted to stopping 'after the House is up' (an inexpiable crime in Jane's eyes), and a complete walking reservoir of spirits and water.

The old Peer—or rather, the old man—for his peerage is of comparatively recent date—has a huge tumbler of hot punch brought him; and the other damns and drinks, and drinks and damns, and smokes. Members arrive every moment in a great bustle to report that 'The Chancellor of the Exchequer's up', and to get glasses of brandy-and-water to sustain them during the division; people who have ordered supper countermand it, and prepare to go downstairs, when suddenly a bell is heard to ring with tremendous violence, and a cry of 'Di-vi-sion!' is heard in the passage. This is enough; away rush the Members pell-mell. The room is cleared in an instant; the noise rapidly dies away; you hear the creaking of the last boot on the last stair, and are left alone with the leviathan of rump-steaks.

Originally two Sketches
The House. The Evening Chronicle, March 7th, 1835
Bellamy's. The Evening Chronicle, April 11th, 1835
Sketches by Boz, Second Series, 1837

Gin-Shops

It is a remarkable circumstance, that different trades appear to
partake of the disease to which elephants and dogs are especially
liable, and to run stark, staring, raving mad, periodically. The
great distinction between the animals and the trades is that the
former run mad with a certain degree of propriety—they are very
regular in their irregularities. We know the period at which the
emergency will arise, and provide against it accordingly. If an
elephant run mad, we are all ready for him—kill or cure—pills or
bullets, calomel in conserve of roses, or lead in a musket-barrel.
If a dog happen to look unpleasantly warm in the summer months,
and to trot about the shady side of the streets with a quarter of a
yard of tongue hanging out of his mouth, a thick leather muzzle,
which has been previously prepared in compliance with the
thoughtful injunctions of the Legislature, is instantly clapped
over his head, by way of making him cooler, and he either looks
remarkably unhappy for the next six weeks, or becomes legally
insane, and goes mad, as it were, by Act of Parliament. But these
trades are as eccentric as comets; nay, worse, for no one can calcu-
late on the recurrence of the strange appearances which betoken
the disease. Moreover, the contagion is general, and the quickness
with which it diffuses itself, almost incredible.

We will cite two or three cases in illustration of our meaning.
Six or eight years ago the epidemic began to display itself among
the linen-drapers and haberdashers. The primary symptoms were
an inordinate love of plate-glass, and a passion for gas-lights and
gilding. The disease gradually progressed, and at last attained
a fearful height. Quiet dusty old shops in different parts of town
were pulled down; spacious premises with stuccoed fronts and
gold letters were erected instead; floors were covered with

Turkey carpets; roofs supported by massive pillars; doors knocked into windows, a dozen squares of glass into one; one shopman into a dozen; and there is no knowing what would have been done, if it had not been fortunately discovered, just in time, that the Commissioners of Bankruptcy were as competent to decide such cases as the Commissioners of Lunacy, and that a little confinement and gentle examination did wonders. The disease abated. It died away. A year or two of comparative tranquillity ensued. Suddenly it burst out again amongst the chemists; the symptoms were the same, with the addition of a strong desire to stick the royal arms over the shop door, and a great rage for mahogany, varnish, and expensive floorcloth. Then the hosiers were infected, and began to pull down their shop fronts with frantic recklessness. The mania again died away, and the public began to congratulate themselves on its entire disappearance, when it burst forth with tenfold violence among the publicans, and keepers of 'wine vaults'. From that moment it has spread among them with unprecedented rapidity, exhibiting a concatenation of all the previous symptoms; onward it has rushed to every part of town, knocking down all the old public houses, and depositing splendid mansions, stone balustrades, rosewood fittings, immense lamps, and illuminated clocks, at the corner of every street.

The extensive scale on which these places are established, and the ostentatious manner in which the business of even the smallest among them is divided into branches, is amusing. A handsome plate of ground glass in one door directs you 'To the Counting-house'; another to the 'Bottle Department'; a third to the 'Wholesale Department'; a fourth to 'The Wine Promenade'; and so forth, until we are in daily expectation of meeting with a 'Brandy Bell', or a 'Whiskey Entrance'. Then, ingenuity is exhausted in devising attractive titles for the different descriptions of gin; and the dram-drinking portion of the community as they gaze upon the gigantic black and white announcements, which are only to be equalled in size by the figures beneath them, are left in a state of pleasing hesitation between 'The Cream of the Valley', 'The Out and Out', 'The No Mistake', 'The Good for Mixing',

'The Real Knock-me-down', 'The celebrated Butter Gin', 'The regular Flare-up', and a dozen other, equally inviting and whole-some *liqueurs*. Although places of this description are to be met with in every second street, they are invariably numerous and splendid in precise proportion to the dirt and poverty of the sur-rounding neighbourhood. The gin-shops in and near Drury Lane, Holborn, St Giles's, Covent Garden, and Clare Market, are the handsomest in London. There is more of filth and squalid misery near those great thoroughfares than in any part of this mighty city.

We will endeavour to sketch the bar of a large gin-shop, and its ordinary customers, for the edification of such of our readers as may not have had opportunities of observing such scenes; and on the chance of finding one well suited to our purpose, we will make for Drury Lane, through the narrow streets and dirty courts which divide it from Oxford Street, and that classical spot adjoining the brewery at the bottom of Tottenham Court Road, best known to the initiated as the 'Rookery'.

The filthy and miserable appearance of this part of London can hardly be imagined by those (and there are many such) who have not witnessed it. Wretched houses with broken windows patched with rags and paper: every room let out to a different family, and in many instances to two or even three—fruit and 'sweet-stuff' manufacturers in the cellars, barbers and red-herring vendors in the front parlours, cobblers in the back; a bird-fancier on the first floor, three families on the second, starvation in the attics, Irishmen in the passage, a 'musician' in the front kitchen, and a char-woman and five hungry children in the back one—filth everywhere—a gutter before the houses and a drain behind—clothes drying and slops emptying, from the windows; girls of fourteen or fifteen, with matted hair, walking about barefoot, and in white greatcoats, almost their only covering; boys of all ages, in coats of all sizes and no coats at all; men and women, in every variety of scanty and dirty apparel, lounging, scolding, drinking, smoking, squabbling, fighting, and swearing,.

You turn the corner. What a change! All is light and brilliancy. The hum of many voices issues from that splendid gin-shop which forms the commencement of the two streets opposite; and the gay building with the fantastically ornamented parapet, the illuminated clock, the plate-glass windows surrounded by stucco rosettes, and its profusion of gas-lights in richly gilt burners, is perfectly dazzling when contrasted with the darkness and dirt we have just left. The interior is even gayer than the exterior. A bar of French-polished mahogany, elegantly carved, extends the whole width of the place; and there are two side-aisles of great casks, painted green and gold, enclosed within a light brass rail, and bearing such inscriptions as 'Old Tom, 549'; 'Young Tom, 360'; 'Samson, 1421'—the figures agreeing, we presume, with 'gallons', understand. Beyond the bar is a lofty and spacious saloon, full of the same enticing vessels, with a gallery running round it, equally well furnished. On the counter, in addition to the usual spirit apparatus, are two or three little baskets of cakes and biscuits, which are carefully secured at the top with wicker-work, to prevent their contents being unlawfully abstracted. Behind it are two showily dressed damsels with large necklaces, dispensing the spirits and 'compounds'. They are assisted by the ostensible proprietor of the concern, a stout coarse fellow in a fur cap, put on very much on one side to give him a knowing air, and to display his sandy whiskers to the best advantage.

The two old washerwomen, who are seated on the little bench to the left of the bar, are rather overcome by the head-dresses and haughty demeanour of the youg ladies who officiate. They receive their half-quartern of gin and peppermint, with consider-able deference, prefacing a request for 'one of them soft biscuits' with a 'Jist be good enough, ma'am'. They are quite astonished at the impudent air of the young fellow in a brown coat and bright buttons, who, ushering in his two companions, and walking up to the bar in as careless a manner as if he had been used to green and gold ornaments all his life, winks at one of the young ladies with singular coolness, and calls for a 'kervorten and a three-out-glass', just as if the place were his own. 'Gin for you, sir?' says the young lady when she has drawn it: carefully looking every way but the right one, to show that the wink had no effect upon her. 'For me, Mary, my dear,' replies the gentleman in brown. 'My name an't Mary as it happens,' says the young girl, rather relaxing as she delivers the change. 'Well, if it an't, it ought to be,' responds the irresistible one; 'all the Marys as ever *I* see, was handsome gals.' Here the young lady, not precisely remembering how blushes are managed in such cases, abruptly ends the flirtation by addressing the female in the faded feathers who has just entered, and who, after stating explicitly, to prevent any subsequent misunderstanding, that 'this gentleman pays', calls for 'a glass of port wine and a bit of sugar'.

Those two old men who came in 'just to have a drain', finished their third quartern a few seconds ago; they have made themselves crying drunk: and the fat comfortable-looking elderly women, who had 'a glass of rum-srub' each, having chimed in with their complaints on the hardness of the times, one of the women has agreed to stand a glass round, jocularly observing that 'grief never mended no broken bones, and as good people's wery scarce, what I says is, make the most on 'em, and that's all about it!' a sentiment which appears to afford unlimited satisfaction to those who have nothing to pay.

It is growing late, and the throng of men, women, and children, who have been constantly going in and out, dwindles down to two or three occasional stragglers—cold, wretched-looking creatures, in the last stage of emaciation and disease. The knot of Irish labourers at the lower end of the place, who have been alternately shaking hands with, and threatening the life of each other, for the last hour, become furious in their disputes, and finding it impossible to silence one man, who is particularly anxious to adjust the difference, they resort to the expedient of knocking him down and jumping on him afterwards. The man in the fur cap, and the potboy rush out; a scene of riot and confusion ensues; half the Irishmen get shut out, and the other half get shut in; the potboy is knocked among the tubs in no time; the landlord hits everybody, and everybody hits the landlord; the barmaids scream; the police come in; the rest is a confused mixture of arms, legs, staves, torn coats, shouting, and struggling. Some of the party are borne off to the station-house, and the remainder slink home to beat their wives for complaining, and kick the children for daring to be hungry.

We have sketched this subject very slightly, not only because our limits compel us to do so, but because, if it were pursued farther, it would be painful and repulsive. Well-disposed gentlemen, and charitable ladies, would alike turn with coldness and disgust from a description of the drunken besotted men, and wretched broken-down miserable women, who form no inconsiderable portion of the frequenters of these haunts; forgetting, in the pleasant consciousness of their own rectitude, the poverty of the one, and the temptation of the other. Gin-drinking is a great vice in England, but wretchedness and dirt are a greater; and until you improve the homes of the poor, or persuade a half-famished wretch not to seek relief in the temporary oblivion of his own misery, with the pittance which, divided among his family, would furnish a morsel of bread for each, gin-shops will increase in number and splendour. If Temperance Societies would suggest an antidote against hunger, filth, and foul air, or could establish dispensaries for the gratuitous distribution of bottles of Lethe-water, gin-palaces would be numbered among the things that were.

The Evening Chronicle, February 7th, 1835
Sketches by Boz, Volume 1, 1836

Astley's

We never see any very large, staring, black Roman capitals, in a book, or shop window, or placarded on a wall, without their immediately recalling to our mind an indistinct and confused recollection of the time when we were first initiated in the mysteries of the alphabet. We almost fancy we see the pin's point following the letter, to impress its form more strongly on our bewildered imagination; and wince involuntarily, as we remember the hard knuckles with which the reverend old lady who instilled into our mind the first principles of education for ninepence per week, or ten and sixpence per quarter, was wont to poke our juvenile head occasionally, by way of adjusting the confusion of ideas in which we were generally involved. The same kind of feeling pursues us in many other instances, but there is no place which recalls so strongly our recollections of childhood as Astley's. It was not a 'Royal Amphitheatre' in those days, nor had Ducrow arisen to shed the light of classic taste and portable gas over the sawdust of the circus; but the whole character of the place was the same, the pieces were the same, the clown's jokes were the same, the riding-masters were equally grand, the comic performers equally witty, the tragedians equally hoarse, and the 'highly trained chargers' equally spirited. Astley's has altered for the better— we have changed for the worse. Our histrionic taste is gone, and with shame we confess that we are far more delighted and amused with the audience than with the pageantry we once so highly appreciated.

We like to watch a regular Astley's party in the Easter or Midsummer holidays—pa and ma, and nine or ten children, varying from five foot six to two foot eleven: from fourteen years of age to four. We had just taken our seat in one of the boxes, in the

centre of the house, the other night, when the next was occupied
by just such a party as we should have attempted to describe, had
we depicted our *beau ideal* of a group of Astley's visitors.

First of all, there came three little boys and a little girl, who,
in pursuance of pa's directions, issued in a very audible voice from
the box door, occupied the front row; then two more little girls
were ushered in by a young lady, evidently the governess. Then
came three more little boys, dressed like the first, in blue jackets
and trousers, with lay-down shirt-collars: then a child in a braided
frock, and high state of astonishment, with very large round eyes,
opened to their utmost width, was lifted over the seats—a
process which occasioned a considerable display of little pink
legs—then came ma and pa, and then the eldest son, a boy of
fourteen years old, who was evidently trying to look as if he did
not belong to the family.

The first five minutes were occupied in taking the shawls off
the little girls, and adjusting the bows which ornamented their
hair; then it was providentially discovered that one of the little
boys was seated behind a pillar and could not see, so the governess
was stuck behind the pillar, and the boy lifted into her place. Then
pa drilled the boys, and directed the stowing away of their pocket-
handkerchiefs, and ma having first nodded and winked to the
governess to pull the girls' frocks a little more off their shoulders,
stood up to review the little troop—an inspection which appeared
to terminate much to her own satisfaction, for she looked with a
complacent air at pa, who was standing up at the further end of
the seat. Pa returned the glance, and blew his nose very em-
phatically; and the poor governess peeped out from behind the
pillar, and timidly tried to catch ma's eye, with a look expressive
of her high admiration of the whole family. Then two of the little
boys who had been discussing the point whether Astley's was
more than twice as large as Drury Lane, agreed to refer it to
'George' for his decision; at which 'George', who was no other
than the young gentleman before noticed, waxed indignant, and
remonstrated in no very gentle terms on the gross impropriety of
having his name repeated in so loud a voice at a public place, on
which all the children laughed very heartily, and one of the little

boys wound up by expressing his opinion, that 'George began to think himself quite a man now', whereupon both pa and ma laughed, too; and George (who carried a dress cane and was cultivating whiskers) muttered that 'William always was encouraged in his impertinence'; and assumed a look of profound contempt, which lasted the whole evening.

The play began, and the interest of the little boys knew no bounds. Pa was clearly interested, too, although he very unsuccessfully endeavoured to look as if he wasn't. As for ma, she was perfectly overcome by the drollery of the principal comedian, and laughed till every one of the immense bows on her ample cap trembled, at which the governess peeped out from behind the pillar again, and whenever she could catch ma's eye, put her handkerchief to her mouth, and appeared, as in duty bound, to be in convulsions of laughter also. Then when the man in the splendid armour vowed to rescue the lady or perish in the attempt, the little boys applauded vehemently, especially one little fellow who was apparently on a visit to the family, and had been carrying on a child's flirtation, the whole evening, with a small coquette of twelve years old, who looked like a model of her mamma on a reduced scale; and who, in common with the other little girls (who, generally speaking, have even more coquettishness about them than much older ones), looked very properly shocked when the knight's squire kissed the princess's confidential chambermaid.

When the scenes in the circle commenced, the children were more delighted than ever; and the wish to see what was going forward completely conquering pa's dignity, he stood up in the box, and applauded as loudly as any of them. Between each feat of horsemanship the governess leant across to ma, and retailed the clever remarks of the children on that which had preceded: and ma, in the openness of her heart, offered the governess an acidulated drop, and the governess, gratified to be taken notice of, retired behind her pillar again with a brighter countenance: and the whole party seemed quite happy, except the exquisite in the back of the box, who, being too grand to take any interest in the children, and too insignificant to be taken notice of by anybody else, occupied himself, from time to time, in rubbing the place where the whiskers ought to be, and was completely alone in his glory.

We defy anyone who has been to Astley's two or three times, and is consequently capable of appreciating the perseverance with which precisely the same jokes are repeated night after night, and season after season, not to be amused with one part of the performances at least—we mean the scenes in the circle. For ourself, we know that when the hoop, composed of jets of gas, is let down, the curtain drawn up for the convenience of the half-price on their ejectment from the ring, the orange-peel cleared away, and the sawdust shaken, with mathematical precision, into a complete circle, we feel as much enlivened as the youngest child present; and actually join in the laugh which follows the clown's shrill shout of 'Here we are!' just for old acquaintance's sake. Nor can we quite divest ourself of our old feeling of reverence for the riding-master, who follows the clown with a long whip in his hand, and bows to the audience with graceful dignity. He is none of your second-rate riding-masters in nankeen dressing-gowns, with brown frogs, but the regular gentleman-attendant on the principal riders, who always wears a military uniform with a tablecloth inside the breast of the coat, in which costume he forcibly reminds one of a fowl trussed for roasting. He is—but why should we attempt to describe that of which no description can convey an adequate idea? Everybody knows the man, and everybody remembers his polished boots, his graceful demeanour, stiff, as some misjudging persons have in their jealousy considered it, and the splendid head of black hair, parted high on the forehead, to impart to the countenance an appearance of deep thought and poetic melancholy. His soft and pleasing voice, too, is in perfect unison with his noble bearing, as he humours the clown by indulging in a little badinage; and the striking recollection of his own dignity, with which he exclaims, 'Now, sir, if you please, inquire for Miss Woolford, sir', can never be forgotten. The graceful air, too, with which he introduces Miss Woolford into the arena, and, after assisting her to the saddle, follows her fairy courser round the circle, can never fail to create a deep impression in the bosom of every female servant present.

When Miss Woolford, and the horse, and the orchestra, all
stop together to take breath, he urbanely takes part in some such
dialogue as the following (commenced by the clown): 'I say, sir!'
—'Well, sir?' (it's always conducted in the politest manner).—
'Did you ever happen to hear I was in the army, sir?'—'No, sir.'
—'Oh, yes, sir—I can go through my exercise, sir.'—'Indeed,
sir!'—'Shall I do it now, sir?'—'If you please, sir; come, sir—
make haste' (a cut with the long whip, and 'Ha' done now—I
don't like it', from the clown). Here the clown throws himself on
the ground, and goes through a variety of gymnastic convulsions,
doubling himself up, and untying himself again, and making himself look very like a man in the most hopeless extreme of human
agony, to the vociferous delight of the gallery, until he is interrupted by a second cut from the long whip, and a request to see
'what Miss Woolford's stopping for'? On which, to the inex-
pressible mirth of the gallery, he exclaims, 'Now, Miss Woolford, what can I come for to go, for to fetch, for to bring, for to
carry, for to do for you, ma'am?' On the lady's announcing with
a sweet smile that she wants the two flags, they are, with sundry
grimaces, procured and handed up; the clown facetiously observing after the performance of the latter ceremony—'He, he, oh! I
say, sir, Miss Woolford knows me; she smiled at me.' Another
cut from the whip, a burst from the orchestra, a start from the
horse, and round goes Miss Woolford again on her graceful performance, to the delight of every member of the audience, young
or old. The next pause affords an opportunity for similar witti-
cisms, the only additional fun being that of the clown making
ludicrous grimaces at the riding-master every time his back is
turned; and finally quitting the circle by jumping over his head,
having previously directed his attention another way.

Did any of our readers ever notice the class of people who hang
about the stage-doors of our minor theatres in the day-time? You
will rarely pass one of these entrances without seeing a group of
three or four men conversing on the pavement, with an indescribable public-house-parlour swagger, and a kind of conscious air,
peculiar to people of this description. They always seem to think
they are exhibiting; the lamps are ever before them. That young

fellow in the faded brown coat, and very full light green trousers, pulls down the wristbands of his check shirt, as ostentatiously as if it were of the finest linen, and cocks the white hat of the summer-before-last as knowingly over his right eye, as if it were a purchase of yesterday. Look at the dirty white Berlin gloves, and the cheap silk handkerchief stuck in the bosom of his threadbare coat. Is it possible to see him for an instant, and not come to the conclusion that he is the walking gentleman who wears a blue surtout, clean collar, and white trousers, for half an hour, and then shrinks into his worn-out scanty clothes: who has to boast night after night of his splendid fortune, with the painful consciousness of a pound a week and his boots to find; to talk of his father's mansion in the country, with a dreary recollection of his own two-pair back, in the New Cut; and to be envied and flattered as the favoured lover of a rich heiress, remembering all the while that the ex-dancer at home is in the family way, and out of an engagement?

Next to him, perhaps, you will see a thin pale man, with a very long face, in a suit of shining black, thoughtfully knocking that part of his boot which once had a heel, with an ash stick. He is the man who does the heavy business, such as prosy fathers, virtuous servants, curates, landlords, and so forth.

By the way, talking of fathers, we should very much like to see some piece in which all the dramatis personæ were orphans. Fathers are invariably great nuisances on the stage, and always have to give the hero or heroine a long explanation of what was done before the curtain rose, usually commencing with 'It is now nineteen years, my dear child, since your blessed mother (here the old villain's voice falters) confided you to my charge. You were then an infant,' &c &c. Or else they have to discover, all of a sudden, that somebody whom they have been in constant com-munication with, during three long acts, without the slightest suspicion, is their own child: in which case they exclaim, 'Ah! what do I see? This bracelet! That smile! These documents! Those eyes! Can I believe my senses?—It must be!—Yes—it is, it is my child!'—'My father!' exclaims the child; and they fall into each other's arms, and look over each other's shoulders, and the audience give three rounds of applause.

To return from this digression, we were about to say that these are the sort of people whom you see talking, and attitudinizing, outside the stage-doors of our minor theatres. At Astley's they are always more numerous than at any other place. There is generally a groom or two, sitting on the window-sill, and two or three dirty shabby-genteel men in checked neckerchiefs, and sallow linen, lounging about, and carrying, perhaps, under one arm, a pair of stage shoes badly wrapped up in a piece of old news-paper. Some years ago we used to stand looking, open-mouthed, at these men, with a feeling of mysterious curiosity, the very recollection of which provokes a smile at the moment we are writing. We could not believe that the beings of light and ele-gance, in milk-white tunics, salmon-coloured legs, and blue scarfs, who flitted on sleek cream-coloured horses before our eyes at night, with all the aid of lights, music, and artificial flowers, could be the pale, dissipated-looking creatures we beheld by day.

We can hardly believe it now. Of the lower class of actors we have seen something, and it requires no great exercise of imagina-tion to identify the walking gentleman with the 'dirty swell', the comic singer with the public-house chairman, or the leading tra-gedian with drunkenness and distress; but these other men are mysterious beings, never seen out of the ring, never beheld but in the costume of gods and sylphs. With the exception of Ducrow, who can scarcely be classed among them, who ever knew a rider at Astley's, or saw him but on horseback? Can our friend in the military uniform ever appear in threadbare attire, or descend to the comparatively unwadded costume of everyday life? Impos-sible! We cannot—we will not—believe it.

The Evening Chronicle, May 9th, 1835
Sketches by Boz, Volume 1, 1835

The Prisoners' Van

We were passing the corner of Bow Street, on our return from a
lounging excursion the other afternoon, when a crowd, assembled
round the door of the Police Office, attracted our attention. We
turned up the street accordingly. There were thirty or forty
people, standing on the pavement and half across the road; and a
few stragglers were patiently stationed on the opposite side of the
way—all evidently waiting in expectation of some arrival. We
waited too, a few minutes, but nothing occurred; so we turned
round to an unshorn, sallow-looking cobbler, who was standing
next us with his hands under the bib of his apron, and put the
usual question of 'What's the matter?' The cobbler eyed us from
head to foot, with superlative contempt, and laconically replied
'Nuffin'.

Now, we were perfectly aware that if two men stop in the street
to look at any given object, or even to gaze in the air, two hundred
men will be assembled in no time; but as we knew very well that
no crowd of people could by possibility remain in a street for five
minutes without getting up a little amusement among themselves,
unless they had some absorbing object in view, the natural inquiry
next in order was, 'What are all these people waiting here for?'
—'Her Majesty's carriage,' replied the cobbler. This was still
more extraordinary. We could not imagine what earthly business
Her Majesty's carriage could have at the Public Office, Bow
Street. We were beginning to ruminate on the possible causes of
such an uncommon appearance, when a general exclamation from
all the boys in the crowd of 'Here's the wan!' caused us to raise
our heads, and look up the street.

The covered vehicle, in which prisoners are conveyed from the
police offices to the different prisons, was coming along at full

BREWER'S DRAYMAN.

speed. It then occurred to us, for the first time, that Her Majesty's carriage was merely another name for the prisoners' van, conferred upon it, not only by reason of the superior gentility of the term, but because the aforesaid van is maintained at Her Majesty's expense: having been originally started for the exclusive accommodation of ladies and gentlemen under the necessity of visiting the various houses of call known by the general denomination of 'Her Majesty's Gaols'.

The van drew up at the office door, and the people thronged round the steps, just leaving a little alley for the prisoners to pass through. Our friend the cobbler, and the other stragglers, crossed over, and we followed their example. The driver, and another man who had been seated by his side in front of the vehicle, dismounted, and were admitted into the office. The office door was closed after them, and the crowd were on the tiptoe of expectation.

After a few minutes' delay, the door again opened, and the two first prisoners appeared. They were a couple of girls, of whom the elder could not be more than sixteen, and the younger of whom had certainly not attained her fourteenth year. That they were sisters was evident from the resemblance which still subsisted between them, though two additional years of depravity had fixed their brand upon the elder girl's features, as legibly as if a red-hot iron had seared them. They were both gaudily dressed, the younger one especially; and, although there was a strong similarity between them in both respects, which was rendered the more obvious by their being handcuffed together, it is impossible to conceive a greater contrast than the demeanour of the two presented. The younger girl was weeping bitterly—not for display, or in the hope of producing effect, but for very shame; her face was buried in her handkerchief: and her whole manner was but too expressive of bitter and unavailing sorrow.

'How long are you for, Emily?' screamed a red-faced woman in the crowd. 'Six weeks and labour,' replied the elder girl with a flaunting laugh; 'and that's better than the stone jug anyhow; the mill's a deal better than the Sessions, and here's Bella a-going too for the first time. Hold up your head, you chicken,' she continued, boisterously tearing the other girl's handkerchief away. 'Hold up your head, and show 'em your face. I an't jealous, but I'm blessed if I an't game!'—'That's right, old gal,' exclaimed a man in a paper cap, who, in common with the greater part of the crowd, had been inexpressibly delighted with this little incident. —'Right!' replied the girl; 'ah, to be sure; what's the odds, eh?'— 'Come! In with you,' interrupted the driver. 'Don't you be in a hurry, coachman,' replied the girl, 'and recollect I want to be set down in Cold Bath Fields—large house with a high garden-wall in front; you can't mistake it. Hallo! Bella, where are you going to—you'll pull my precious arm off!' This was addressed to the younger girl, who, in her anxiety to hide herself in the caravan, had ascended the steps first, and forgotten the strain upon the handcuff. 'Come down, and let's show you the way.' And after jerking the miserable girl down with a force which made her stagger on the pavement, she got into the vehicle, and was followed by her wretched companion.

These two girls had been thrown upon London streets, their vices and debauchery, by a sordid and rapacious mother. What the younger girl was then, the elder had been once; and what the elder then was, the younger must soon become. A melancholy prospect, but how surely to be realized; a tragic drama, but how often acted! Turn to the prisons and police offices of London— nay, look into the very streets themselves. These things pass before our eyes, day after day, and hour after hour—they have become such matters of course, that they are utterly disregarded. The progress of these girls in crime will be as rapid as the flight of a pestilence, resembling it too in its baneful influence and wide-spreading infection. Step by step, how many wretched females, within the sphere of every man's observation, have become involved in a career of vice, frightful to contemplate; hopeless at its commencement, loathsome and repulsive in its course; friendless, forlorn, and unpitied, at its miserable conclusion!

There were other prisoners—boys of ten, as hardened in vice as men of fifty—a houseless vagrant, going joyfully to prison as a place of food and shelter, handcuffed to a man whose prospects were ruined, character lost, and family rendered destitute, by his first offence. Our curiosity, however, was satisfied. The first group had left an impression on our mind we would gladly have avoided, and would willingly have effaced.

The crowd dispersed; the vehicle rolled away with its load of guilt and misfortune; and we saw no more of the Prisoners' Van.

The Evening Chronicle, November 29th, 1835
Sketches by Boz, Volume 1, 1836 (shortened)

Meditations in Monmouth Street

We have always entertained a particular attachment towards Monmouth Street, as the only true and real emporium for second-hand wearing apparel. Monmouth Street is venerable from its antiquity, and respectable from its usefulness. Holywell Street we despise; the red-headed and red-whiskered Jews who forcibly haul you into their squalid houses, and thrust you into a suit of clothes, whether you will or not, we detest.

The inhabitants of Monmouth Street are a distinct class; a peaceable and retiring race, who immure themselves for the most part in deep cellars, or small back parlours, and who seldom come forth into the world, except in the dusk and coolness of the evening, when they may be seen seated, in chairs on the pavement, smoking their pipes, or watching the gambols of their engaging children as they revel in the gutter, a happy troop of infantine scavengers. Their countenances bear a thoughtful and a dirty cast, certain indications of their love of traffic; and their habitations are distinguished by that disregard of outward appearance and neglect of personal comfort, so common among people who are constantly immersed in profound speculations, and deeply engaged in sedentary pursuits.

We have hinted at the antiquity of our favourite spot. 'A Monmouth Street laced coat' was a byword a century ago; and still we find Monmouth Street the same. Pilot greatcoats with wooden buttons have usurped the place of the ponderous laced coats with full skirts; embroidered waistcoats with large flaps have yielded to double-breasted checks with roll-collars; and three-cornered hats of quaint appearance have given place to the low crowns and broad brims of the coachman school; but it is the times that have changed, not Monmouth Street. Through every alteration and every change, Monmouth Street has still remained the burial-place of the fashions; and such, to judge from all present appearances, it will remain until there are no more fashions to bury.

We love to walk among these extensive groves of the illustrious dead, and to indulge in the speculations to which they give rise; now fitting a deceased coat, then a dead pair of trousers, and anon the mortal remains of a gaudy waistcoat, upon some being of our own conjuring up, and endeavouring, from the shape and fashion of the garment itself, to bring its former owner before our mind's eye. We have gone on speculating in this way, until whole rows of coats have started from their pegs, and buttoned up, of their own accord, round the waists of imaginary wearers; lines of trousers have jumped down to meet them; waistcoats have almost burst with anxiety to put themselves on; and half an acre of shoes have suddenly found feet to fit them, and gone stumping down the street with a noise which has fairly awakened us from our pleasant reverie, and driven us slowly away, with a bewildered stare, an object of astonishment to the good people of Monmouth Street, and of no slight suspicion to the policemen at the opposite street corner.

We were occupied in this manner the other day, endeavouring to fit a pair of lace-up half-boots on an ideal personage, for whom, to say the truth, they were a full couple of sizes too small, when our eyes happened to alight on a few suits of clothes ranged outside a shop window, which it immediately struck us, must at different periods have all belonged to, and been worn by, the same individual, and had now, by one of those strange conjunctions of circumstances which will occur sometimes, come to be exposed together for sale in the same shop. The idea seemed a fantastic one, and we looked at the clothes again with a firm determination not to be easily led away. No, we were right; the more we looked, the more we were convinced of the accuracy of our previous impression. There was the man's whole life written as legibly on those clothes, as if we had his autobiography engrossed on parchment before us.

The first was a patched and much-soiled skeleton suit, one of those straight blue cloth cases in which small boys used to be

confined, before belts and tunics had come in, and old notions had
gone out: an ingenious contrivance for displaying the full sym-
metry of a boy's figure, by fastening him into a very tight jacket,
with an ornamental row of buttons over each shoulder, and then
buttoning his trousers over it, so as to give his legs the appearance of being hooked on, just under the armpits. This was the
boy's dress. It had belonged to a town boy, we could see; there
was a shortness about the legs and arms of the suit; and a bagging
at the knees, peculiar to the rising youth of London streets. A
small day-school he had been at, evidently. If it had been a regular
boys' school they wouldn't have let him play on the floor so much,
and rub his knees so white. He had an indulgent mother too, and
plenty of halfpence, as the numerous smears of some sticky sub-
stance about the pockets, and just below the chin, which even the
salesman's skill could not succeed in disguising, sufficiently betokened. They were decent people, but not overburdened with
riches, or he would not have so far outgrown the suit when he
passed into those corduroys with the round jacket; in which he
went to a boys' school, however, and learnt to write—and in ink
of pretty tolerable blackness, too, if the place where he used to
wipe his pen might be taken as evidence.

A black suit and the jacket changed into a diminutive coat. His
father had died, and the mother had got the boy a message-lad's
place in some office. A long-worn suit that one; rusty and threadbare before it was laid aside, but clean and free from soil to the
last. Poor woman! We could imagine her assumed cheerfulness
over the scanty meal, and the refusal of her own small portion,
that her hungry boy might have enough. Her constant anxiety for
his welfare, her pride in his growth mingled sometimes with the
thought, almost too acute to bear, that as he grew to be a man his
old affection might cool, old kindnesses fade from his mind, and
old promises be forgotten—the sharp pain that even then a careless word or a cold look would give her—all crowded on our
thoughts as vividly as if the very scene were passing before us.

These things happen every hour, and we all know it; and yet
we felt as much sorrow when we saw, or fancied we saw—it makes
no difference which—the change that began to take place now, as

if we had just conceived the bare possibility of such a thing for the first time. The next suit, smart but slovenly; meant to be gay, and yet not half so decent as the threadbare apparel; redolent of the idle lounge, and the blackguard companions, told us, we thought, that the widow's comfort had rapidly faded away. We could imagine that coat—imagine! we could see it; we *had* seen it a hundred times—sauntering in company with three or four other coats of the same cut, about some place of profligate resort at night.

We dressed, from the same shop window in an instant, half a dozen boys of from fifteen to twenty; and putting cigars into their mouths, and their hands into their pockets, watched them as they sauntered down the street, and lingered at the corner, with the obscene jest, and the oft-repeated oath. We never lost sight of them, till they had cocked their hats a little more on one side, and swaggered into the public house; and then we entered the desolate home, where the mother sat late in the night, alone; we watched her, as she paced the room in feverish anxiety, and every now and then opened the door, looked wistfully into the dark and empty street, and again returned, to be again and again disappointed. We beheld the look of patience with which she bore the brutish threat, nay, even the drunken blow; and we heard the agony of tears that gushed from her very heart, as she sank upon her knees in her solitary and wretched apartment.

A long period had elapsed, and a greater change had taken place, by the time of casting off the suit that hung above. It was that of a stout, broad-shouldered, sturdy-chested man; and we knew at once, as anybody would, who glanced at that broad-skirted green coat, with the large metal buttons, that its wearer seldom walked forth without a dog at his heels, and some idle ruffian, the very counterpart of himself, at his side. The vices of the boy had grown with the man, and we fancied his home then—if such a place deserve the name.

We saw the bare and miserable room, destitute of furniture, crowded with his wife and children, pale, hungry, and emaciated; the man cursing their lamentations, staggering to the tap-room, from whence he had just returned, followed by his wife and a sickly infant, clamouring for bread; and heard the street-wrangle and noisy recrimination that his striking her occasioned. And then imagination led us to some metropolitan workhouse, situated in the midst of crowded streets and alleys, filled with noxious vapours, and ringing with boisterous cries, where an old and feeble woman, imploring pardon for her son, lay dying in a close dark room, with no child to clasp her hand, and no pure air from heaven to fan her brow. A stranger closed the eyes that settled into a cold unmeaning glare, and strange ears received the words that murmured from the white and half-closed lips.

A coarse round frock, with a worn cotton neckerchief, and other articles of clothing of the commonest description, completed the history. A prison, and the sentence—banishment or the gallows. What would the man have given then, to be once again the contented humble drudge of his boyish years; to have been restored to life, but for a week, a day, an hour, a minute, only for so long a time as would enable him to say one word of passionate regret to, and hear one sound of heartfelt forgiveness from, the cold and ghastly form that lay rotting in the pauper's grave! The children wild in the streets, the mother a destitute widow; both deeply tainted with the deep disgrace of the husband and father's name, and impelled by sheer necessity, down the precipice that had led him to a lingering death, possibly of many years' duration, thousands of miles away. We had no clue to the end of the tale; but it was easy to guess its termination.

We took a step or two farther on, and by way of restoring the naturally cheerful tone of our thoughts, began fitting visionary feet and legs into a cellar-board full of boots and shoes, with a speed and accuracy that would have astonished the most expert artist in leather living. There was one pair of boots in particular— a jolly, good-tempered, hearty-looking pair of tops that excited our warmest regard; and we had got a fine, red-faced, jovial fellow of a market-gardener into them before we had made their acquaintance half a minute. They were just the very thing for him. There were his huge fat legs bulging over the tops, and fitting them too tight to admit of his tucking in the loops he had pulled them on by; and his knee-cords with an interval of stocking; and his blue apron tucked up round his waist; and his red neckerchief

OLD CLOTHES MAN.

and blue coat, and a white hat stuck on one side of his head; and
there he stood with a broad grin on his great red face, whistling
away, as if any other idea but that of being happy and comfortable
had never entered his brain.

This was the very man after our own heart; we knew all about
him; we had seen him coming up to Covent Garden in his green
chaise-cart, with the fat tubby little horse, half a thousand times;
and even while we cast an affectionate look upon his boots, at that
instant, the form of a coquettish servant-maid suddenly sprung
into a pair of Denmark satin shoes that stood beside them, and we
at once recognized the very girl who accepted his offer of a ride,
just on this side the Hammersmith suspension-bridge, the very
last Tuesday morning we rode into town from Richmond.

A very smart female, in a showy bonnet, stepped into a pair of
grey cloth boots, with black fringe and binding, that were studi-
ously pointing out their toes on the other side of the top-boots,
and seemed very anxious to engage his attention, but we didn't
observe that our friend the market-gardener appeared at all capti-
vated with these blandishments; for beyond giving a knowing
wink when they first began, as if to imply that he quite understood
their end and object, he took no further notice of them. His indifference, however, was amply recompensed by the excessive
gallantry of a very old gentleman with a silver-headed stick, who
tottered into a pair of large list shoes, that were standing in one
corner of the board, and indulged in a variety of gestures expressive of his admiration of the lady in the cloth boots, to the im-
measurable amusement of a young fellow we put into a pair of
long-quartered pumps, who we thought would have split the coat
that slid down to meet him, with laughing.

We had been looking on at this little pantomime with great
satisfaction for some time, when, to our unspeakable astonishment, we perceived that the whole of the characters, including a
numerous *corps de ballet* of boots and shoes in the background, into
which we had been hastily thrusting as many feet as we could press
into the service, were arranging themselves in order for dancing;
and some music striking up at the moment, to it they went without delay. It was perfectly delightful to witness the agility of the

market-gardener. Out went the boots, first on one side, then on the other, then cutting, then shuffling, then setting to the Denmark satins, then advancing, then retreating, then going round, and then repeating the whole of the evolutions again, without appearing to suffer in the least from the violence of the exercise.

Nor were the Denmark satins a bit behindhand, for they jumped and bounded about in all directions; and though they were neither so regular, nor so true to the time as the cloth boots, still, as they seemed to do it from the heart, and to enjoy it more, we candidly confess that we preferred their style of dancing to the other. But the old gentleman in the list shoes was the most amusing object in the whole party; for, besides his grotesque attempts to appear youthful, and amorous, which were sufficiently entertaining in themselves, the young fellow in the pumps managed so artfully that every time the old gentleman advanced to salute the lady in the cloth boots, he trod with his whole weight on the old fellow's toes, which made him roar with anguish, and rendered all the others like to die of laughing.

We were in the full enjoyment of these festivities when we heard a shrill, and by no means musical voice, exclaim, 'Hope you'll know me agin, imperence!' and on looking intently forward to see from whence the sound came, we found that it proceeded, not from the young lady in the cloth boots, as we had at first been inclined to suppose, but from a bulky lady of elderly appearance who was seated in a chair at the head of the cellar-steps, apparently for the purpose of superintending the sale of the articles arranged there.

A barrel-organ, which had been in full force close behind us, ceased playing; the people we had been fitting into the shoes and boots took to flight at the interruption; and as we were conscious that in the depth of our meditations we might have been rudely staring at the old lady for half an hour without knowing it, we took to flight too, and were soon immersed in the deepest obscurity of the adjacent 'Dials'.

The Morning Chronicle, September 24th, 1836
The Evening Chronicle, September 26th, 1836
Sketches by Boz, Second Series, 1837

Scotland Yard

Scotland Yard is a small—a very small—tract of land, bounded
on one side by the River Thames, on the other by the gardens of
Northumberland House: abutting at one end on the bottom of
Northumberland Street, at the other on the back of Whitehall
Place. When this territory was first accidentally discovered by a
country gentleman who lost his way in the Strand, some years
ago, the original settlers were found to be a tailor, a publican,
two eating-house keepers, and a fruit-pie maker; and it was also
found to contain a race of strong and bulky men, who repaired to
the wharves in Scotland Yard regularly every morning, about five
or six o'clock, to fill heavy wagons with coal, with which they
proceeded to distant places up the country, and supplied the inhabitants with fuel. When they had emptied their wagons, they
again returned for a fresh supply; and this trade was continued
throughout the year.

As the settlers derived their subsistence from ministering to
the wants of these primitive traders, the articles exposed for sale,
and the places where they were sold, bore strong outward marks
of being expressly adapted to their tastes and wishes. The tailor
displayed in his window a Lilliputian pair of leather gaiters, and
a diminutive round frock, while each doorpost was appropriately
garnished with a model of a coal-sack. The two eating-house
keepers exhibited joints of a magnitude, and puddings of a solid-
ity,which coalheavers alone could appreciate; and the fruit-pie
maker displayed on his well-scrubbed window-board large white
compositions of flour and dripping, ornamented with pink stains,
giving rich promise of the fruit within, which made their huge
mouths water, as they lingered past.

But the choicest spot in all Scotland Yard was the old public house in the corner. Here, in a dark wainscoted room of ancient appearance, cheered by the glow of a mighty fire, and decorated with an enormous clock, whereof the face was white, and the figures black, sat the lusty coalheavers, quaffing large draughts of Barclay's best, and puffing forth volumes of smoke, which wreathed heavily above their heads, and involved the room in a thick dark cloud. From this apartment might their voices be heard on a winter's night, penetrating to the very bank of the river, as they shouted out some sturdy chorus, or roared forth the burden of a popular song; dwelling upon the last few words with a strength and length of emphasis which made the very roof tremble above them.

Here, too, would they tell old legends of what the Thames was in ancient times, when the Patent Shot Manufactory wasn't built, and Waterloo Bridge had never been thought of; and then they would shake their heads with portentous looks, to the deep edification of the rising generation of heavers, who crowded round them, and wondered where all this would end; whereat the tailor would take his pipe solemnly from his mouth, and say, how that he hoped it might end well, but he very much doubted whether it would or not, and couldn't rightly tell what to make of it—a mysterious expression of opinion, delivered with a semi-pro-phetic air, which never failed to elicit the fullest concurrence of the assembled company; and so they would go on drinking and wondering till ten o'clock came, and with it the tailor's wife to fetch him home, when the little party broke up, to meet again in the same room, and say and do precisely the same things, on the following evening at the same hour.

About this time the barges that came up the river began to bring vague rumours to Scotland Yard of somebody in the city having been heard to say that the Lord Mayor had threatened in so many words to pull down the old London Bridge and build up a new one. At first these rumours were disregarded as idle tales, wholly destitute of foundation, for nobody in Scotland Yard doubted that if the Lord Mayor contemplated any such dark de-sign, he would just be clapped up in the Tower for a week or two, and then killed off for high treason.

By degrees, however, the reports grew stronger, and more frequent, and at last a barge, laden with numerous chaldrons of the best Wallsend, brought up the positive intelligence that several of the arches of the old bridge were stopped, and that preparations were actually in progress for constructing the new one. What an excitement was visible in the old tap-room on that memorable night! Each man looked into his neighbour's face, pale with alarm and astonishment, and read therein an echo of the sentiments which filled his own breast. The oldest heaver present proved to demonstration, that the moment the piers were removed all the water in the Thames would run clean off and leave a dry gully in its place. What was to become of the coal-barges— of the trade of Scotland Yard—of the very existence of its population? The tailor shook his head more sagely than usual, and grimly pointing to a knife on the table, bid them wait and see what happened. He said nothing—not he; but if the Lord Mayor didn't fall a victim to popular indignation, why he would be rather astonished; that was all.

They did wait; barge after barge arrived, and still no tidings of the assassination of the Lord Mayor. The first stone was laid: it was done by a Duke—the King's brother. Years passed away, and the bridge was opened by the King himself. In course of time the piers were removed; and when the people in Scotland Yard got up next morning in the confident expectation of being able to step over to Pedlar's Acre without wetting the soles of their shoes, they found to their unspeakable astonishment that the water was just where it used to be.

A result so different from that which they had anticipated from this first improvement produced its full effect upon the inhabitants of Scotland Yard. One of the eating-house keepers began to court public opinion, and to look for customers among a new class of people. He covered his little dining-tables with white cloths, and got a painter's apprentice to inscribe something about hot joints from twelve to two in one of the little panes of his shop window. Improvement began to march with rapid strides to the very threshold of Scotland Yard. A new market sprung up at Hungerford, and the Police Commissioners established their office in Whitehall Place. The traffic in Scotland Yard increased; fresh Members were added to the House of Commons, the Metropolitan Representatives found it a near cut, and many other foot passengers followed their example.

We marked the advance of civilization, and beheld it with a sigh. The eating-house keeper who manfully resisted the innovation of tablecloths was losing ground every day, as his opponent gained it, and a deadly feud sprung up between them. The genteel one no longer took his evening's pint in Scotland Yard, but drank gin and water at a 'parlour' in Parliament Street. The fruit-pie maker still continued to visit the old room, but he took to smoking cigars, and began to call himself a pastrycook, and to read the papers. The old heavers still assembled round the ancient fireplace, but their talk was mournful: and the loud song and the joyous shout were heard no more.

And what is Scotland Yard now? How have its old customs changed; and how has the ancient simplicity of its inhabitants faded away! The old tottering public house is converted into a spacious and lofty 'wine-vaults'; gold leaf has been used in the construction of the letters which emblazon its exterior, and the poet's art has been called into requisition, to intimate that if you drink a certain description of ale you must hold fast by the rail. The tailor exhibits in his window the pattern of a foreign-looking brown surtout, with silk buttons, a fur collar, and fur cuffs. He wears a stripe down the outside of each leg of his trousers: and we have detected his assistants (for he has assistants now) in the act of sitting on the shop-board in the same uniform.

At the other end of the little row of houses a bootmaker has established himself in a brick box, with the additional innovation of a first floor; and here he exposes for sale boots—real Wellington boots—an article which a few years ago none of the original inhabitants had ever seen or heard of. It was but the other day, that a dressmaker opened another little box in the middle of the row; and when we thought that the spirit of change could produce no alteration beyond that, a jeweller appeared, and not content with exposing gilt rings and copper bracelets out of number, put up an announcement, which still sticks in his window, that 'ladies' ears may be pierced within'. The dressmaker employs a young lady who wears pockets in her apron; and the tailor informs the public that gentlemen may have their own materials made up.

Amidst all this change, and restlessness, and innovation, there remains but one old man who seems to mourn the downfall of this ancient place. He holds no converse with human kind, but, seated on a wooden bench at the angle of the wall which fronts the crossing from Whitehall Place, watches in silence the gambols of his sleek and well-fed dogs. He is the presiding genius of Scotland Yard. Years and years have rolled over his head; but in fine weather or in foul, hot or cold, wet or dry, hail, rain, or snow, he is still in his accustomed spot. Misery and want are depicted in his countenance; his form is bent by age, his head is grey with length of trial, but there he sits from day to day, brooding over the past; and thither he will continue to drag his feeble limbs, until his eyes have closed upon Scotland Yard, and upon the world together.

A few years hence, and the antiquary of another generation looking into some mouldy record of the strife and passions that agitated the world in these times, may glance his eye over the pages we have just filled: and not all his knowledge of the history of the past, not all his black-letter lore, or his skill in book-collecting, not all the dry studies of a long life, or the dusty volumes that have cost him a fortune, may help him to the whereabouts, either of Scotland Yard or of any one of the landmarks we have mentioned in describing it.

> *The Morning Chronicle*, October 4th, 1836
> *The Evening Chronicle*, October 5th, 1836
> *Sketches by Boz*, Second Series, 1837
> (etched title, 1836)

The Theatrical
Young Gentleman

All gentlemen who love the drama—and there are few gentlemen who are not attached to the most intellectual and rational of all our amusements—do not come within this definition. As we have no mean relish for theatrical entertainments ourself, we are disinterestedly anxious that this should be perfectly understood.

The theatrical young gentleman has early and important information on all theatrical topics. 'Well,' says he, abruptly, when you meet him in the street, 'here's a pretty to-do. Flimkins has thrown up his part in the melodrama at the Surrey.'—'And what's to be done?' you inquire with as much gravity as you can counterfeit. 'Ah, that's the point,' replies the theatrical young gentleman, looking very serious; 'Boozle declines it; positively declines it. From all I am told, I should say it was decidedly in Boozle's line, and that he would be very likely to make a great hit in it; but he objects on the ground of Flimkins having been put up in the part first, and says no earthly power shall induce him to take the character. It's a fine part, too—excellent business, I'm told. He has to kill six people in the course of the piece, and to fight over a bridge in red fire, which is as safe a card, you know, as can be. Don't mention it; but I hear that the last scene, when he is first poisoned, and then stabbed, by Mrs Flimkins as Vengedora, will be the greatest thing that has been done these many years.' With this piece of news, and laying his finger on his lips as a caution for you not to excite the town with it, the theatrical young gentleman hurries away.

The theatrical young gentleman, from often frequenting the different theatrical establishments, has pet and familiar names for them all. Thus Covent Garden is the garden, Drury Lane the lane, the Victoria the vic, and the Olympic the pic. Actresses, too, are always designated by their surnames only, as Taylor, Nisbett, Faucit, Honey; that talented and lady-like girl Sheriff, that clever little creature Horton, and so on. In the same manner he prefixes Christian names when he mentions the actors, as Charley Young, Jemmy Buckstone, Fred Yates, Paul Bedford. When he is at a loss for a Christian name, the word 'old' applied indiscrimately answers quite as well: as old Charley Matthews at Vestris's, old Harley, and old Braham. He has a great knowledge of the private proceedings of actresses, especially of their getting married, and can tell you in a breath half a dozen who have changed their names without avowing it. Whenever an alteration of this kind is made in the playbills, he will remind you that he let you into the secret six months ago.

The theatrical young gentleman has a great reverence for all that is connected with the stage department of the different theatres. He would, at any time, prefer going a street or two out of his way to omitting to pass a stage entrance, into which he always looks with a curious and searching eye. If he can only identify a popular actor in the street, he is in a perfect transport of delight; and no sooner meets him than he hurries back, and walks a few paces in front of him, so that he can turn round from time to time, and have a good stare at his features. He looks upon a theatrical-fund dinner as one of the most enchanting festivities ever known; and thinks that to be a member of the Garrick Club, and see so many actors in their plain clothes, must be one of the highest gratifications the world can bestow.

The theatrical young gentleman is a constant half-price visitor at one or other of the theatres, and has an infinite relish for all pieces which display the fullest resources of the establishment. He likes to place implicit reliance upon the playbills when he goes to see a show-piece, and works himself up to such a pitch of enthusiasm, as not only to believe (if the bills say so) that there are three hundred and seventy-five people on the stage at one time in the last scene, but is highly indignant with you, unless you believe it also. He considers that if the stage be opened from the footlights to the back wall, in any new play, the piece is a triumph

of dramatic writing, and applauds accordingly. He has a great
notion of trap-doors, too; and thinks any character going down
or coming up a trap (no matter whether he be an angel or a
demon—they both do it occasionally) one of the most interesting
feats in the whole range of scenic illusion.

Besides these acquirements, he has several veracious accounts
to communicate of the private manners and customs of different
actors, which, during the pauses of a quadrille, he usually com-
municates to his partner, or imparts to his neighbour at a supper-
table. Thus he is advised that Mr Liston always had a footman in
gorgeous livery waiting at the side-scene with a brandy bottle and
tumbler, to administer half a pint or so of spirit to him every time
he came off, without which assistance he must infallibly have
fainted. He knows for a fact that, after an arduous part, Mr George
Bennett is put between two feather beds, to absorb the perspiration; and is credibly informed that Mr Baker has, for many years,
submitted to a course of lukewarm toast-and-water, to qualify him
to sustain his favourite characters. He looks upon Mr Fitz Ball as
the principal dramatic genius and poet of the day; but holds that
there are great writers extant besides him—in proof whereof he
refers you to various dramas and melodramas recently produced,
of which he takes in all the sixpenny and threepenny editions as
fast as they appear.

The theatrical young gentleman is a great advocate for violence
of emotion and redundancy of action. If a father has to curse a
child upon the stage, he likes to see it done in the thorough-going
style, with no mistake about it: to which end it is essential that
the child should follow the father on her knees, and be knocked
violently over on her face by the old gentleman as he goes into
a small cottage, and shuts the door behind him. He likes to see a
blessing invoked upon the young lady, when the old gentleman
repents, with equal earnestness, and accompanied by the usual
conventional forms, which consist of the old gentleman looking
anxiously up into the clouds, as if to see whether it rains, and then
spreading an imaginary tablecloth in the air over the young lady's
head—soft music playing all the while. Upon these, and other
points of a similar kind, the theatrical young gentleman is a great

critic indeed. He is likewise very acute in judging of natural expressions of the passions, and knows precisely the frown, wink, nod, or leer, which stands for any one of them, or the means by which it may be converted into any other: as jealousy, with a good stamp of the right foot, becomes anger; or wildness, with the hands clasped before the throat, instead of tearing the wig, is passionate love. If you venture to express a doubt of the accuracy of any of these portraitures, the theatrical young gentleman assures you, with a haughty smile, that it always has been done in that way, and he supposes they are not going to change it at this time of day to please you; to which, of course, you meekly reply that you suppose not.

There are innumerable disquisitions of this nature, in which the theatrical young gentleman is very profound, especially to ladies whom he is most in the habit of entertaining with them; but as we have no space to recapitulate them at greater length, we must rest content with calling the attention of the young ladies in general to the theatrical young gentlemen of their own acquaintance.

Sketches of Young Gentlemen, 1838
(published anonymously)

Doctors' Commons

Walking without any definite object through St Paul's Churchyard, a little while ago, we happened to turn down a street entitled
'Paul's Chain', and keeping straight forward for a few hundred
yards, found ourself, as a natural consequence, in Doctors' Commons. Now Doctors' Commons being familiar by name to everybody, as the place where they grant marriage-licences to love-sick
couples, and divorces to unfaithful ones, register the wills of
people who have any property to leave, and punish hasty gentlemen who call ladies by unpleasant names, we no sooner discovered
that we were really within its precincts than we felt a laudable
desire to become better acquainted therewith; and as the first
object of our curiosity was the Court, whose decrees can even
unloose the bonds of matrimony, we procured a direction to it,
and bent our steps thither without delay.

Crossing a quiet and shady courtyard, paved with stone, and
frowned upon by old red-brick houses, on the doors of which were
painted the names of sundry learned civilians, we paused before
a small, green-baized, brass-headed-nailed door which, yielding
to our gentle push, at once admitted us into an old quaint-looking
apartment, with sunken windows, and black carved wainscoting,
at the upper end of which, seated on a raised platform, of semi-
circular shape, were about a dozen solemn-looking gentlemen, in
crimson gowns and wigs.

At a more elevated desk in the centre, sat a very fat and red-
faced gentleman, in tortoise-shell spectacles, whose dignified
appearance announced the judge; and round a long green-baized
table below, something like a billiard-table without the cushions
and pockets, were a number of very self-important-looking personages, in stiff neckcloths, and black gowns with white fur

collars, whom we at once set down as proctors. At the lower end of the billiard-table was an individual in an arm-chair, and a wig, whom we afterwards discovered to be the registrar; and seated behind a little desk, near the door, were a respectable-looking man in black, of about twenty stone weight or thereabouts, and a fat-faced, smirking, civil-looking body, in a black gown, black kid gloves, knee shorts, and silks, with a shirt-frill in his bosom, curls on his head, and a silver staff in his hand, whom we had no difficulty in recognizing as the officer of the Court. The latter, indeed, speedily set our mind at rest upon this point, for, advancing to our elbow and opening a conversation forthwith, he had communicated to us, in less than five minutes, that he was the apparitor, and the other the court-keeper; that this was the Arches Court, and therefore the counsel wore red gowns, and the proctors fur collars; and that when the other Courts sat there, they didn't wear red gowns or fur collars either; with many other scraps of intelligence equally interesting. Besides these two officers, there was a little thin old man, with long grizzly hair, crouched in a remote corner, whose duty, our communicative friend informed us, was to ring a large hand-bell when the Court opened in the morning, and who, for aught his appearance betokened to the contrary, might have been similarly employed for the last two centuries at least.

The red-faced gentleman in the tortoise-shell spectacles had got all the talk to himself just then, and very well he was doing it, too, only he spoke very fast, but that was habit; and rather thick, but that was good living. So we had plenty of time to look about us. There was one individual who amused us mightily. This was one of the bewigged gentlemen in the red robes, who was straddling before the fire in the centre of the Court, in the attitude of the brazen Colossus, to the complete exclusion of everybody else. He had gathered up his robe behind, in much the same manner as a slovenly woman would her petticoats on a very dirty day, in order that he might feel the full warmth of the fire. His wig was put on all awry, with the tail straggling about his neck; his scanty grey trousers and short black gaiters, made in the worst possible style, imparted an additional inelegant appearance to his uncouth person; and his limp, badly starched shirt-collar almost obscured his eyes. We shall never be able to claim any credit as a physiognomist again, for, after a careful scrutiny of this gentleman's countenance, we had come to the conclusion that it bespoke nothing but conceit and silliness when our friend with the silver staff whispered in our ear that he was no other than a doctor of civil law, and heaven knows what besides. So of course we were mistaken, and he must be a very talented man. He conceals it so well though—perhaps with the merciful view of not astonishing ordinary people too much—that you would suppose him to be one of the stupidest dogs alive.

The gentleman in the spectacles having concluded his judgment, and a few minutes having been allowed to elapse, to afford time for the buzz in the Court to subside, the registrar called on the next cause, which was 'the office of the Judge promoted by Bumple against Sludberry'. A general movement was visible in the Court at this announcement, and the obliging functionary with silver staff whispered us that 'there would be some fun now, for this was a brawling case'.

We were not rendered much the wiser by this piece of information, till we found by the opening speech of the counsel for the promoter that, under a half-obsolete statute of one of the Edwards, the Court was empowered to visit with the penalty of excommunication, any person who should be proved guilty of the crime of 'brawling', or 'smiting', in any church, or vestry adjoining thereto; and it appeared, by some eight-and-twenty affidavits, which were duly referred to, that on a certain night, at a certain vestry-meeting, in a certain parish particularly set forth, Thomas Sludberry, the party appeared against in that suit, had made use of, and applied to Michael Bumple, the promoter, the words 'You be blowed'; and that, on the said Michael Bumple and others remonstrating with the said Thomas Sludberry, on the impropriety of his conduct, the said Thomas Sludberry repeated the aforesaid expression, 'You be blowed'; and furthermore desired and requested to know, whether the said Michael Bumple 'wanted anything for himself'; adding, 'that if the said Michael Bumple did want anything for himself, he, the said Thomas Sludberry, was the man to give it him'; at the same time making use of other heinous and sinful expressions, all of which, Bumple submitted, came within the intent and meaning of the Act; and therefore he, for the soul's health and chastening of Sludberry, prayed for sentence of excommunication against him accordingly.

Upon these facts a long argument was entered into, on both sides, to the great edification of a number of persons interested in the parochial squabbles, who crowded the Court; and when some very long and grave speeches had been made *pro* and *con*, the red-faced gentleman in the tortoise-shell spectacles took a review of the case, which occupied half an hour more, and then pronounced upon Sludberry the awful sentence of excommunication for a fortnight, and payment of the costs of the suit. Upon this, Sludberry, who was a little, red-faced, sly-looking ginger-beer seller, addressed the Court, and said, if they'd be good enough to take off the costs, and excommunicate him for the term of his natural life instead, it would be much more convenient to him, for he never went to church at all. To this appeal the gentleman in the spectacles made no other reply than a look of virtuous indignation; and Sludberry and his friends retired. As the man with the silver staff informed us that the Court was on the point of rising, we retired, too—pondering, as we walked away, upon the beautiful spirit of these ancient ecclesiastical laws, the kind and neighbourly feelings they are calculated to awaken, and the strong attachment to religious institutions which they cannot fail to engender.

We were so lost in these meditations that we had turned into the street, and run up against a doorpost, before we recollected where we were walking. On looking upwards to see what house we had stumbled upon, the words 'Prerogative Office', written in large characters, met our eye; and as we were in a sight-seeing humour and the place was a public one, we walked in.

The room into which we walked was a long, busy-looking place, partitioned off, on either side, into a variety of little boxes, in which a few clerks were engaged in copying or examining deeds. Down the centre of the room were several desks nearly breast high, at each of which three or four people were standing, poring over large volumes. As we knew that they were searching for wills, they attracted our attention at once.

It was curious to contrast the lazy indifference of the attorneys' clerks who were making a search for some legal purpose, with the air of earnestness and interest which distinguished the strangers to the place, who were looking up the will of some deceased relative; the former pausing every now and then with an impatient yawn, or raising their heads to look at the people who passed up and down the room; the latter stooping over the book, and running down column after column of names in the deepest abstraction.

There was one little dirty-faced man in a blue apron, who after a whole morning's search, extending some fifty years back, had just found the will to which he wished to refer, which one of the officials was reading to him in a low hurried voice from a thick vellum book with large clasps. It was perfectly evident that the more the clerk read, the less the man with the blue apron understood about the matter. When the volume was first brought down, he took off his hat, smoothed down his hair, smiled with great self-satisfaction, and looked up in the reader's face with the air of a man who had made up his mind to recollect every word he heard. The first two or three lines were intelligible enough; but then the technicalities began, and the little man began to look rather dubious. Then came a whole string of complicated trusts, and he was regularly at sea. As the reader proceeded, it was quite apparent that it was a hopeless case, and the little man, with his mouth open and his eyes fixed upon his face, looked on with an expression of bewilderment and perplexity irresistibly ludicrous.

A little farther on, a hard-featured old man with a deeply-wrinkled face, was intently perusing a lengthy will with the aid of a pair of horn spectacles: occasionally pausing from his task, and slyly noting down some brief memorandum of the bequests contained in it. Every wrinkle about his toothless mouth, and sharp keen eyes, told of avarice and cunning. His clothes were nearly threadbare, but it was easy to see that he wore them from choice and not from necessity; all his looks and gestures down to the very small pinches of snuff which he every now and then took from a little tin canister, told of wealth, and penury, and avarice.

As he leisurely closed the register, put up his spectacles, and folded his scraps of paper in a large leathern pocket-book, we thought what a nice hard bargain he was driving with some poverty-stricken legatee, who, tired of waiting year after year, until some life-interest should fall in, was selling his chance, just as it began to grow most valuable, for a twelfth part of its worth. It was a good speculation—a very safe one. The old man stowed his pocket-book carefully in the breast of his greatcoat, and hobbled away with a leer of triumph. That will had made him ten years younger at the lowest computation.

Having commenced our observations, we should certainly have extended them to another dozen of people at least, had not a sudden shutting up and putting away of the worm-eaten old books warned us that the time for closing the office had arrived; and thus deprived us of a pleasure, and spared our readers an infliction.

We naturally fell into a train of reflection as we walked homewards, upon the curious old records of likings and dislikings; of jealousies and revenges; of affection defying the power of death, and hatred pursued beyond the grave, which these depositories contain; silent but striking tokens, some of them, of excellence of heart, and nobleness of soul; melancholy examples, others, of the worst passions of human nature. How many men, as they lay speechless and helpless on the bed of death, would have given worlds but for the strength and power to blot out the silent evidence of animosity and bitterness which now stands registered against them in Doctors' Commons!

The Morning Chronicle, October 11th, 1836
The Evening Chronicle, October 12th, 1836
Sketches by Boz, Second Series, 1837
(etched title 1836)

A Visit to Newgate

'The force of habit' is a trite phrase in everybody's mouth; and
it is not a little remarkable that those who use it most as applied
to others unconsciously afford in their own persons singular examples of the power which habit and custom exercise over the
minds of men, and of the little reflection they are apt to bestow
on subjects with which every day's experience has rendered them
familiar. If Bedlam could be suddenly removed like another
Aladdin's palace, and set down on the space now occupied by
Newgate, scarcely one man out of a hundred, whose road to
business every morning lies through Newgate Street, or the Old
Bailey, would pass the building without bestowing a hasty glance
on its small, grated windows, and a transient thought upon the
condition of the unhappy beings immured in its dismal cells; and
yet these same men, day by day, and hour by hour, pass and re-
pass this gloomy depository of the guilt and misery of London,
in one perpetual stream of life and bustle, utterly unmindful of the
throng of wretched creatures pent up within—nay, not even
knowing, or if they do, not heeding, the fact, that as they pass one
particular angle of the massive wall with a light laugh or a merry
whistle they stand within one yard of a fellow creature, bound and
helpless, whose hours are numbered, from whom the last feeble
ray of hope has fled for ever, and whose miserable career will
shortly terminate in a violent and shameful death. Contact with
death, even in its least terrible shape, is solemn and appalling.
How much more awful is it to reflect on this near vicinity to the
dying—to men in full health and vigour, in the flower of youth or
the prime of life, with all their faculties and perceptions as acute
and perfect as your own; but dying, nevertheless—dying as
surely—with the hand of death imprinted upon them as indelibly

—as if mortal disease had wasted their frames to shadows, and corruption had already begun!

It was with some such thoughts as these that we determined, not many weeks since, to visit the interior of Newgate—in an amateur capacity, of course; and, having carried our intention into effect, we proceed to lay its results before our readers, in the hope —founded more upon the nature of the subject than on any presumptuous confidence in our own descriptive powers—that this paper may not be found wholly devoid of interest. We have only to premise that we do not intend to fatigue the reader with any statistical accounts of the prison; they will be found at length in numerous reports of numerous committees, and a variety of authorities of equal weight. We took no notes, made no memoranda, measured none of the yards, ascertained the exact number of inches in no particular room: are unable even to report of how many apartments the gaol is composed.

We saw the prison, and saw the prisoners; and what we did see, and what we thought, we will tell at once in our own way.

Having delivered out credentials to the servant who answered our knock at the door of the governor's house, we were ushered into the 'office', a little room, on the right-hand side as you enter, with two windows looking into the Old Bailey, fitted up like an ordinary attorney's office, or merchant's counting-house, with the usual fixtures—a wainscoted partition, a shelf or two, a desk, a couple of stools, a pair of clerks, an almanack, a cloak, and a few maps. After a little delay, occasioned by sending into the interior of the prison for the officer whose duty it was to conduct us, that functionary arrived; a respectable-looking man of about two or three and fifty, in a broad-brimmed hat, and full suit of black, who, but for his keys, would have looked quite as much like a clergyman as a turnkey. We were disappointed; he had not even top-boots on. Following our conductor by a door opposite to that at which we had entered, we arrived at a small room, without any other furniture than a little desk, with a book for visitors' autographs, and a shelf, on which were a few boxes for papers, and casts of the heads and faces of the two notorious murderers, Bishop and Williams, the former, in particular, exhibiting a style

of head and set of features which might have afforded sufficient
moral grounds for his instant execution at any time, even had
there been no other evidence against him. Leaving this room
also, by an opposite door, we found ourself in the lodge which
opens on the Old Bailey; one side of which is plentifully garnished
with a choice collection of heavy sets of irons, including those
worn by the redoubtable Jack Sheppard—genuine; and those *said*
to have been graced by the sturdy limbs of the no less celebrated
Dick Turpin—doubtful. From this lodge a heavy oaken gate,
bound with iron, studded with nails of the same material, and
guarded by another turnkey, opens on a few steps, if we remember
right, which terminate in a narrow and dismal stone passage,
running parallel with the Old Bailey, and leading to the different
yards, through a number of tortuous and intricate windings,
guarded in their turn by huge gates and gratings, whose appearance is sufficient to dispel at once the slightest hope of escape that
any new-comer may have entertained; and the very recollection
of which, on eventually traversing the place again, involves one
in a maze of confusion.

It is necessary to explain here that the buildings in the prison,
or in other words the different wards—form a square, of which
the four sides abut respectively on the Old Bailey, the old College
of Physicians (now forming a part of Newgate Market), the
Sessions House, and Newgate Street. The intermediate space is
divided into several paved yards, in which the prisoners take such
air and exercise as can be had in such a place. These yards, with
the exception of that in which prisoners under sentence of death
are confined (of which we shall presently give a more detailed
description), run parallel with Newgate Street, and consequently
from the Old Bailey, as it were, to Newgate Market. The women's
side is in the right wing of the prison nearest the Sessions House.
As we were introduced into this part of the building first, we will
adopt the same order, and introduce our readers to it also.

Turning to the right, then, down the passage to which we just
now adverted, omitting any mention of intervening gates—for if
we noticed every gate that was unlocked for us to pass through,
and locked again as soon as we had passed, we should require a

DUSTMAN.

gate at every comma—we came to a door composed of thick bars of wood, through which were discernible, passing to and fro in a narrow yard, some twenty women: the majority of whom, however, as soon as they were aware of the presence of strangers, retreated to their wards. One side of this yard is railed off at a considerable distance, and formed into a kind of iron cage, about five feet ten inches in height, roofed at the top, and defended in front by iron bars, from which the friends of the female prisoners communicate with them. In one corner of this singular-looking den was a yellow, haggard, decrepit old woman, in a tattered gown that had once been black, and the remains of an old straw bonnet, with faded ribbon of the same hue, in earnest conversation with a young girl—a prisoner, of course—of about two-and-twenty. It is impossible to imagine a more poverty-stricken object, or a creature so borne down in soul and body, by excess of misery and destitution, as the old woman. The girl was a good-looking robust female, with a profusion of hair streaming about in the wind—for she had no bonnet on—and a man's silk pocket-handkerchief loosely thrown over a most ample pair of shoulders. The old woman was talking in that low, stifled tone of voice which tells so forcibly of mental anguish; and every now and then burst into an irrepressible sharp, abrupt cry of grief, the most distressing sound that ears can hear. The girl was perfectly unmoved. Hardened beyond all hope of redemption, she listened doggedly to her mother's entreaties, whatever they were: and, beyond inquiring after 'Jem', and eagerly catching at the few halfpence her miserable parent had brought her, took no more apparent interest in the conversation than the most unconcerned spectators. Heaven knows there were enough of them, in the persons of the other prisoners in the yard, who were no more concerned by what was passing before their eyes, and within their hearing, than if they were blind and deaf. Why should they be? Inside the prison, and out, such scenes were too familiar to them to excite even a passing thought, unless of ridicule or contempt for feelings which they had long since forgotten.

A little farther on a squalid-looking woman in a slovenly, thick-bordered cap, with her arms muffled in a large red shawl, the fringed ends of which straggled nearly to the bottom of a dirty white apron, was communicating some instructions to *her* visitor—her daughter evidently. The girl was thinly clad, and shaking with the cold. Some ordinary word of recognition passed between her and her mother when she appeared at the grating, but neither hope, condolence, regret, nor affection was expressed on either side. The mother whispered her instructions, and the girl received them with her pinched-up half-starved features twisted into an expression of careful cunning. It was some scheme for the woman's defence that she was disclosing, perhaps; and a sullen smile came over the girl's face for an instant, as if she were pleased: not so much at the probability of her mother's liberation, as at the chance of her 'getting off' in spite of her prosecutors. The dialogue was soon concluded; and with the same careless indifference with which they had approached each other, the mother turned towards the inner end of the yard, and the girl to the gate at which she had entered.

The girl belonged to a class—unhappily but too extensive—the very existence of which should make men's hearts bleed. Barely past her childhood, it required but a glance to discover that she was one of those children, born and bred in neglect and vice, who have never known what childhood is: who have never been taught to love and court a parent's smile, or to dread a parent's frown. The thousand nameless endearments of childhood, its gaiety and its innocence, are alike unknown to them. They have entered at once upon the stern realities and miseries of life, and to their better nature it is almost hopeless to appeal in after-times, by any of the references which will awaken, if it be only for a moment, some good feeling in ordinary bosoms, however corrupt they may have become. Talk to *them* of parental solicitude, the happy days of childhood, and the merry games of infancy! Tell them of hunger and the streets, beggary and stripes, the gin-shop, the station-house, and the pawnbroker's, and they will understand you.

Two or three women were standing at different parts of the grating, conversing with their friends, but a very large proportion of the prisoners appeared to have no friends at all, beyond such of their old companions as might happen to be within the walls. So, passing hastily down the yard, and pausing only for an instant to notice the little incidents we have just recorded, we were conducted up a clean and well-lighted flight of stone stairs to one of the wards. There are several in this part of the building, but a description of one is a description of the whole.

It was a spacious, bare, whitewashed apartment, lighted, of course, by windows looking into the interior of the prison, but far more light and airy than one could reasonably expect to find in such a situation. There was a large fire with a deal table before it, round which ten or a dozen women were seated on wooden forms at dinner. Along both sides of the room ran a shelf; below it, at regular intervals, a row of large hooks were fixed in the wall, on each of which was hung the sleeping mat of a prisoner: her rug and blanket being folded up, and placed on the shelf above. At night, these mats are placed on the floor, each beneath the hook on which it hangs during the day; and the ward is thus made to answer the purposes both of a day-room and sleeping apartment. Over the fireplace was a large sheet of pasteboard, on which were displayed a variety of texts from Scripture, which were also scattered about the room in scraps about the size and shape of the copy-slips which are used in schools. On the table was a sufficient provision of a kind of stewed beef and brown bread, in pewter dishes, which are kept perfectly bright, and displayed on shelves in great order and regularity when they are not in use.

The women rose hastily, on our entrance, and retired in a hurried manner to either side of the fireplace. They were all cleanly—many of them decently—attired, and there was nothing peculiar, either in their appearance or demeanour. One or two resumed the needlework which they had probably laid aside at the commencement of their meal; others gazed at the visitors with listless curiosity; and a few retired behind their companions to the very end of the room, as if desirous to avoid even the casual observation of the strangers. Some old Irish women, both in this and other wards, to whom the thing was no novelty, appeared perfectly indifferent to our presence, and remained standing close to the seats from which they had just risen; but the general feeling among the females seemed to be one of uneasiness during the period of our stay among them: which was very brief. Not a word was uttered during the time of our remaining unless, indeed, by the wardswoman in reply to some question which we put to the turnkey who accompanied us. In every ward on the female side, a wardswoman is appointed to preserve order, and a similar regulation is adopted among the males. The wardsmen and wardswomen are all prisoners, selected for good conduct. They alone are allowed the privilege of sleeping on bedsteads; a small stump bedstead being placed in every ward for that purpose. On both sides of the gaol is a small receiving-room, to which prisoners are conducted on their first reception, and whence they cannot be removed until they have been examined by the surgeon of the prison.*

Retracing our steps to the dismal passage in which we found ourselves at first (and which, by the by, contains three or four dark cells for the accommodation of refractory prisoners), we were led through a narrow yard to the 'school'—a portion of the prison set apart for boys under fourteen years of age. In a tolerable-sized room, in which were writing-materials and some copybooks, was the schoolmaster, with a couple of his pupils; the remainder having been fetched from an adjoining apartment, the whole were drawn up in line for our inspection. There were fourteen of them in all, some with shoes, some without; some in pinafores without jackets, others in jackets without pinafores, and one in scarce anything at all. The whole number, without an exception we believe, had been committed for trial on charges of pocketpicking; and fourteen such terrible little faces were never beheld. There was not one redeeming feature among them—not a glance of honesty—not a wink expressive of anything but the gallows and the hulks, in the whole collection. As to anything like shame or contrition, that was entirely out of the question. They were evidently quite gratified at being thought worth the trouble of

---

* The regulations of the prison relative to the confinement of prisoners during the day, their sleeping at night, their taking their meals, and other matters of gaol economy, have been all altered—greatly for the better—since this sketch was first published. Even the construction of the prison itself has been changed.

looking at; their idea appeared to be that we had come to see Newgate as a grand affair, and that they were an indispensable part of the show; and every boy as he 'fell in' to the line actually seemed as pleased and important as if he had done something excessively meritorious in getting there at all. We never looked upon a more disagreeable sight, because we never saw fourteen such hopeless creatures of neglect, before.

On either side of the school-yard is a yard for men, in one of which—that towards Newgate Street—prisoners of the more respectable class are confined. Of the other, we have little description to offer, as the different wards necessarily partake of the same character. They are provided, like the wards on the women's side, with mats and rugs, which are disposed of in the same manner during the day; the only very striking difference between their appearance and that of the wards inhabited by the females is the utter absence of any employment. Huddled together on two opposite forms, by the fireside, sit twenty men perhaps; here, a boy in livery; there, a man in a rough greatcoat and top-boots; farther on, a desperate-looking fellow in his shirt-sleeves, with an old Scotch cap upon his shaggy head; near him again, a tall ruffian, in a smock-frock; next to him, a miserable being of distressed appearance, with his head resting on his hand—all alike in one respect, all idle and listless. When they do leave the fire, sauntering moodily about, lounging in the window, or leaning against the wall, vacantly swinging their bodies to and fro. With the exception of a man reading an old newspaper, in two or three instances, this was the case in every ward we entered.

The only communication these men have with their friends is through two close iron gratings, with an intermediate space of about a yard in width between the two, so that nothing can be handed across, nor can the prisoner have any communication by touch with the person who visits him. The married men have a separate grating at which to see their wives, but its construction is the same.

The prison chapel is situated at the back of the governor's house: the latter having no windows looking into the interior of the prison. Whether the associations connected with the place—

the knowledge that here a portion of the burial service is, on some dreadful occasions, performed over the quick and not upon the dead—cast over it a still more gloomy and sombre air than art has imparted to it, we know not, but its appearance is very striking. There is something in a silent and deserted place of worship, solemn and impressive at any time; and the very dissimilarity of this one from any we have been accustomed to only enhances the impression. The meanness of its appointments—the bare and scanty pulpit, with the paltry painted pillars on either side—the women's gallery with its great heavy curtain—the men's with its unpainted benches and dingy front—the tottering little table at the altar, with the commandments on the wall above it, scarcely legible through lack of paint, and dust and damp—so unlike the velvet and gilding, the marble and wood, of a modern church—are strange and striking. There is one object, too, which rivets the attention and fascinates the gaze, and from which we may turn horror-stricken in vain, for the recollection of it will haunt us, waking and sleeping, for a long time afterwards. Immediately below the reading-desk, on the floor of the chapel, and forming the most conspicuous object in its little area, is *the condemned pew*; a huge black pen, in which the wretched people who are singled out for death are placed on the Sunday preceding their execution, in sight of all their fellow prisoners, from many of whom they may have been separated but a week before, to hear prayers for their own souls, to join in the responses of their own burial service, and to listen to an address, warning their recent companions to take example by their fate, and urging themselves, while there is yet time—nearly four-and-twenty hours—to 'turn, and flee from the wrath to come'! Imagine what have been the feelings of the men whom that fearful pew has enclosed, and of whom, between the gallows and the knife, no mortal remnant may now remain! Think of the hopeless clinging to life to the last, and the wild despair, far exceeding in anguish the felon's death itself, by which they have heard the certainty of their speedy transmission to another world, with all their crimes upon their heads, rung into their ears by the officiating clergyman!

At one time—and at no distant period either—the coffins of

the men about to be executed were placed in that pew, upon the
seat by their side, during the whole service. It may seem incredible, but it is true. Let us hope that the increased spirit of civilization and humanity which abolished this frightful and degrading
custom may extend itself to other usages equally barbarous;
usages which have not even the plea of utility in their defence, as
every year's experience has shown them to be more and more
inefficacious.

Leaving the chapel, descending to the passage so frequently
alluded to, and crossing the yard before noticed as being allotted
to prisoners of a more respectable description than the generality
of men confined here, the visitor arrives at a thick iron gate of
great size and strength. Having been admitted through it by the
turnkey on duty, he turns sharp round to the left, and pauses
before another gate; and, having passed this last barrier, he stands
in the most terrible part of this gloomy building—the condemned ward.

The press-yard, well known by name to newspaper readers,
from its frequent mention in accounts of executions, is at the
corner of the building, and next to the ordinary's house, in Newgate Street: running from Newgate Street, towards the centre of
the prison, parallel with Newgate Market. It is a long, narrow
court, of which a portion of the wall in Newgate Street forms one
end and the gate the other. At the upper end, on the left hand—
that is, adjoining the wall in Newgate Street—is a cistern of
water, and at the bottom a double grating (of which the gate
itself forms a part) similar to that before described. Through these
grates the prisoners are allowed to see their friends; a turnkey
always remaining in the vacant space between, during the whole
interview. Immediately on the right as you enter is a building containing the press-room, day-room, and cells; the yard is on every
side surrounded by lofty walls guarded by *chevaux de frise*; and
the whole is under the constant inspection of vigilant and experienced turnkeys.

In the first apartment into which we were conducted—which
was at the top of a staircase, and immediately over the press-room
—were five-and-twenty or thirty prisoners, all under sentence

of death, awaiting the result of the recorder's report—men of all ages and appearances, from a hardened old offender with swarthy face and grizzly beard of three days' growth to a handsome boy, not fourteen years old, and of singularly youthful appearance even for that age, who had been condemned for burglary. There was nothing remarkable in the appearance of these prisoners. One or two decently dressed men were brooding with a dejected air over the fire; several little groups of two or three had been engaged in conversation at the upper end of the room, or in the windows; and the remainder were crowded round a young man seated at a table, who appeared to be engaged in teaching the younger ones to write. The room was large, airy, and clean. There was very little anxiety or mental suffering depicted in the countenance of any of the men; they had all been sentenced to death, it is true, and the recorder's report had not yet been made, but we question whether there was a man among them, notwithstanding, who did not *know* that although he had undergone the ceremony, it never was intended that his life should be sacrificed. On the table lay a Testament, but there were no tokens of its having been in recent use.

In the press-room below were three men, the nature of whose offence rendered it necessary to separate them even from their companions in guilt. It is a long, sombre room, with two windows sunk into the stone wall, and here the wretched men are pinioned on the morning of their execution, before moving towards the scaffold. The fate of one of these prisoners was uncertain, some mitigatory circumstances having come to light since his trial, which had been humanely represented in the proper quarter. The other two had nothing to expect from the mercy of the crown; their doom was sealed; no plea could be urged in extenuation of their crime, and they well knew that for them there was no hope in this world. 'The two short ones,' the turnkey whispered, 'were dead men.'

The man to whom we have alluded as entertaining some hopes of escape was lounging, at the greatest distance he could place between himself and his companions, in the window nearest to the door. He was probably aware of our approach, and had assumed an air of courageous indifference; his face was purposely averted towards the window, and he stirred not an inch while we were present. The other two men were at the upper end of the room. One of them, who was imperfectly seen in the dim light, had his back towards us, and was stooping over the fire, with his right arm on the mantelpiece, and his head sunk upon it. The other was leaning on the sill of the farthest window. The light fell full upon him, and communicated to his pale, haggard face, and disordered hair, an appearance which, at that distance, was ghastly. His cheek rested upon his hand; and with his face a little raised, and his eyes wildly staring before him, he seemed to be unconsciously intent on counting the chinks in the opposite wall. We passed this room again afterwards. The first man was pacing up and down the court with a firm military step—he had been a soldier in the foot-guards—and a cloth cap jauntily thrown on one side of his head. He bowed respectfully to our conductor, and the salute was returned. The other two still remained in the positions we have described, and were as motionless as statues.*

A few paces up the yard, and forming a continuation of the building in which are the two rooms we have just quitted, lie the condemned cells. The entrance is by a narrow and obscure stair-case leading to a dark passage, in which a charcoal stove casts a lurid tint over the objects in its immediate vicinity, and diffuses something like warmth around. From the left-hand side of this passage, the massive door of every cell on the story opens; and from it alone can they be approached. There are three of these passages, and three of these ranges of cells, one above the other; but in size, furniture and appearance, they are all precisely alike. Prior to the recorder's report being made, all the prisoners under sentence of death are removed from the day-room at five o'clock in the afternoon, and locked up in these cells, where they are allowed a candle until ten o'clock; and here they remain until seven next morning. When the warrant for a prisoner's execution arrives, he is removed to the cells and confined in one of them until he leaves it for the scaffold. He is at liberty to walk in the

---

* These two men were executed shortly afterwards. The other was respited during His Majesty's pleasure.

yard; but, both in his walks and in his cell, he is constantly attended by a turnkey who never leaves him on any pretence.

We entered the first cell. It was a stone dungeon, eight feet
long by six wide, with a bench at the upper end, under which
were a common rug, a bible, and prayer-book. An iron candle-
stick was fixed into the wall at the side; and a small high window
in the back admitted as much air and light as could struggle in
between a double row of heavy, crossed iron bars. It contained
no other furniture of any description.

Conceive the situation of a man, spending his last night on
earth in this cell. Buoyed up with some vague and undefined hope
of reprieve, he knew not why—indulging in some wild and visionary idea of escaping, he knew not how—hour after hour of the
three preceding days allowed him for preparation, has fled with
a speed which no man living would deem possible, for none but
this dying man can know. He has wearied his friend with entreaties, exhausted the attendants with importunities, neglected
in his feverish restlessness the timely warnings of his spiritual
consoler; and, now that the illusion is at last dispelled, now that
eternity is before him and guilt behind, now that his fears of death
amount almost to madness, and an overwhelming sense of his
helpless, hopeless state rushes upon him, he is lost and stupefied,
and has neither thoughts to turn to, nor power to call upon, the
Almighty Being, from whom alone he can seek mercy and forgiveness, and before whom his repentance can alone avail.

Hours have glided by, and still he sits upon the same stone
bench with folded arms, heedless alike of the fast-decreasing time
before him and the urgent entreaties of the good man at his side.
The feeble light is wasting gradually, and the deathlike stillness
of the street without, broken only by the rumbling of some passing
vehicle which echoes mournfully through the empty yards, warns
him that the night is waning fast away. The deep bell of St Paul's
strikes—one! He heard it; it has roused him. Seven hours left!
He paces the narrow limits of his cell with rapid strides, cold
drops of terror starting on his forehead, and every muscle of his
frame quivering with agony. Seven hours! He suffers himself to
be led to his seat, mechanically takes the bible which is placed in

his hand, and tries to read and listen. No: his thoughts will
wander. The book is torn and soiled by use—and like the book
he read his lessons in, at school, just forty years ago! He has never
bestowed a thought upon it, perhaps, since he left it as a child:
and yet the place, the time, the room—nay, the very boys he
played with, crowd as vividly before him as if they were scenes
of yesterday; and some forgotten phrase, some childish word,
rings in his ears like the echo of one uttered but a minute since.
The voice of the clergyman recalls him to himself. He is reading
from the sacred book its solemn promises of pardon for repentance, and its awful denunciation of obdurate men. He falls upon
his knees and clasps his hands to pray. Hush! what sound was
that? He starts upon his feet. It cannot be two yet. Hark! Two
quarters have struck; the third—the fourth. It is! Six hours left.
Tell him not of repentance! Six hours' repentance for eight times
six years of guilt and sin! He buries his face in his hands, and
throws himself on the bench.

Worn with watching and excitement, he sleeps, and the same
unsettled state of mind pursues him in his dreams. An insupportable load is taken from his breast; he is walking with his wife in a
pleasant field, with the bright sky above them, and a fresh and
boundless prospect on every side—how different from the stone
walls of Newgate! She is looking—not as she did when he saw
her for the last time in that dreadful place, but as she used when
he loved her—long, long ago, before misery and ill-treatment
had altered her looks, and vice had changed his nature, and she is
leaning upon his arm, and looking up into his face with tenderness
and affection—and he does *not* strike her now, nor rudely shake
her from him. And oh! how glad he is to tell her all he had forgotten in that last hurried interview, and to fall on his knees
before her and fervently beseech her pardon for all the unkindness
and cruelty that wasted her form and broke her heart! The scene
suddenly changes. He is on his trial again: there are the judge and
jury, and prosecutors, and witnesses, just as they were before.
How full the court is—what a sea of heads—with a gallows, too,
and a scaffold—and how all those people stare at *him*! Verdict,
'Guilty'. No matter; he will escape.

The night is dark and cold, the gates have been left open, and in an instant he is in the street, flying from the scene of his imprisonment like the wind. The streets are cleared, the open fields are gained and the broad wide country lies before him. Onward he dashes in the midst of darkness, over hedge and ditch, through mud and pool, bounding from spot to spot with a speed and lightness, astonishing even to himself. At length he pauses; he must be safe from pursuit now; he will stretch himself on that bank and sleep till sunrise.

A period of unconsciousness succeeds. He wakes, cold and wretched. The dull grey light of morning is stealing into the cell, and falls upon the form of the attendant turnkey. Confused by his dreams, he starts from his uneasy bed in momentary uncertainty. It is but momentary. Every object in the narrow cell is too frightfully real to admit of doubt or mistake. He is the condemned felon again, guilty and despairing; and in two hours more will be dead.

Sketches by Boz, Volume 1, 1836
(specially written for this)

The Chinese Junk

Drive down to the Blackwall railway, and for the matter of eighteenpence you are at the Chinese Empire in no time. In half a score of minutes the tiles and chimney-pots, backs of squalid houses, frowsty pieces of waste ground, narrow courts and streets, swamps, ditches, masts of ships, gardens of duckweed, and unwholesome little bowers of scarlet beans, whirl away in a flying dream, and nothing is left but China. How the flowery region ever came into this latitude and longitude is the first thing one asks; and it is not certainly the least of the marvel. As Aladdin's palace was transported hither and thither by the rubbing of a lamp, so the crew of Chinamen aboard the *Keying* devoutly believed that their good ship would turn up, quite safe, at the desired port, if they only tied red rags enough upon the mast, rudder and cable. Somehow they did not succeed. Perhaps they ran short of rag; at any rate, they hadn't enough on board to keep them above water; and to the bottom they would undoubtedly have gone but for the skill and coolness of a dozen English sailors, who brought them over the ocean in safety. Well, if there be one thing in the world that his extraordinary craft is not at all like, that thing is a ship of any kind. So narrow, so long, so grotesque; so low in the middle, so high at each end, like a China pen-tray; with no rigging, with nowhere to go to aloft; with mats for sails, great warped cigars for masts, gaudy dragons and sea-monsters disporting themselves from stem to stern, and *on* the stern a gigantic cock of impossible aspect defying the world (as well he may) to produce his equal—it would look more at home at the top of a public building, or at the top of a mountain, or down in a mine, than afloat on the water. As for the Chinese lounging on the deck, the most extravagant imagination would never dare to suppose them to be mariners. Imagine a ship's crew, without a profile among them, in gauze pinafores and plaited hair; wearing stiff clogs a quarter of a foot thick in the sole; and lying at night in little scented boxes, like backgammon men or chess-pieces, or mother-of-pearl counters! But by Jove! even this is nothing to your surprise when you go down into the cabin. There you get into a torture of perplexity. As, what became of all those lanterns hanging to the roof when the Junk was out at sea? Whether they dangled there, banging and beating against each other, like so many jesters' baubles? Whether the idol Chin Tee, of the eighteen arms, enshrined in a celestial Punch's Show, in the place of honour, ever tumbled out in heavy weather? Whether the incense and the joss stick still burnt before her, with a faint perfume and a little thread of smoke, while the mighty waves were roaring all around? Whether that preposterous tissue-paper umbrella in the corner was always spread, as being a convenient maritime instrument for walking about the decks with in a storm? Whether all the cool and shiny little chairs and tables were continually sliding about and bruising each other, and if not why not? Whether anybody on the voyage ever read those two books printed in characters like bird-cages and fly-traps? Whether the Mandarin passenger, He Sing, who had never been ten miles from home in his life before, lying sick on a bamboo couch in a private china closet of his own (where he is now perpetually writing autographs for inquisitive barbarians), ever began to doubt the potency of the Goddess of the Sea, whose counterfeit presentment, like a flowery monthly nurse, occupies the sailors' joss-house in the second gallery? Whether it is possible that the said Mandarin, or the artist of the ship, Sam Sing, Esquire, R.A. of Canton, *can* ever go ashore without a walking-staff of cinnamon, agreeably to the usage of their likenesses in British tea-shops? Above all, whether the hoarse old ocean could ever have been seriously in earnest with this floating toy-shop; or had merely played with it in lightness of spirit—roughly, but meaning no harm—as the bull did with another kind of china-shop on St Patrick's Day in the morning.

From a Letter to John Forster. The Examiner, June 24th, 1848 (MS. in the Forster Collection, Victoria and Albert Museum)

The Amusements
of the People

As one half of the world is said not to know how the other half
lives, so it may be affirmed that the upper half of the world
neither knows nor greatly cares how the lower half amuses itself.
Believing that it does not care, mainly because it does not
know, we purpose occasionally recording a few facts on this
subject.

The general character of the lower class of dramatic amusements is a very significant sign of a people, and a very good test
of their intellectual condition. We design to make our readers
acquainted in the first place with a few of our experiences under
this head in the metropolis.

It is probable that nothing will ever root out from among the
common people an innate love they have for dramatic entertainment in some form or other. It would be a very doubtful benefit
to society, we think, if it could be rooted out. The Polytechnic
Institution in Regent Street, where an infinite variety of ingenious models are exhibited and explained, and where lectures com-
prising a quantity of useful information on many practical subjects are delivered, is a great public benefit and a wonderful place,
but we think a people formed *entirely* in their hours of leisure by
Polytechnic Institutions would be an uncomfortable community.
We would rather not have to appeal to the generous sympathies
of a man of five-and-twenty, in respect of some affliction of which
he had had no personal experience, who had passed all his holidays, when a boy, among cranks and cogwheels. We should be
more disposed to trust him if he had been brought into occasional
contact with a Maid and a Magpie; if he had made one or two
diversions into the Forest of Bondy; or had even gone the length
of a Christmas Pantomime. There is a range of imagination in most

of us, which no amount of steam-engines will satisfy; and which
The-great-exhibition-of-the-works-of-industry-of-all-nations,
itself, will probably leave unappeased. The lower we go, the
more natural it is that the best-relished provision for this should
be found in dramatic entertainments; as at once the most obvious,
the least troublesome, and the most real, of all escapes out of
the literal world. Joe Whelks, of the New Cut, Lambeth, is not
much of a reader, has no great store of books, no very com-
modious room to read in, no very decided inclination to read, and
no power at all of presenting vividly before his mind's eye what
he reads about. But, put Joe in the gallery of the Victoria Theatre;
show him doors and windows in the scene that will open and shut,
and that people can get in and out of; tell him a story with these
aids, and by the help of live men and women dressed up, confiding
to him their innermost secrets, in voices audible half a mile off;
and Joe will unravel a story through all its entanglements, and
sit there as long after midnight as you have anything left to show
him. Accordingly, the Theatres to which Mr Whelks resorts are
always full; and whatever changes of fashion the drama knows
elsewhere, it is always fashionable in the New Cut.

The question, then, might not unnaturally arise, one would
suppose, whether Mr Whelks's education is at all susceptible of
improvement, through the agency of his theatrical tastes. How
far it is improved at present, our readers shall judge for themselves.

In affording them the means of doing so, we wish to disclaim
any grave imputation on those who are concerned in ministering
to the dramatic gratification of Mr Whelks. Heavily taxed,
wholly unassisted by the State, deserted by the gentry, and quite
unrecognized as a means of public instruction, the higher English
Drama has declined. Those who would live to please Mr Whelks
must please Mr Whelks to live. It is not the Manager's province
to hold the Mirror up to Nature, but to Mr Whelks—the only
person who acknowledges him. If, in like manner, the actor's
nature, like the dyer's hand, become subdued to what he works in,
the actor can hardly be blamed for it. He grinds hard at his vocation, is often steeped in direful poverty, and lives, at the best, in a

CHIMNEY SWEEPER.

little world of mockeries. It is bad enough to give away a great estate six nights a week, and want a shilling; to preside at imaginary banquets, hungry for a mutton chop; to smack the lips over a tankard of toast and water, and declaim about the mellow produce of the sunny vineyard on the banks of the Rhine; to be a rattling young lover, with the measles at home; and to paint sorrow over with burnt cork and rouge; without being called upon to despise his vocation, too. If he can utter the trash to which he is condemned, with any relish, so much the better for him, Heaven knows; and peace be with him!

A few weeks ago, we went to one of Mr Whelks's favourite Theatres, to see an attractive Melo-Drama called MAY MORN-ING, OR THE MYSTERY OF 1715, AND THE MURDER! We had an idea that the former of these titles might refer to the month in which either the Mystery or the Murder happened, but we found it to be the name of the heroine, the pride of Keswick Vale; who was 'called May Morning' (after a common custom among the English Peasantry) 'from her bright eyes and merry laugh'. Of this young lady, it may be observed, in passing, that she sub-sequently sustained every possible calamity of human existence, in a white muslin gown with blue tucks; and that she did every conceivable and inconceivable thing with a pistol that could any-how be effected by that description of fire-arms.

The Theatre was extremely full. The prices of admission were, to the boxes, a shilling; to the pit, sixpence; to the gallery, three-pence. The gallery was of enormous dimensions (among the company, in the front row, we observed Mr Whelks); and over-flowing with occupants. It required no close observation of the attentive faces, rising one above another, to the very door in the roof, and squeezed and jammed in, regardless of all discomforts, even there, to impress a stranger with a sense of its being highly desirable to lose no possible chance of effecting any mental im-provement in that great audience.

The company in the pit were not very clean or sweet-savoured, but there were some good-humoured young mechanics among them, with their wives. These were generally accompanied by 'the baby', insomuch that the pit was a perfect nursery. No effect made on the stage was so curious as the looking down on the quiet faces of these babies fast asleep, after looking up at the staring sea of heads in the gallery. There were a good many cold fried soles in the pit, besides; and a variety of flat stone bottles, of all portable sizes.

The audience in the boxes was of much the same character (babies and fish excepted) as the audience in the pit. A private in the foot-guards sat in the next box; and a personage who wore pins on his coat instead of buttons, and was in such a damp habit of living as to be quite mouldy, was our nearest neighbour. In several parts of the house we noticed some young pickpockets of our acquaintance; but as they were evidently there as private individuals, and not in their public capacity, we were little disturbed by their presence. For we consider the hours of idleness passed by this class of society as so much gain to society at large; and we do not join in a whimsical sort of lamentation that is generally made over them, when they are found to be unoccupied.

As we made these observations the curtain rose, and we were presently in possession of the following particulars.

Sir George Elmore, a melancholy Baronet with every appearance of being in that advanced stage of indigestion in which Mr Morrison's patients usually are, when they happen to hear, through Mr Moat, of the surprising effects of his Vegetable Pills, was found to be living in a very large castle, in the society of one round table, two chairs, and Captain George Elmore, 'his supposed son, the Child of Mystery, and the Man of Crime'. The Captain, in addition to an undutiful habit of bullying his father on all occasions, was a prey to many vices: foremost among which may be mentioned his desertion of his wife, 'Estella de Neva, a Spanish lady', and his determination unlawfully to possess himself of May Morning; M. M. being then on the eve of marriage to Will Stanmore, a cheerful sailor, with very loose legs.

The strongest evidence, at first, of the Captain's being the Child of Mystery and the Man of Crime was deducible from his boots, which, being very high and wide, and apparently made of sticking-plaister, justified the worst theatrical suspicions to his disadvantage. And indeed he presently turned out as ill as could

be desired : getting into May Morning's Cottage by the window
after dark; refusing to 'unhand' May Morning when required to
do so by that lady; waking May Morning's only surviving parent,
a blind old gentleman with a black ribbon over his eyes, whom we
shall call Mr Stars, as his name was stated in the bill thus * * * * * *;
and showing himself desperately bent on carrying off May Morning by force of arms. Even this was not the worst of the Captain;
for, being foiled in his diabolical purpose—temporarily by means
of knives and pistols, providentially caught up and directed at him
by May Morning, and finally, for the time being, by the advent of
Will Stanmore—he caused one Slink, his adherent, to denounce
Will Stanmore as a rebel, and got that cheerful mariner carried
off, and shut up in prison. At about the same period of the Captain's career there suddenly appeared in his father's castle a dark-
complexioned lady of the name of Manuella, 'a Zingara Woman
from the Pyrenean mountains; the wild wanderer of the heath,
and the pronouncer of the prophecy', who threw the melancholy
baronet, his supposed father, into the greatest confusion by asking
him what he had upon his conscience, and by pronouncing mysterious rhymes concerning the Child of Mystery and the Man of
Crime, to a low trembling of fiddles. Matters were in this state
when the Theatre resounded with applause, and Mr Whelks fell
into a fit of unbounded enthusiasm, consequent on the entrance of
'Michael the Mendicant'.

At first we referred something of the cordiality with which
Michael the Mendicant was greeted to the fact of his being 'made
up' with an excessively dirty face, which might create a bond of
union between himself and a large majority of the audience. But
it soon came out that Michael the Mendicant had been hired in old
time by Sir George Elmore, to murder his (Sir George Elmore's)
elder brother—which he had done; notwithstanding which little
affair of honour, Michael was in reality a very good fellow; quite
a tender-hearted man; who, on hearing of the Captain's determination to settle Will Stanmore, cried out, 'What! more
bel-ood!' and fell flat—overpowered by his nice sense of humanity. In like manner, in describing that small error of judgment into
which he had allowed himself to be tempted by money, this

gentleman exclaimed, 'I ster-ruck him down, and fel-ed in er-
orror!' and further he remarked, with honest pride, 'I have liveder
as a beggar—a roadersider vaigerant, but no ker-rime since then
has stained these hands!' All these sentiments of the worthy man
were hailed with showers of applause; and when, in the excitement of his feelings on one occasion, after a soliloquy, he 'went
off' *on his back*, kicking and shuffling along the ground, after the
manner of bold spirits in trouble, who object to be taken to the
station-house, the cheering was tremendous.

And to see how little harm he had done, after all! Sir George
Elmore's elder brother was NOT dead. Not he! He recovered,
after this sensitive creature had 'fel-ed in er-orror', and, putting
a black ribbon over his eyes to disguise himself, went and lived
in a modest retirement with his only child. In short, Mr Stars was
the identical individual! When Will Stanmore turned out to be
the wrongful Sir George Elmore's son, instead of the Child of
Mystery and Man of Crime, who turned out to be Michael's son
(a change having been effected, in revenge, by the lady from the
Pyrenean mountains, who became the Wild Wanderer of the
Heath, in consequence of the wrongful Sir George Elmore's per-
fidy to her and desertion of her), Mr Stars went up to the Castle,
and mentioned to his murdering brother how it was. Mr Stars
said it was all right; he bore no malice; he had kept out of the way,
in order that his murdering brother (to whose numerous virtues
he was no stranger) might enjoy the property; and now he would
propose that they should make it up and dine together. The
murdering brother immediately consented, embraced the Wild
Wanderer, and it is supposed set instructions to Doctors'
Commons for a licence to marry her. After which, they were all
very comfortable indeed. For it is not much to try to murder your
brother for the sake of his property, if you only suborn such a
delicate assassin as Michael the Mendicant!

All this did not tend to the satisfaction of the Child of Mystery
and Man of Crime, who was so little pleased by the general happiness, that he shot Will Stanmore, now joyfully out of prison and
going to be married directly to May Morning, and carried off
the body, and May Morning to boot, to a lone hut. Here, Will

Stanmore, laid out for dead at fifteen minutes past twelve, p.m., arose at seventeen minutes past, infinitely fresher than most daisies, and fought two strong men single-handed. However, the Wild Wanderer, arriving with a party of male wild wanderers, who were always at her disposal—and the murdering brother arriving arm-in-arm with Mr Stars—stopped the combat, confounded the Child of Mystery and Man of Crime, and blessed the lovers.

The adventures of RED RIVEN THE BANDIT concluded the moral lesson of the evening. But, feeling by this time a little fatigued, and believing that we already discerned in the countenance of Mr Whelks a sufficient confusion between right and wrong to last him for one night, we retired: the rather as we intended to meet him, shortly, at another place of dramatic entertainment for the people.

Household Words, March 30th, 1850

On Duty
with Inspector Field

How goes the night? Saint Giles's clock is striking nine. The weather is dull and wet, and the long lines of street lamps are blurred, as if we saw them through tears. A damp wind blows and rakes the pieman's fire out, when he opens the door of his little furnace, carrying away an eddy of sparks.

Saint Giles's clock strikes nine. We are punctual. Where is Inspector Field? Assistant Commissioner of Police is already here, enwrapped in oilskin cloak, and standing in the shadow of Saint Giles's steeple. Detective Sergeant, weary of speaking French all day to foreigners unpacking at the Great Exhibition, is already here. Where is Inspector Field?

Inspector Field is, tonight, the guardian genius of the British Museum. He is bringing his shrewd eye to bear on every corner of its solitary galleries, before he reports 'all right'. Suspicious of the Elgin marbles, and not to be done by cat-faced Egyptian giants with their hands upon their knees. Inspector Field, sagacious, vigilant, lamp in hand, throwing monstrous shadows on the walls and ceilings, passes through the spacious rooms. If a mummy trembled in an atom of its dusty covering, Inspector Field would say, 'Come out of that, Tom Green. I know you!' If the smallest 'Gonoph' about town were crouching at the bottom of a classic bath, Inspector Field would nose him with a finer scent than the ogre's, when adventurous Jack lay trembling in his kitchen copper. But all is quiet, and Inspector Field goes warily on, making little outward show of attending to anything in particular, just recognizing the Ichthyosaurus as a familiar acquaintance, and wondering, perhaps, how the detectives did it in the days before the Flood.

Will Inspector Field be long about his work? He may be half an hour longer. He sends his compliments by police constable, and proposes that we meet at Saint Giles's Station House, across the road. Good. It were as well to stand by the fire, there, as in the shadow of Saint Giles's steeple.

Anything doing here tonight? Not much. We are very quiet. A lost boy, extremely calm and small, sitting by the fire, whom we now confide to a constable to take home, for the child says that if you show him Newgate Street, he can show you where he lives —a raving drunken woman in the cells, who has screeched her voice away, and has hardly power enough left to declare, even with the passionate help of her feet and arms, that she is the daughter of a British officer, and strike her blind and dead, but she'll write a letter to the Queen! but who is soothed with a drink of water—in another cell, a quiet woman, with a child at her breast, for begging—in another, her husband in a smock-frock, with a basket of watercresses—in another, a pickpocket—in another, a meek tremulous old pauper man who has been out for a holiday 'and has took but a little drop, but it has overcome him after so many months in the house'—and that's all as yet. Presently, a sensation at the Station House door. Mr Field, gentlemen!

Inspector Field comes in, wiping his forehead, for he is of a burly figure, and has come fast from the ores and metals of the deep mines of the earth, and from the Parrot Gods of the South Sea Islands, and from the birds and beetles of the tropics, and from the Arts of Greece and Rome, and from the Sculptures of Nineveh, and from the traces of an elder world, when these were not. Is Rogers ready? Rogers is ready, strapped and greatcoated, with a flaming eye in the middle of his waist, like a deformed Cyclops. Lead on, Rogers, to Rats' Castle!

How many people may there be in London who, if we had brought them deviously and blindfold, to this street, fifty paces from the Station House, and within call of Saint Giles's church, would know it for a not remote part of the city in which their lives are passed? How many, who amidst this compound of sickening smells, these heaps of filth, these tumbling houses, with all their

vile contents, animate and inanimate, slimily overflowing into the
black road, would believe that they breathe *this* air? How much
Red Tape may there be, that could look round on the faces which
now hem us in—for our appearance here has caused a rush from
all points to a common centre—the lowering foreheads, the
sallow cheeks, the brutal eyes, the matted hair, the infected,
vermin-haunted heaps of rags—and say, 'I have thought of this.
I have not dismissed the thing. I have neither blustered it away,
nor frozen it away, nor tied it up and put it away, nor smoothly
said pooh, pooh! to it when it has been shown to me'?

This is not what Rogers wants to know, however. What
Rogers wants to know is, whether you *will* clear the way here,
some of you, or whether you won't; because if you don't do it
right on end, he'll lock you up! 'What! *You* are there, are you,
Bob Miles? You haven't had enough of it yet, haven't you? You
want three months more, do you? Come away from that gentleman! What are you creeping round there for?'

'What am I a doing, thinn, Mr Rogers?' says Bob Miles, appearing, villainous, at the end of a lane of light, made by the
lantern.

'I'll let you know pretty quick, if you don't hook it. *Will* you
hook it?'

A sycophantic murmur rises from the crowd. 'Hook it, Bob,
when Mr Rogers and Mr Field tells you! Why don't you hook
it, when you are told to?'

The most importunate of the voices strikes familiarly on Mr
Roger's ear. He suddenly turns his lantern on the owner.

'What! *You* are there, are you, Mister Click? You hook it too
—come!'

'What for?' says Mr Click, discomfited.

'You hook it, will you!' says Mr Rogers with stern emphasis.

Both Click and Miles *do* 'hook it', without another word, or, in
plainer English, sneak away.

'Come up there, my men!' says Inspector Field to two constables on duty who have followed. 'Keep together, gentlemen;
we are going down here. Heads!'

Saint Giles's church strikes half-past ten. We stoop low, and creep down a precipitous flight of steps into a dark close cellar. There is a fire. There is a long deal table. There are benches. The cellar is full of company, chiefly very young men in various conditions of dirt and raggedness. Some are eating supper. There are no girls or women present. Welcome to Rats' Castle, gentlemen, and to this company of noted thieves!

'Well, my lads! How are you, my lads? What have you been doing today? Here's some company come to see you, my lads! *There's* a plate of beefsteak, sir, for the supper of a fine young man! And there's a mouth for a steak, sir! Why, I should be too proud of such a mouth as that, if I had it myself! Stand up and show it, sir! Take off your cap. There's a fine young man for a nice little party, sir! An't he?'

Inspector Field is the bustling speaker. Inspector Field's eye is the roving eye that searches every corner of the cellar as he talks. Inspector Field's hand is the well-known hand that has collared half the people here, and motioned their brothers, sisters, fathers, mothers, male and female friends, inexorably to New South Wales. Yet Inspector Field stands in this den, the Sultan of the place. Every thief here cowers before him, like a schoolboy before his schoolmaster. All watch him, all answer when addressed, all laugh at his jokes, all seek to propitiate him. This cellar company alone—to say nothing of the crowd surrounding the entrance from the street above, and making the steps shine with eyes—is strong enough to murder us all, and willing enough to do it; but let Inspector Field have a mind to pick out one thief here, and take him; let him produce that ghostly truncheon from his pocket, and say, with his business-air, 'My lad, I want you!' and all Rats' Castle shall be stricken with paralysis, and not a finger move against him, as he fits the handcuffs on!

Where's the Earl of Warwick?—Here he is, Mr Field! Here's the Earl of Warwick, Mr Field!—Oh, there you are, my Lord. Come for'ard. There's a chest, sir, not to have a clean shirt on. An't it? Take your hat off, my Lord. Why, I should be ashamed if I was you—and an Earl, too—to show myself to a gentleman with my hat on!—The Earl of Warwick laughs and uncovers. All the company laugh. One pickpocket, especially, laughs with great enthusiasm. Oh, what a jolly game it is, when Mr Field comes down—and don't want nobody!

So, *you* are here, too, are you, you tall, grey, soldierly-looking, grave man, standing by the fire?—Yes, sir. Good evening, Mr Field!—Let us see. You lived servant to a nobleman once?—Yes, Mr Field.—And what is it you do now; I forget?—Well, Mr Field, I job about as well as I can. I left my employment on account of delicate health. The family is still kind to me. Mr Wix of Piccadilly is also very kind to me when I am hard up. Likewise Mr Nix of Oxford Street. I get a trifle from them occasionally, and rub on as well as I can, Mr Field. Mr Field's eye rolls enjoyingly, for this man is a notorious begging-letter writer.—Good night, my lads!—Good night, Mr Field, and thank'ee, sir!

Clear the street here, half a thousand of you! Cut it, Mrs Stalker—none of that—we don't want you! Rogers of the flaming eye, lead on to the tramps' lodging-house!

A dream of baleful faces attends to the door. Now, stand back all of you! In the rear Detective Sergeant plants himself, composedly whistling, with his strong right arm across the narrow passage. Mrs Stalker, I am something'd that need not be written here, if you won't get yourself into trouble, in about half a minute, if I see that face of yours again!

Saint Giles's church clock, striking eleven, hums through our hand from the dilapidated door of a dark outhouse as we open it, and are stricken back by the pestilent breath that issues from within. Rogers to the front with the light, and let us look!

Ten, twenty, thirty—who can count them! Men, women, children, for the most part naked, heaped upon the floor like maggots in a cheese! Ho! In that dark corner yonder! Does anybody lie there? Me, sir, Irish me, a widder, with six children. And yonder? Me, sir, Irish me, with me wife and eight poor babes. And to the left there? Me, sir, Irish me, along with two more Irish boys as is me friends. And to the right there? Me, sir, and the Murphy fam'ly, numbering five blessed souls. And what's this, coiling, now, about my foot? Another Irish me, pitifully in want of shaving, whom I have awakened from sleep—and across my other foot lies his wife—and by the shoes of Inspector Field

lie their three eldest—and their youngest are at present squeezed
between the open door and the wall. And why is there no one on
that little mat before the sullen fire? Because O'Donovan, with
his wife and daughter, is not come in from selling Lucifers! Nor on
the bit of sacking in the nearest corner? Bad luck! Because that
Irish family is late tonight, a-cadging in the streets!

They are all awake now, the children excepted, and most of
them sit up, to stare. Wheresoever Mr Rogers turns the flaming
eye, there is a spectral figure rising, unshrouded, from a grave
of rags. Who is the landlord here?—I am, Mr Field! says a
bundle of ribs and parchment against the wall, scratching itself.—
Will you spend this money fairly, in the morning, to buy coffee
for 'em all?—Yes, sir, I will!—Oh, he'll do it, sir, he'll do it fair.
He's honest! cry the spectres. And with thanks and Good Night
sink into their graves again.

Thus, we make our New Oxford Streets, and our other new
streets, never heeding, never asking, where the wretches whom
we clear out, crowd. With such scenes at our doors, with all the
plagues of Egypt tied up with bits of cobweb in kennels so near
our homes, we timorously make our Nuisance Bills and Boards
of Health, nonentities, and think to keep away the Wolves of
Crime and Filth, by our electioneering ducking to little vestry-
men and our gentlemanly handling of Red Tape!

Intelligence of the coffee-money has got abroad. The yard is
full, and Rogers of the flaming eye is beleaguered with entreaties
to show other lodging houses. Mine next! Mine! Mine! Rogers,
military, obdurate, stiff-necked, immovable, replies not, but leads
away; all falling back before him. Inspector Field follows. Detective Sergeant, with his barrier of arm across the little passage,
deliberately waits to close the procession. He sees behind him,
without any effort, and exceedingly disturbs one individual far in
the rear by coolly calling out, 'It won't do, Mr Michael! Don't
try it!'

After council holden in the street, we enter other lodging-
houses, public houses, many lairs and holes; all noisome and
offensive; none so filthy and so crowded as where Irish are. In one,
the Ethiopian party are expected home presently—were in

Oxford Street when last heard of—shall be fetched, for our delight, within ten minutes. In another, one of the two or three Professors who draw Napoleon Buonaparte and a couple of mackerel, on the pavement, and then let the work of art out to a speculator, is refreshing after his labours. In another, the vested interest of the profitable nuisance has been in one family for a hundred years, and the landlord drives in comfortably from the country to his snug little stew in town. In all, Inspector Field is received with warmth. Coiners and smashers droop before him; pickpockets defer to him; the gentle sex (not very gentle here) smile upon him. Half drunken hags check themselves in the midst of pots of beer, or pints of gin, to drink to Mr Field, and pressingly to ask the honour of his finishing the draught. One beldame in rusty black has such admiration for him that she runs a whole street's length to shake him by the hand; tumbling into a heap of mud by the way, and still pressing her attentions when her very form has ceased to be distinguishable through it. Before the power of the law, the power of superior sense—for common thieves are fools beside these men—and the power of a perfect mastery of their character, the garrison of Rats' Castle and the adjacent Fortresses make but a skulking show indeed when reviewed by Inspector Field.

Saint Giles's clock says it will be midnight in half an hour, and Inspector Field says we must hurry to the Old Mint in the Borough. The cab-driver is low-spirited, and has a solemn sense of his responsibility. Now, what's your fare, my lad?—Oh, *you* know, Inspector Field, what's the good of asking *me*!

Say, Parker, strapped and greatcoated, and waiting in dim Borough doorway by appointment, to replace the trusty Rogers whom we left deep in Saint Giles's, are you ready? Ready, Inspector Field, and at a motion of my wrist behold my flaming eye.

This narrow street, sir, is the chief part of the Old Mint, full of low lodging-houses, as you see by the transparent canvas-lamps and blinds, announcing beds for travellers! But it is greatly changed, friend Field, from my former knowledge of it; it is infinitely quieter and more subdued than when I was here last, some seven years ago? Oh yes! Inspector Haynes, a first-rate man, is on this station now and plays the Devil with them!

Well, my lads! How are you tonight, my lads? Playing cards here, eh? Who wins?—Why, Mr Field, I, the sulky gentleman with the damp flat side-curls, rubbing my bleared eye with the end of my neckerchief which is like a dirty eel-skin, am losing just at present, but I suppose I must take my pipe out of my mouth, and be submissive to *you*—I hope I see you well, Mr Field?—Aye, all right, my lad. Deputy, who have you got upstairs? Be pleased to show the rooms!

Why Deputy, Inspector Field can't say. He only knows that the man who takes care of the beds and lodgers is always called so. Steady, O Deputy, with the flaring candle in the blacking-bottle, for this is a slushy backyard, and the wooden staircase outside the house creaks and has holes in it.

Again, in these confined intolerable rooms, burrowed out like the holes of rats or the nests of insect-vermin, but fuller of intolerable smells, are crowds of sleepers, each on his foul truckle-bed coiled up beneath a rug. Halloa here! Come! Let us see you! Show your face! Pilot Parker goes from bed to bed and turns their slumbering heads towards us, as a salesman might turn sheep. Some wake up with an execration and a threat.—What! who spoke? Oh! If it's the accursed glaring eye that fixes me, go where I will, I am helpless. Here! I sit up to be looked at. Is it me you want? Not you, lie down again! and I lie down, with a woeful growl.

Wherever the turning lane of light becomes stationary for a moment some sleeper appears at the end of it, submits himself to be scrutinized, and fades away into the darkness.

There should be strange dreams here, Deputy. They sleep sound enough, says Deputy, taking the candle out of the blacking-bottle, snuffing it with his fingers, throwing the snuff into the bottle, and corking it up with the candle; that's all *I* know. What is the inscription, Deputy, on all the discoloured sheets? A precaution against loss of linen. Deputy turns down the rug of an unoccupied bed and discloses it. STOP THIEF!

To lie at night, wrapped in the legend of my slinking life; to take the cry that pursues me, waking, to my breast in sleep; to

have it staring at me, and clamouring for me, as soon as consciousness returns; to have it for my first-foot on New Year's
Day, my Valentine, my birthday salute, my Christmas greeting,
my parting with the old year. STOP THIEF!

And to know that I *must* be stopped, come what will. To know
that I am no match for this individual energy and keenness, or
this organized and steady system! Come across the street, here,
and, entering by a little shop, and yard, examine these intricate
passages and doors, contrived for escape, flapping and counter-
flapping, like the lids of the conjurer's boxes. But what avail they?
Who gets in by a nod, and shows their secret working to us?
Inspector Field.

Don't forget the old Farm House, Parker! Parker is not the
man to forget it. We are going there, now. It is the old Manor
House of these parts, and stood in the country once. Then, perhaps, there was something, which was not the beastly street, to
see from the shattered low fronts of the overhanging wooden
houses we are passing under—shut up now, pasted over with bills
about the literature and drama of the Mint, and mouldering away.
This long paved yard was a paddock or a garden once, or a court
in front of the Farm House. Perchance, with a dovecot in the
centre, and fowls pecking about—with fair elm trees, then, where
discoloured chimney-stacks and gables are now—noisy, then,
with rooks which have yielded to a different sort of rookery. It's
likelier than not, Inspector Field thinks, as we turn into the common kitchen, which is in the yard, and many paces from the house.

Well, my lads and lasses, how are you all? Where's Blackey,
who has stood near London Bridge these five-and-twenty years,
with a painted skin to represent disease?—Here he is, Mr Field!
—How are you, Blackey?—Jolly, sa! Not playing the fiddle tonight, Blackey?—Not a night, sa! A sharp, smiling youth, the
wit of the kitchen, interposes. He an't musical tonight, sir. I've
been giving him a moral lecture; I've been a-talking to him about
his latter end, you see. A good many of these are my pupils, sir.
This here young man (smoothing down the hair of one near him,
reading a Sunday paper) is a pupil of mine. I'm a-teaching of him
to read, sir. He's a promising cove, sir. He's a smith, he is, and

gets his living by the sweat of the brow, sir. So do I, myself, sir. This young woman is my sister, Mr Field. *She's* getting on very well too. I've a deal of trouble with 'em, sir, but I'm richly rewarded, now I see 'em all a-doing so well, and growing up so creditable. That's a great comfort, that is, an't it, sir?—In the midst of the kitchen (the whole kitchen is in ecstasies with this impromptu 'chaff') sits a young, modest, gentle-looking creature, with a beautiful child in her lap. She seems to belong to the company, but is so strangely unlike it. She has such a pretty, quiet face and voice, and is so proud to hear the child admired—thinks you would hardly believe that he is only nine months old! Is she as bad as the rest, I wonder? Inspectorial experience does not engender a belief contrariwise, but prompts the answer, Not a ha-porth of difference!

There is a piano going in the old Farm House as we approach. It stops. Landlady appears. Has no objections, Mr Field, to gentlemen being brought, but wishes it were at earlier hours, the lodgers complaining of ill-conwenience. Inspector Field is polite and soothing—knows his woman and the sex. Deputy (a girl in this case) shows the way up a heavy broad old staircase, kept very clean, into clean rooms where many sleepers are, and where painted panels of an older time look strangely on the truckle beds. The sight of whitewash and the smell of soap—two things we seem by this time to have parted from in infancy—make the old Farm House a phenomenon, and connect themselves with the so curiously misplaced picture of the pretty mother and child long after we have left it,—long after we have left, besides, the neighbouring nook with something of a rustic flavour in it yet, where once, beneath a low wooden colonnade still standing as of yore, the eminent Jack Sheppard condescended to regale himself, and where, now, two old bachelor brothers in broad hats (who are whispered in the Mint to have made a compact long ago that if either should ever marry he must forfeit his share of the joint property) still keep a sequestered tavern, and sit o' nights smoking pipes in the bar, among ancient bottles and glasses, as our eyes behold them.

How goes the night now? Saint George of Southwark answers

with twelve blows upon his bell. Parker, good night, for Williams is already waiting over in the region of Ratcliffe Highway, to show the houses where the sailors dance.

I should like to know where Inspector Field was born. In Ratcliffe Highway, I would have answered with confidence, but for his being equally at home wherever we go. *He* does not trouble his head as I do, about the river at night. *He* does not care for its creeping, black and silent, on our right there, rushing through sluice-gates, lapping at piles and posts and iron rings, hiding strange things in its mud, running away with suicides and accidentally drowned bodies faster than midnight funeral should, and acquiring such various experience between its cradle and its grave. It has no mystery for *him*. Is there not the Thames Police?

Accordingly, Williams leads the way. We are a little late, for some of the houses are already closing. No matter. You show us plenty. All the landlords know Inspector Field. All pass him, freely and good-humouredly, wheresoever he wants to go. So thoroughly are all these houses open to him and our local guide that, granting that sailors must be entertained in their own way—as I suppose they must, and have a right to be—I hardly know how such places could be better regulated. Not that I call the company very select; or the dancing very graceful—even so graceful as that of the German Sugar Bakers, whose assembly, by the Minories, we stopped to visit—but there is watchful maintenance of order in every house, and swift expulsion where need is. Even in the midst of drunkenness, both of the lethargic kind and the lively, there is sharp landlord supervision, and pockets are in less peril than out of doors. These houses show, singularly, how much of the picturesque and romantic there truly is in the sailor, requiring to be especially addressed. All the songs (sung in a hailstorm of halfpence, which are pitched at the singer without the least tenderness for the time or tune—mostly from great rolls of copper carried for the purpose—and which he occasionally dodges like shot as they fly near his head) are of the sentimental sea sort. All the rooms are decorated with nautical subjects. Wrecks, engagements, ships on fire, ships passing lighthouses on iron-bound coasts, ships blowing up, ships going down, ships running ashore, men lying out upon the main-yard in a gale of wind, sailors and ships in every variety of peril, constitute the illustrations of fact. Nothing can be done in the fanciful way, without a thumping boy upon a scaly dolphin.

How goes the night now? Past one. Black and Green are waiting in Whitechapel to unveil the mysteries of Wentworth Street. Williams, the best of friends must part. Adieu!

Are not Black and Green ready at the appointed place? Oh yes! They glide out of shadow as we stop. Imperturbable Black opens the cab door; Imperturbable Green takes a mental note of the driver. Both Green and Black then open, each his flaming eye, and marshal us the way that we are going.

The lodging-house we want is hidden in a maze of streets and courts. It is fast shut. We knock at the door, and stand hushed looking up for a light at one or other of the begrimed old lattice windows in its ugly front, when another constable comes up— supposes that we want 'to see the school'. Detective Sergeant meanwhile has got over a rail, opened a gate, dropped down an area, overcome some other little obstacles, and tapped at a window. Now returns. The landlord will send a deputy immediately.

Deputy is heard to stumble out of bed. Deputy lights a candle, draws back a bolt or two, and appears at the door. Deputy is a shivering shirt and trousers by no means clean, a yawning face, a shock head much confused externally and internally. We want to look for someone. You may go up with the light, and take 'em all, if you like, says Deputy, resigning it, and sitting down upon a bench in the kitchen with his ten fingers sleepily twisting in his hair.

Holloa here! Now then! Show yourselves. That'll do. It's not you. Don't disturb yourself any more! So on, through a labyrinth of airless rooms, each man responding, like a wild beast, to the keeper who has tamed him, and who goes into his cage. What, you haven't found him, then? says Deputy, when we come down. A woman mysteriously sitting up all night in the dark by the smouldering ashes of the kitchen fire, says it's only tramps and cadgers here; it's gonophs over the way. A man mysteriously walking about the kitchen all night in the dark, bids her hold her tongue. We come out. Deputy fastens the door and goes to bed again.

Black and Green, you know Bark, lodging-house keeper and receiver of stolen goods?—Oh yes, Inspector Field.—Go to Bark's next.

Bark sleeps in an inner wooden hutch, near his street door. As we parley on the step with Bark's Deputy, Bark growls in his bed. We enter, and Bark flies out of bed. Bark is a red villain and a wrathful, with a sanguine throat that looks very much as if it were expressly made for hanging, as he stretches it out, in pale defiance, over the half-door of his hutch. Bark's parts of speech are of an awful sort—principally adjectives. I won't, says Bark, have no adjective police and adjective strangers in my adjective premises! I won't, by adjective and substantive! Give me my trousers, and I'll send the whole adjective police to adjective and substantive! Give me, says Bark, my adjective trousers! I'll put an adjective knife in the whole bileing of 'em. I'll punch their adjective heads. I'll rip up their adjective substantives. Give me my adjective trousers! says Bark, and I'll spike the bileing of 'em!

Now, Bark, what's the use of this? Here's Black and Green, Detective Sergeant, and Inspector Field. You know we will come in.—I know you won't! says Bark. Somebody give me my adjective trousers! Bark's trousers seem difficult to find. He calls for them as Hercules might for his club. Give me my adjective trousers! says Bark, and I'll spile the bileing of 'em.

Inspector Field holds that it's all one whether Bark likes the visit or don't like it. He, Inspector Field, is an Inspector of the Detective Police, Detective Sergeant *is* Detective Sergeant, Black and Green are constables in uniform. Don't you be a fool, Bark, or you know it will be the worse for you.—I don't care, says Bark. Give me my adjective trousers!

At two o'clock in the morning we descend into Bark's low kitchen, leaving Bark to foam at the mouth above, and Imperturbable Black and Green to look at him. Bark's kitchen is crammed full of thieves, holding a *conversazione* there by lamplight. It is by far the most dangerous assembly we have seen yet.

Stimulated by the ravings of Bark, above, their looks are sullen, but not a man speaks. We ascend again. Bark has got his trousers, and is in a state of madness in the passage with his back against a door that shuts off the upper staircase. We observe, in other respects, a ferocious individuality in Bark. Instead of 'STOP THIEF!' on his linen, he prints 'STOLEN FROM BARK's!'

Now, Bark, we are going upstairs!—No, you ain't!—You refuse admission to the police, do you, Bark?—Yes, I do! I refuse it to all the adjective police, and to all the adjective substantives. If the adjective coves in the kitchen was men, they'd come up now, and do for you! Shut me that there door! says Bark, and suddenly we are enclosed in the passage. They'd come up and do for you! cries Bark, and waits. Not a sound in the kitchen! They'd come up and do for you! cries Bark again, and waits. Not a sound in the kitchen! We are shut up, half a dozen of us, in Bark's house in the innermost recesses of the worst part of London, in the dead of the night—the house is crammed with notorious robbers and ruffians —and not a man stirs. No, Bark. They know the weight of the law, and they know Inspector Field and Co. too well!

We leave bully Bark to subside at leisure out of his passion and his trousers, and, I dare say, to be inconveniently reminded of this little brush before long. Black and Green do ordinary duty here, and look serious.

As to White, who waits on Holborn Hill to show the courts that are eaten out of Rotten Gray's Inn Lane, where other lodging-houses are, and where (in one blind alley) the Thieves' Kitchen and Seminary for the teaching of the art to children is, the night has so worn away, being now

almost at odds with morning, which is which,

that they are quiet, and no light shines through the chinks in the shutters. As undistinctive Death will come here, one day, sleep comes now. The wicked cease from troubling sometimes, even in this life.

Household Words, June 14th, 1851

Arcadian London

Being in a humour for complete solitude and uninterrupted meditation this autumn, I have taken a lodging for six weeks in the
most unfrequented part of England—in a word, in London.

The retreat into which I have withdrawn myself is Bond Street.
From this lonely spot I make pilgrimages into the surrounding
wilderness, and traverse extensive tracts of the Great Desert.
The first solemn feeling of isolation overcome, the first oppres-
sive consciousness of profound retirement conquered, I enjoy that
sense of freedom, and feel reviving within me that latent wildness
of the original savage, which has been (upon the whole, somewhat frequently) noticed by Travellers.

My lodgings are at a hatter's—my own hatter's. After exhibiting no articles in his window, for some weeks, but seaside
wide-awakes, shooting caps, and a choice of rough waterproof
head-gear for the moors and mountains, he has put upon the heads
of his family as much of this stock as they could carry, and has taken
them off to the Isle of Thanet. His young man alone remains—
and remains alone—in the shop. The young man has let out the
fire at which the irons are heated, and saving his strong sense of
duty, I see no reason why he should take the shutters down.

Happily for himself and for his country, the young man is a
Volunteer; most happily for himself, or I think he would become
the prey of a settled melancholy. For, to live surrounded by human
hats, and alienated from human heads to fit them on, is surely a
great endurance. But, the young man, sustained by practising his
exercise, and by constantly furbishing up his regulation plume (it
is unnecessary to observe that, as a hatter, he is in a cock's-feather
corps), is resigned, and uncomplaining. On a Saturday, when he
closes early and gets his knickerbockers on, he is even cheerful. I

[148]

am gratefully particular in this reference to him, because he is my companion through many peaceful hours. My hatter has a desk up certain steps behind his counter, enclosed like the clerk's desk at church. I shut myself into this place of seclusion after breakfast, and meditate. At such times I observe the young man loading an imaginary rifle with the greatest precision, and maintaining a most galling and destructive fire upon the national enemy. I thank him publicly for his companionship and his patriotism.

The simple character of my life, and the calm nature of the scenes by which I am surrounded, occasion me to rise early. I go forth in my slippers, and promenade the pavement. It is pastoral to feel the freshness of the air in the uninhabited town, and to appreciate the shepherdess character of the few milkwomen who purvey so little milk that it would be worth nobody's while to adulterate it, if anybody were left to undertake the task. On the crowded sea-shore, the great demand for milk, combined with the strong local temptation of chalk, would betray itself in the lowered quality of the article. In Arcadian London I derive it from the cow.

The Arcadian simplicity of the metropolis altogether, and the primitive ways into which it has fallen in this autumnal Golden Age, make it entirely new to me. Within a few hundred yards of my retreat is the house of a friend who maintains a most sumptuous butler. I never, until yesterday, saw that butler out of superfine black broadcloth. Until yesterday I never saw him off duty, never saw him (he is the best of butlers) with the appearance of having any mind for anything but the glory of his master and his master's friends. Yesterday morning, walking in my slippers near the house of which he is the prop and ornament—a house now a waste of shutters—I encountered that butler, also in his slippers, and in a shooting suit of one colour, and in a low-crowned straw hat, smoking an early cigar. He felt that we had formerly met in another state of existence, and that we were translated into a new sphere. Wisely and well, he passed me without recognition. Under his arm he carried the morning paper, and shortly afterwards I saw him sitting on a rail in the pleasant open landscape of Regent Street, perusing it at his ease under the ripening sun.

My landlord having taken his whole establishment to be salted down, I am waited on by an elderly woman labouring under a chronic sniff, who, at the shadowy hour of half past nine o'clock of every evening, gives admittance at the street door to a meagre and mouldy old man whom I have never yet seen detached from a flat pint of beer in a pewter pot. The meagre and mouldy old man is her husband, and the pair have a dejected consciousness that they are not justified in appearing on the surface of the earth. They come out of some hole when London empties itself, and go in again when it fills. I saw them arrive on the evening when I myself took possession, and they arrived with the flat pint of beer, and their bed in a bundle. The old man is a weak old man, and appeared to me to get the bed down the kitchen stairs by tumbling down with and upon it. They make their bed in the lowest and remotest corner of the basement, and they smell of bed, and have no possession but bed: unless it be (which I rather infer from an undercurrent of flavour in them) cheese. I know their name, through the chance of having called the wife's attention, at half past nine on the second evening of our acquaintance, to the circumstance of there being someone at the house door; when she apologetically explained, 'It's only Mr Klem.' What becomes of Mr Klem all day, or when he goes out, or why, is a mystery I cannot penetrate; but at half past nine he never fails to turn up on the doorstep with the flat pint of beer. And the pint of beer, flat as it is, is so much more important than himself that it always seems to my fancy as if it had found him drivelling in the street, and had humanely brought him home. In making his way below, Mr Klem never goes down the middle of the passage, like another Christian, but shuffles against the wall, as if entreating me to take notice that he is occupying as little space as possible in the house; and, whenever I come upon him face to face, he backs from me in fascinated confusion. The most extraordinary circumstance I have traced, in connection with this aged couple, is, that there is a Miss Klem, their daughter, apparently ten years older than either of them, who has also a bed, and smells of it, and carries it about the earth at dusk, and hides it in deserted houses. I came into this piece of knowledge

FOOTMAN.

through Mrs Klem's beseeching me to sanction the sheltering of
Miss Klem under that roof for a single night, 'between her takin'
care of the upper part in Pall Mall which the family of his back,
and a 'ouse in Serjameses Street, which the family of leaves towng
ter-morrer'. I gave my gracious consent (having nothing that I
know of to do with it), and in the shadowy hours Miss Klem became perceptible on the doorstep, wrestling with a bed in a bundle.
Where she made it up for the night I cannot positively state, but
I think, in a sink. I know that, with the instinct of a reptile or an
insect, she stowed it and herself away in deep obscurity. In the
Klem family I have noticed another remarkable gift of nature, and
that is the power they possess of converting everything into flue.
Such broken victuals as they take by stealth appear (whatever the
nature of the viands) invariably to generate flue; and even the
nightly pint of beer, instead of assimilating naturally, strikes me
as breaking out in that form, equally on the shabby gown of Mrs
Klem, and the threadbare coat of her husband.

Mrs Klem has no idea of my name—as to Mr Klem he has no
idea of anything—and only knows me as her good gentleman.
Thus, if doubtful whether I am in my room or no, Mrs Klem taps
at the door and says, 'Is my good gentleman here?' Or, if a
messenger desiring to see me were consistent with my solitude,
she would show him in with 'Here is my good gentleman.' I find
this to be a generic custom. For, I meant to have observed before
now, that in its Arcadian time all my part of London is indistinctly
pervaded by the Klem species. They creep about with beds, and go
to bed in miles of deserted houses. They hold no companionship,
except that sometimes, after dark, two of them will emerge from
opposite houses, and meet in the middle of the road as on neutral
ground, or will peep from adjoining houses over an interposing
barrier of area railings, and compare a few reserved mistrustful
notes respecting their good ladies or good gentlemen. This I have
discovered in the course of various solitary rambles I have taken
Northward from my retirement, along the awful perspectives of
Wimpole Street, Harley Street, and similar frowning regions.
Their effect would be scarcely distinguishable from that of the
primeval forests, but for the Klem stragglers; these may be dimly

observed, when the heavy shadows fall, flitting to and fro, putting up the door-chain, taking in the pint of beer, lowering like phantoms at the dark parlour windows, or secretly consorting underground with the dust-bin and the water cistern.

In the Burlington Arcade, I observe, with peculiar pleasure, a primitive state of manners to have superseded the baneful influences of ultra-civilization. Nothing can surpass the innocence of the ladies' shoe-shops, the artificial-flower repositories, and the head-dress depots. They are in strange hands at this time of the year—hands of unaccustomed persons, who are imperfectly acquainted with the prices of the goods, and contemplate them with unsophisticated delight and wonder. The children of these virtuous people exchange familiarities in the Arcade, and temper the asperity of the two tall beadles. Their youthful prattle blends in an unwonted manner with the harmonious shade of the scene, and the general effect is as of the voices of birds in a grove. In this happy restoration of the golden time, it has been my privilege even to see the bigger beadle's wife. She brought him his dinner in a basin, and he ate it in his arm-chair, and afterwards fell asleep like a satiated child. At Mr Truefitt's, the excellent hairdresser's, they are learning French to beguile the time; and even the few solitaries left on guard at Mr Atkinson's, the perfumer's round the corner (generally the most inexorable gentleman in London, and the most scornful of three-and-sixpence), condescend a little, as they drowsily bide or recall their turn for chasing the ebbing Neptune on the ribbed sea-sand. From Messrs Hunt and Roskell's, the jewellers, all things are absent but the precious stones, and the gold and silver, and the soldierly pensioner at the door with his decorated breast. I might stand night and day, for a month to come, in Savile Row, with my tongue out, yet not find a doctor to look at it for love or money. The dentists' instruments are rusting in their drawers, and their horrible cool parlours, where people pretend to read the Every-Day Book, and not to be afraid, are doing penance for their grimness in white sheets. The lightweight of shrewd appearance, with one eye always shut up, as if he were eating a sharp gooseberry in all seasons, who usually stands at the gateway of the livery stables on very little legs under a very large waistcoat, has gone to Doncaster. Of such undesigning aspect is his guileless yard now, with its gravel and scarlet-beans, and the yellow brake housed under a glass roof in a corner, that I almost believe I could not be taken in there, if I tried. In the places of business of the great tailors, the cheval-glasses are dim and dusty for lack of being looked into. Ranges of brown-paper coat and waistcoat bodies look as funereal as if they were the hatchments of the customers with whose names they are inscribed; the measuring tapes hang idle on the wall; the order-taker, left on the hopeless chance of someone looking in, yawns in the last extremity over the book of patterns, as if he were trying to read that entertaining library. The hotels in Brook Street have no one in them, and the staffs of servants stare disconsolately for next season out of all the windows. The very man who goes about like an erect turtle, between two boards recommendatory of the Sixteen-Shilling Trousers, is aware of himself as a hollow mockery, and eats filberts while he leans his hinder shell against a wall.

Among these tranquillizing objects it is my delight to walk and meditate. Soothed by the repose around me, I wander insensibly to considerable distances, and guide myself back by the stars. Thus, I enjoy the contrast of a few still partially inhabited and busy spots, where all the lights are not fled, where all the garlands are not dead, whence all but I have not departed. Then does it appear to me that in this age three things are clamorously required of Man in the miscellaneous thoroughfares of the metropolis. Firstly, that he have his boots cleaned. Secondly, that he eat a penny ice. Thirdly, that he get himself photographed. Then do I speculate. What have those seam-worn artists been who stand at the photograph doors in Greek caps, sample in hand, and mysteriously salute the public—the female public with a pressing tenderness—to come in and be 'took'? What did they do with their greasy blandishments before the era of cheap photography? Of what class were their previous victims, and how victimized? And how did they get, and how did they pay for, that large collection of likenesses, all purporting to have been taken inside, with the taking of none of which had that establishment any more to do than with the taking of Delhi?

But, these are small oases, and I am soon back again in metropolitan Arcadia. It is my impression that much of its serene and
peaceful character is attributable to the absence of customary
Talk. How do I know but there may be subtle influences in Talk,
to vex the souls of men who don't hear it? How do I know but that
Talk, five, ten, twenty miles off, may get into the air and disagree
with me? If I rise from my bed, vaguely troubled and wearied and
sick of my life, in the session of Parliament, who shall say that my
noble friend, my right reverend friend, my right honourable
friend, my honourable friend, my honourable and learned friend,
or my honourable and gallant friend, may not be responsible for
that effect upon my nervous system? Too much Ozone in the air,
I am informed and fully believe (though I have no idea what it is),
would affect me in a marvellously disagreeable way; why may
not too much Talk? I don't see or hear the Ozone; I don't see or
hear the Talk. And there is so much Talk; so much too much;
such loud cry, and such scant supply of wool; such a deal of fleec-
ing, and so little fleece! Hence, in the Arcadian season, I find it a
delicious triumph to walk down to deserted Westminster, and see
the Courts shut up; to walk a little farther, and see the Two
Houses shut up; to stand in the Abbey Yard, like the New Zea-
lander of the grand English History (concerning which unfortunate man a whole rookery of mares' nests is generally being
discovered), and gloat upon the ruins of Talk. Returning to my
primitive solitude, and lying down to sleep, my grateful heart
expands with the consciousness that there is no adjourned Debate,
no ministerial explanation, nobody to give notice of intention to
ask the noble Lord at the head of Her Majesty's Government
five-and-twenty bootless questions in one, no term-time with
legal argument, no Nisi Prius with eloquent appeal to British
Jury; and the air will tomorrow, and tomorrow, and tomorrow
remain untroubled by this superabundant generating of Talk. In
a minor degree it is a delicious triumph to me to go into the club,
and see the carpets up, and the Bores and the other dust dispersed
to the four winds. Again, New Zealander-like, I stand on the cold
hearth, and say in the solitude, 'Here I watched Bore A1, with
voice always mysteriously low, and head always mysteriously

drooped, whispering political secrets into the ears of Adam's confiding children. Accursed be his memory for ever and a day!'

But, I have all this time been coming to the point, that the happy nature of my retirement is most sweetly expressed in its being the abode of Love. It is, as it were, an inexpensive Agapemone: nobody's speculation: everybody's profit. The one great result of the resumption of primitive habits, and (convertible terms) the not having much to do, is, the abounding of Love.

The Klem species are incapable of the softer emotions; probably, in that low nomadic race, the softer emotions have all degenerated into flue. But, with this exception, all the sharers of my retreat make love.

I have mentioned Savile Row. We all know the Doctor's servant. We all know what a respectable man he is, what a hard dry man, what a firm man, what a confidential man: how he lets us into the waiting-room, like a man who knows minutely what is the matter with us, but from whom the rack should not wring the secret. In the prosaic 'season', he has distinctly the appearance of a man conscious of money in the Savings Bank, and taking his stand on his respectability with both feet. At that time it is as impossible to associate him with relaxation, or any human weakness as it is to meet his eye without feeling guilty of indisposition. In the blest Arcadian time, how changed! I have seen him in a pepper-and-salt jacket—jacket—and drab trousers, with his arm round the waist of a bootmaker's housemaid, smiling in open day. I have seen him at the pump by the Albany, unsolicitedly pumping for two fair young creatures, whose figures, as they bent over their cans, were—if I may be allowed an original expression—a model for a sculptor. I have seen him trying the piano in the Doctor's drawing-room with his forefinger, and have heard him humming tunes in praise of lovely women. I have seen him seated on a fire-engine, and going (obviously in search of excitement) to a fire. I saw him, one moonlight evening, when the peace and purity of our Arcadian west were at their height, polk with the lovely daughter of a cleaner of gloves, from the doorsteps of his own residence, across Savile Row, round by Clifford Street and Old

Burlington Street, back to Burlington Gardens. Is this the Golden Age revived, or Iron London?

The Dentist's servant. Is that man no mystery to us, no type of invisible power? The tremendous individual knows (who else does?) what is done with the extracted teeth; he knows what goes on in the little room where something is always being washed or filed; he knows what warm spicy infusion is put into the comfortable tumbler from which we rinse our wounded mouth, with a gap in it that feels a foot wide; he knows whether the thing we spit into is a fixture communicating with the Thames, or could be cleared away for a dance; he sees the horrible parlour when there are no patients in it, and he could reveal, if he would, what becomes of the Every-Day Book then. The conviction of my coward conscience, when I see that man in a professional light, is, that he knows all the statistics of my teeth and gums, my double teeth, my single teeth, my stopped teeth, and my sound. In this Arcadian rest, I am fearless of him as of a harmless, powerless creature in a Scotch cap, who adores a young lady in a voluminous crinoline at a neighbouring billiard-room, and whose passion would be uninfluenced if every one of her teeth were false. They may be. He takes them all on trust.

In secluded corners of the place of my seclusion there are little shops withdrawn from public curiosity, and never two together, where servants' perquisites are bought. The cook may dispose of grease at these modest and convenient marts; the butler, of bottles; the valet and lady's-maid, of clothes; most servants, indeed, of most things they may happen to lay hold of. I have been told that in sterner times loving correspondence, otherwise interdicted, may be maintained by letter through the agency of some of these useful establishments. In the Arcadian autumn no such device is necessary. Everybody loves, and openly and blamelessly loves. My landlord's young man loves the whole of one side of the way of Old Bond Street, and is beloved several doors up New Bond Street besides. I never look out of window but I see kissing of hands going on all around me. It is the morning custom to glide from shop to shop, and exchange tender sentiments; it is the evening custom for couples to stand hand-in-hand at house doors, or roam, linked in that flowery manner, through the unpeopled streets. There is nothing else to do but love; and what there is to do is done.

In unison with this pursuit, a chaste simplicity obtains in the domestic habits of Arcadia. Its few scattered people dine early, live moderately, sup socially, and sleep soundly. It is rumoured that the beadles of the Arcade, from being the mortal enemies of boys, have signed with tears an address to Lord Shaftesbury, and subscribed to a ragged school. No wonder! For they might turn their heavy maces into crooks, and tend sheep in the Arcade, to the purling of the water-carts as they give the thirsty streets much more to drink than they can carry.

A happy Golden Age, and a serene tranquillity. Charming picture, but it will fade. The iron age will return; London will come back to town. If I show my tongue then in Savile Row for half a minute, I shall be prescribed for: the Doctor's man and the Dentist's man will then pretend that these days of unprofessional innocence never existed. Where Mr and Mrs Klem and their bed will be at that time, passes human knowledge; but my hatter hermitage will then know them no more, nor will it then know me. The desk at which I have written these meditations will retributively assist at the making out of my account, and the wheels of gorgeous carriages and the hoofs of high-stepping horses will crush the silence out of Bond Street—will grind Arcadia away, and give it to the elements in granite powder.

All the Year Round, September 29th, 1860
The Uncommercial Traveller, First Series, 1861

Wapping Workhouse

My day's no-business beckoning me to the East End of London, I had turned my face to that point of the metropolitan compass on leaving Covent Garden, and had got past the India House, thinking in my idle manner of Tippoo Sahib and Charles Lamb, and had got past my little Wooden Midshipman, after affectionately patting him on one leg of his knee-shorts for old acquaintance' sake, and had got past Aldgate Pump, and had got past the Saracen's Head (with an ignominious rash of posting-bills disfiguring his swarthy countenance), and had strolled up the empty yard of his ancient neighbour the Black or Blue Boar, or Bull, who departed this life I don't know when, and whose coaches are all gone I don't know where; and I had come out again into the age of railways, and I had got past Whitechapel Church, and was—rather inappropriately for an Uncommercial Traveller—in the Commercial Road. Pleasantly wallowing in the abundant mud of that thoroughfare, and greatly enjoying the huge piles of building belonging to the sugar refiners, the little masts and vanes in small back-gardens in back-streets, the neighbouring canals and docks, the India vans lumbering along their stone tramway, and the pawnbrokers' shops where hard-up Mates had pawned so many sextants and quadrants, that I should have bought a few cheap if I had the least notion how to use them, I at last began to file off to the right, towards Wapping.

Not that I intended to take boat at Wapping Old Stairs, or that I was going to look at the locality, because I believe (for I don't) in the constancy of the young woman who told her seagoing lover, to such a beautiful old tune, that she had ever continued the same since she gave him the 'baccer-box marked with his name; I am afraid he usually got the worst of those transactions, and was frightfully taken in. No, I was going to Wapping, because an Eastern police magistrate had said, through the morning papers, that there was no classification at the Wapping Workhouse for women, and that it was a disgrace and a shame, and divers other hard names, and because I wished to see how the fact really stood. For, that Eastern police magistrates are not always the wisest men of the East may be inferred from their course of procedure respecting the fancy-dressing and pantomime-posturing at St George's in that quarter: which is usually to discuss the matter at issue, in a state of mind betokening the weakest perplexity, with all parties, concerned and unconcerned, and, for a final expedient, to consult the complainant as to what he thinks ought to be done with the defendant, and take the defendant's opinion as to what he would recommend to be done with himself.

Long before I reached Wapping, I gave myself up as having lost my way, and, abandoning myself to the narrow streets in a Turkish frame of mind, relied on predestination to bring me somehow or other to the place I wanted, if I were ever to get there. When I had ceased for an hour or so to take any trouble about the matter, I found myself on a swing-bridge, looking down at some dark locks in some dirty water. Over against me stood a creature remotely in the likeness of a young man, with a puffed sallow face, and a figure all dirty and shiny and slimy, who may have been the youngest son of his filthy old father, Thames, or the drowned man about whom there was a placard on the granite post like a large thimble, that stood between us.

I asked this apparition what is called the place? Unto which it replied, with a ghastly grin and a sound like gurgling water in its throat:

'Mr Baker's trap.'

As it is a point of great sensitiveness with me on such occasions to be equal to the intellectual pressure of the conversation, I deeply considered the meaning of this speech, while I eyed the apparition—then engaged in hugging and sucking a horizontal iron bar at the top of the locks. Inspiration suggested to me that Mr Baker was the acting coroner of that neighbourhood.

'A common place for suicide,' said I, looking down at the locks.

'Sue?' returned the ghost with a stare. 'Yes! And Poll. Likewise Emily. And Nancy. And Jane'—he sucked the iron between each name—'and all the bileing. Ketches off their bonnets or shorls, takes a run, and headers down here, they doos. Always a headerin' down here, they is. Like one o'clock.'

'And at about that hour of the morning, I suppose?'

'Ah!' said the apparition. '*They* ain't partickler. Two 'ull do for *them*. Three. All times o' night. On'y mind you!' Here the apparition rested his profile on the bar, and gurgled in a sarcastic manner. 'There must be somebody comin'. They don't go a headerin' down here wen there ain't no Bobby nor General Cove fur to hear the splash.'

According to my interpretation of these words, I was myself a General Cove, or member of the miscellaneous public. In which modest character I remarked:

'They are often take out, are they, and restored?'

'I dunno about restored,' said the apparition, who, for some occult reason, very much objected to that word; 'they're carried into the werkiss, and put into a 'ot bath, and brought round. But I dunno about restored,' said the apparition; 'blow *that*!'—and vanished.

As it had shown a desire to become offensive, I was not sorry to find myself alone, especially as the 'werkiss' it had indicated with a twist of its matted head was close at hand. So I left Mr Baker's terrible trap (baited with a scum that was like the soapy rinsing of sooty chimneys), and made bold to ring at the workhouse gate, where I was wholly unexpected and quite unknown.

A very bright and nimble little matron, with a bunch of keys in her hand, responded to my request to see the House. I began to doubt whether the police magistrate was quite right in his facts, when I noticed her quick active little figure and her intelligent eyes.

The traveller (the matron intimated) should see the worst first. He was welcome to see everything. Such as it was, there it all was.

This was the only preparation for our entering 'the Foul wards'. They were in an old building squeezed away in a corner

FISHMONGER.

of a paved yard, quite detached from the more modern and spacious main body of the workhouse. They were in a building most monstrously behind the time—a mere series of garrets or lofts, with every inconvenient and objectionable circumstance in their construction, and only accessible by steep and narrow staircases, infamously ill adapted for the passage upstairs of the sick, or downstairs of the dead.

Abed in these miserable rooms, here on bedsteads, there (for a change, as I understood it) on the floor, were women in every stage of distress and disease. None but those who have attentively observed such scenes can conceive the extraordinary variety of expression still latent under the general monotony and uniformity of colour, attitude, and condition. The form a little coiled up and turned away, as though it had turned its back on this world for ever; the uninterested face, at once lead-coloured and yellow, looking passively upward from the pillow; the haggard mouth a little dropped, the hand outside the coverlet, so dull and indifferent, so light, and yet so heavy; these were on every pallet: but when I stopped beside a bed, and said ever so slight a word to the figure lying there, the ghost of the old character came into the face, and made the Foul ward as various as the fair world. No one appeared to care to live, but no one complained; all who could speak said that as much was done for them as could be done there, that the attendance was kind and patient, that their suffering was very heavy, but they had nothing to ask for. The wretched rooms were as clean and sweet as it is possible for such rooms to be; they would become a pest-house in a single week, if they were ill kept.

I accompanied the brisk matron up another barbarous staircase, into a better kind of loft, devoted to the idiotic and imbecile. There was at least Light in it, whereas the windows in the former wards had been like sides of schoolboys' bird-cages. There was a strong grating over the fire here, and holding a kind of state on either side of the hearth, separated by the breadth of this grating, were two old ladies in a condition of feeble dignity, which was surely the very last and lowest reduction of self-complacency to be found in this wonderful humanity of ours. They were evidently jealous of each other, and passed their whole time (as some people do whose fires are not grated) in mentally disparaging each other, and contemptuously watching their neighbours. One of these parodies on provincial gentlewomen was extremely talkative, and expressed a strong desire to attend the service on Sundays, from which she represented herself to have derived the greatest interest and consolation when allowed that privilege. She gossiped so well, and looked altogether so cheery and harmless, that I began to think this a case for the Eastern magistrate, until I found that, on the last occasion of her attending chapel, she had secreted a small stick, and had caused some confusion in the responses by suddenly producing it and belabouring the congregation.

So, these two old ladies, separated by the breadth of the grating —otherwise they would fly at one another's caps—sat all day long, suspecting one another, and contemplating a world of fits. For everybody else in the room had fits, except the wards-woman; an elderly, able-bodied pauperess, with a large upper lip, and an air of repressing and saving her strength, as she stood with her hands folded before her, and her eyes slowly rolling, biding her time for catching or holding somebody. This civil personage (in whom I regretted to identify a reduced member of my honourable friend Mrs Gamp's family) said, 'They has 'em continiwal, sir. They drops without no more notice than if they was coach horses dropped from the moon, sir. And, when one drops, another drops, and sometimes there'll be as many as four or five on 'em at once, dear me, a rollin' and a tearin', bless you! This young woman, now, has 'em dreadful bad.'

She turned up this young woman's face with her hand as she said it. This young woman was seated on the floor, pondering in the foreground of the afflicted. There was nothing repellent either in her face or head. Many, apparently worse, varieties of epilepsy and hysteria were about her, but she was said to be the worst here. When I had spoken to her a little, she still sat with her face turned up, pondering, and a gleam of the midday sun shone in upon her.

—Whether this young woman, and the rest of these so sorely troubled, as they sit or lie pondering in their confused dull way, ever get mental glimpses, among the motes in the sunlight, of healthy people and healthy things? Whether this young woman, brooding like this in the summer season, ever thinks that somewhere there are trees and flowers, even mountains and the great sea? Whether, not to go so far, this young woman ever has any dim revelation of that young woman—that young woman who is not here, and never will come here; who is courted and caressed, and loved, and has a husband, and bears children, and lives in a home, and who never knows what it is to have this lashing and tearing coming upon her? And whether this young woman, God help her, gives herself up then, and drops like a coach horse from the moon?

I hardly knew whether the voices of infant children, penetrating into so hopeless a place, made a sound that was pleasant or painful to me. It was something to be reminded that the weary world was not all aweary, and was ever renewing itself; but, this young woman was a child not long ago, and a child not long hence might be such as she. Howbeit, the active step and eye of the vigilant matron conducted me past the two provincial gentlewomen (whose dignity was ruffled by the children,), and into the adjacent nursery.

There were many babies here, and more than one handsome young mother. There were ugly young mothers also, and sullen young mothers, and callous young mothers. But, the babies had not appropriated to themselves any bad expression yet, and might have been, for anything that appeared to the contrary, in their soft faces, Princes Imperial and Princesses Royal. I had the pleasure of giving a poetical commission to the baker's man to make a cake with all dispatch, and toss it into the oven for one red-headed young pauper and myself, and felt much the better for it. Without that refreshment I doubt if I should have been in a condition for 'the Refractories', towards whom my quick little matron—for whose adaptation to her office I had by this time conceived a genuine respect—drew me next, and marshalled me the way that I was going.

The Refractories were picking oakum, in a small room giving on a yard. They sat in line on a form, with their backs to a window; before them, a table, and their work. The oldest Refractory was, say, twenty; youngest Refractory, say, sixteen. I have never yet ascertained, in the course of my uncommercial travels, why a Refractory habit should affect the tonsils and uvula; but I have always observed that Refractories of both sexes and every grade, between a Ragged School and the Old Bailey, have one voice, in which the tonsils and uvula gain a diseased ascendancy.

'Five pound, indeed! I hain't a-going fur to pick five pound,' said the Chief of the Refractories, keeping time to herself with her head and chin. 'More than enough to pick what we picks now, in sich a place as this, and on wot we gets here!'

(This was in acknowledgment of a delicate intimation that the amount of work was likely to be increased. It certainly was not heavy then, for one Refractory had already done her day's task—it was barely two o'clock—and was sitting behind it, with a head exactly matching it.)

'A pretty 'Ouse this is, matron, ain't it?' said Refractory Two, 'where a pleeseman's called in if a gal says a word!'

'And wen you're sent to prison for nothink or less!' said the Chief, tugging at her oakum as if it were the matron's hair. 'But any place is better than this; that's one thing, and be thankful!'

A laugh of Refractories, led by Oakum Head with folded arms —who originated nothing, but who was in command of the skir-mishers outside the conversation.

'If any place is better than this,' said my brisk guide in the calmest manner, 'it is a pity you left a good place when you had one.'

'Ho, no, I didn't, matron!' returned the Chief with another pull at her oakum, and a very expressive look at the enemy's forehead. 'Don't say that, matron, cos it's lies!'

Oakum Head brought up the skirmishers again, skirmished, and retired.

'And *I* warn't a-going,' exclaimed Refractory Two, 'though I was in one place for as long as four year—*I* warn't a-going fur to stop in a place that warn't fit for me—there!' And where the family weren't 'spectable characters—there! And where I, fort'nately or hunfort'nately, found that the people weren't what they pretended to make theirselves out to be—there! And where it wasn't their faults, by chalks, if I warn't made bad and ruinated. Hah!'

During this speech Oakum Head had again made a diversion with the skirmishers, and had again withdrawn.

The Uncommercial Traveller ventured to remark that he supposed Chief Refractory and Number Two to be the two young women who had been taken before the magistrate?

'Yes!' said the Chief, 'we har! and the wonder is, that a pleeseman ain't 'ad in now, and we took off agen. You can't open your lips here without a pleeseman.'

Number Two laughed (very uvularly), and the skirmishers followed suit.

'I'm sure I'd be thankful,' protested the Chief, looking sideways at the Uncommercial, 'if I could be got into a place, or got abroad. I'm sick and tired of this precious 'Ouse, I am, with reason.'

So would be, and so was, Number Two. So would be, and so was, Oakum Head. So would be, and so were, skirmishers.

The Uncommercial took the liberty of hinting that he hardly thought it probable that any lady or gentleman, in want of a likely young domestic of retiring manners, would be tempted into the engagement of either of the two leading Refractories, on her own presentation of herself as per sample.

'It ain't no good being nothink else here,' said the Chief.

The Uncommercial thought it might be worth trying.

'Oh no, it ain't!' said the Chief.

'Not a bit of good,' said Number Two.

'And I'm sure I'd be very thankful to be got into a place, or got abroad,' said the Chief.

'And so should I,' said Number Two. 'Truly thankful, I should.'

Oakum Head then rose, and announced as an entirely new idea, the mention of which profound novelty might be naturally expected to startle her unprepared hearers, that she would be very thankful to be got into a place, or got abroad. And, as if she had then said, 'Chorus, ladies!' all the skirmishers struck up to the same purpose. We left them, thereupon, and began a long walk among the women who were simply old and infirm; but whenever, in the course of this same walk, I looked out of any high window that commanded the yard, I saw Oakum Head, with all the other Refractories, looking out at their low window for me, and never failing to catch me, the moment I showed my head.

In ten minutes I had ceased to believe in such fables of a golden time as youth, the prime of life, or a hale old age. In ten minutes all the lights of womankind seemed to have been blown out, and nothing in that way to be left this vault to brag of, but the flickering and expiring snuffs.

And what was very curious was, that these dim old women had one company notion which was the fashion of the place. Every old woman who became aware of a visitor, and was not in bed, hobbled over a form into her accustomed seat, and became one of a line of dim old women confronting another line of dim old women across a narrow table. There was no obligation whatever upon them to range themselves in this way; it was their manner of 'receiving'. As a rule, they made no attempt to talk to one another, or to look at the visitor, or to look at anything, but sat silently working their mouths, like a sort of poor old cows. In some of these wards it was good to see a few green plants; in others, an isolated Refractory acting as nurse, who did well enough in that capacity when separated from her compeers. Every one of these wards, day-room, night-room, or both combined, was scrupulously clean and fresh. I have seen as many such places as most travellers in my line, and I never saw one such better kept.

Among the bedridden there was great patience, great reliance on the books under the pillow, great faith in G O D. All cared for sympathy, but none much cared to be encouraged with hope of recovery; on the whole, I should say, it was considered rather a distinction to have a complication of disorders, and to be in a worse way than the rest. From some of the windows the river could be seen, with all its life and movement: the day was bright, but I came upon no one who was looking out.

In one large ward, sitting by the fire in arm-chairs of distinction, like the President and Vice of the good company, were two old women, upwards of ninety years of age. The younger of the two, just turned ninety, was deaf, but not very, and could easily be made to hear. In her early time she had nursed a child, who was now another old woman, more infirm than herself, inhabiting the very same chamber. She perfectly understood this when the matron told it, and with sundry nods and motions of her forefinger, pointed out the woman in question. The elder of this pair, ninety-three, seated before an illustrated newspaper (but not reading it), was a bright-eyed old soul, really not deaf, wonderfully preserved, and amazingly conversational. She had not long lost her husband, and had been in that place little more than a year. At Boston, in the State of Massachusetts, this poor creature would have been individually addressed, would have been tended in her own room, and would have had her life gently assimilated to a comfortable life out of doors. Would that be much to do in England for a woman who has kept herself out of a workhouse more than ninety rough long years? When Britain first, at Heaven's command, arose, with a great deal of allegorical confusion, from out the azure main, did her guardian angels positively forbid it in the Charter which has been so much besung?

The object of my journey was accomplished when the nimble matron had no more to show me. As I shook hands with her at the gate, I told her that I thought Justice had not used her very well, and that the wise men of the East were not infallible.

Now, I reasoned with myself, as I made my journey home again, concerning those Foul wards. They ought not to exist; no person of common decency and humanity can see them, and doubt it. But what is this Union to do? The necessary alteration would cost several thousands of pounds; it has already to support three workhouses; its inhabitants work hard for their bare lives, and are already rated for the relief of the Poor to the utmost extent of reasonable endurance. One poor parish in this very Union is rated to the amount of FIVE AND SIXPENCE in the pound, at the very same time when the rich parish of St George's, Hanover Square, is rated at about SEVENPENCE in the pound, Paddington at about FOURPENCE, St James's, Westminster, at about TENPENCE! It is only through the equalization of Poor Rates that what is left undone in this wise can be done. Much more is left undone, or is ill done, than I have space to suggest in these notes

of a single uncommercial journey; but, the wise men of the East,
before they can reasonably hold forth about it, must look to the
North and South and West; let them also, any morning before
taking the seat of Solomon, look into the shops and dwellings all
around the Temple, and first ask themselves, 'How much more
can these poor people—many of whom keep themselves with
difficulty enough out of the workhouse—bear?'

I had yet other matter for reflection as I journeyed home, inasmuch as, before I altogether departed from the neighbourhood of
Mr Baker's trap, I had knocked at the gate of the workhouse of
St George's-in-the-East, and had found it to be an establishment
highly creditable to those parts, and thoroughly well administered
by a most intelligent master. I remarked in it an instance of the
collateral harm that obstinate vanity and folly can do. 'This was
the Hall where those old paupers, male and female, whom I had
just seen, met for the Church service, was it?'—'Yes.'—'Did
they sing the Psalms to any instrument?'—'They would like to
very much; they would have an extraordinary interest in doing
so.'—'And could none be got?'—'Well, a piano could even have
been got for nothing, but these unfortunate dissensions——' Ah!
better, far better, my Christian friend in the beautiful garment, to
have left the singing boys alone, and left the multitude to sing for
themselves! You should know better than I, but I think I have
read that they did so, once upon a time, and that 'when they had
sung an hymn', Someone (not in a beautiful garment) went up
unto the Mount of Olives.

It made my heart ache to think of this miserable trifling, in the
streets of a city where every stone seemed to call to me, as I
walked along, 'Turn this way, man, and see what waits to be
done!' So I decoyed myself into another train of thought to ease
my heart. But, I don't know that I did it, for I was so full of
paupers, that it was, after all, only a change to a single pauper,
who took possession of my remembrance instead of a thousand.

'I beg your pardon, sir,' he had said, in a confidential manner,
on another occasion, taking me aside; 'but I have seen better
days.'

'I am very sorry to hear it.'

'Sir, I have a complaint to make against the master.'

'I have no power here, I assure you. And if I had——'

'But allow me, sir, to mention it, as between yourself and a man who has seen better days, sir. The master and myself are both masons, sir, and I make him the sign continually; but, because I am in this unfortunate position, sir, he won't give me the countersign!'

All the Year Round, February 18th, 1860
The Uncommercial Traveller, First Series, 1861

Lively Turtle

I have a comfortable property. What I spend, I spend upon myself; and what I don't spend I save. Those are my principles. I am warmly attached to my principles, and stick to them on all occasions.

I am not, as some people have represented, a mean man. I never denied myself anything that I thought I should like to have. I may have said to myself 'SNOADY'—that is my name—'you will get those peaches cheaper if you wait till next week'; or, I may have said to myself, 'Snoady, you will get that wine for nothing, if you wait till you are asked out to dine'; but I never deny myself anything. If I can't get what I want without buying it, and paying its price for it, I *do* buy it and pay its price for it. I have an appetite bestowed upon me; and, if I balked it, I should consider that I was flying in the face of Providence.

I have no near relation but a brother. If he wants anything of me, he don't get it. All men are my brothers; and I see no reason why I should make his an exceptional case.

I live at a cathedral town where there is an old corporation. I am not in the Church, but it may be that I hold a little place of some sort. Never mind. It may be profitable. Perhaps yes, perhaps no. It may, or it may not, be a sinecure. I don't choose to say. I never enlightened my brother on these subjects, and I consider all men my brothers. The Negro is a man and a brother—should I hold myself accountable for my position in life, *to him*? Certainly not.

I often run up to London. I like London. The way I look at it, is this. London is not a cheap place, but, on the whole, you can get more of the real thing for your money there—I mean the best thing, whatever it is—than you can get in most places. Therefore, I say to the man who has got the money, and wants the thing, 'Go to London for it, and treat yourself.'

When *I* go, I do it in this manner. I go to Mrs Skim's Private Hotel and Commercial Lodging House, near Aldersgate Street, City (it is advertised in *Bradshaw's Railway Guide*, where I first found it), and there I pay, 'for bed and breakfast, with meat, two and ninepence per day, including servants'. Now, I have made a calculation, and I am satisfied that Mrs Skim cannot possibly make much profit out of *me*. In fact, if all her patrons were like me, my opinion is, the woman would be in the *Gazette* next month.

Why do I go to Mrs Skim's when I could go to the Clarendon, you may ask? Let us argue that point. If I went to the Clarendon I could get nothing in bed but sleep; could I? No. Now, sleep at the Clarendon is an expensive article; whereas sleep, at Mrs Skim's, is decidedly cheap. I have made a calculation, and I don't hesitate to say, all things considered, that it's cheap. Is it an inferior article, as compared with the Clarendon sleep, or is it of the same quality? I am a heavy sleeper, and it is of the same quality. Then why should I go to the Clarendon?

But as to breakfast? you may say.—Very well. As to breakfast. I could get a variety of delicacies for breakfast at the Clarendon, that are out of the question at Mrs Skim's. Granted. But I don't want to have them! My opinion is that we are not entirely animal and sensual. Man has an intellect bestowed upon him. If he clogs that intellect by too good a breakfast, how can he properly exert that intellect in meditation, during the day, upon his dinner? That's the point. We are not to enchain the soul. We are to let it soar. It is expected of us.

At Mrs Skim's, I get enough for breakfast (there is no limitation to the bread and butter, though there is to the meat) and not too much. I have all my faculties about me, to concentrate upon the object I have mentioned, and I can say to myself besides, 'Snoady, you have saved six, eight, ten, fifteen shillings, already today. If there is anything you fancy for your dinner, have it. Snoady, you have earned your reward.'

My objection to London is that it is the headquarters of the worst radical sentiments that are broached in England. I consider that it has a great many dangerous people in it. I consider the present publication (if it's *Household Words*) very dangerous, and I write this with the view of neutralizing some of its bad effects. My political creed is, let us be comfortable. We are all very comfortable as we are—*I* am very comfortable as I am—leave us alone!

All mankind are my brothers, and I don't think it Christian—if you come to that—to tell my brother that he is ignorant, or degraded, or dirty, or anything of the kind. I think it's abusive, and low. You meet me with the observation that I am required to love my brother. I reply, 'I do.' I am sure I am always willing to say to my brother, 'My good fellow, I love you very much; go along with you; keep to your own road; leave me to mine; whatever is, is right; whatever isn't, is wrong; don't make a disturbance!' It seems to me that this is at once the whole duty of man, and the only temper to go to dinner in.

Going to dinner in this temper in the City of London, one day not long ago, after a bed at Mrs Skim's, with meat-breakfast and servants included, I was reminded of the observation which, if my memory does not deceive me, was formerly made by somebody on some occasion, that man may learn wisdom from the lower animals. It is a beautiful fact, in my opinion, that great wisdom is to be learnt from that noble animal the Turtle.

I had made up my mind, in the course of the day I speak of, to have a Turtle dinner. I mean a dinner mainly composed of Turtle. Just a comfortable tureen of soup, with a pint of punch; and nothing solid to follow but a tender juicy steak. I like a tender juicy steak. I generally say to myself when I order one, 'Snoady, you have done right.'

When I make up my mind to have a delicacy, expense is no consideration. The question resolves itself, then, into a question of the very best. I went to a friend of mine who is a Member of the Common Council, and with that friend I held the following conversation.

Said I to him, 'Mr Groggles, the best Turtle is where?'

Says he, 'If you want a basin for lunch, my opinion is, you can't do better than drop into Birch's.'

Said I, 'Mr Groggles, I thought you had known me better,

than to suppose me capable of a basin. My intention is to dine. A tureen.'

Says Mr Groggles, without a moment's consideration, and in a determined voice. 'Right opposite the India House, Leadenhall Street.'

We parted. My mind was not inactive during the day, and at six in the afternoon I repaired to the house of Mr Groggles's recommendation. At the end of the passage, leading from the street into the coffee-room, I observed a vast and solid chest, in which I then supposed that a Turtle of unusual size might be deposited. But, the correspondence between its bulk and that of the charge made for my dinner, afterwards satisfied me that it must be the till of the establishment.

I stated to the waiter what had brought me there, and I mentioned Mr Groggles's name. He feelingly repeated after me, 'A tureen of Turtle, and a tender juicy steak.' His manner, added to the manner of Mr Groggles in the morning, satisfied me that all was well. The atmosphere of the coffee-room was odoriferous with Turtle, and the steams of thousands of gallons, consumed within its walls, hung, in savoury grease, upon their surface. I could have inscribed my name with a penknife, if I had been so disposed, in the essence of innumerable Turtles. I preferred to fall into a hungry reverie, brought on by the warm breath of the place, and to think of the West Indies and the Island of Ascension.

My dinner came—and went. I will draw a veil over the meal, I will put the cover on the empty tureen, and merely say that it was wonderful—and that I paid for it.

I sat meditating, when all was over, on the imperfect nature of our present existence, in which we can eat only for a limited time, when the waiter roused me with these words.

Said he to me, as he brushed the crumbs off the table, 'Would you like to see the Turtle, sir?'

'To see what Turtle, waiter?' said I (calmly) to him.

'The tanks of Turtle below, sir,' said he to me.

Tanks of Turtle! Good Gracious! 'Yes!'

The waiter lighted a candle, and conducted me downstairs to a range of vaulted apartments, cleanly whitewashed and illuminated with gas, where I saw a sight of the most astonishing and gratifying description, illustrative of the greatness of my native country. 'Snoady,' was my first observation to myself, 'Rule Britannia. Britannia rules the waves!'

There were two or three hundred Turtle in the vaulted apartment—all alive. Some in tanks, and some taking the air in long dry walks littered down with straw. They were of all sizes; many of them enormous. Some of the enormous ones had entangled themselves with the smaller ones, and pushed and squeezed themselves into corners, with their fins over water-pipes, and their heads downwards, where they were apoplectically struggling and splashing, apparently in the last extremity. Others were calm at the bottom of the tanks; others languidly rising to the surface. The Turtle in the walks littered down with straw were calm and motionless. It was a thrilling sight. I admire such a sight. It rouses my imagination. If you wish to try its effect on yours, make a call right opposite the India House any day you please—dine—pay—and ask to be taken below.

Two athletic young men, without coats, and with the sleeves of their shirts tucked up to the shoulders, were in attendance on these noble animals. One of them, wrestling with the most enormous Turtle in company, and dragging him up to the edge of the tank, for me to look at, presented an idea to me which I never had before. I ought to observe that I like an idea. I say, when I get a new one, 'Snoady, book that!'

My idea, on the present occasion, was—Mr Groggles! It was not a Turtle that I saw, but Mr Groggles. It was the dead image of Mr Groggles. He was dragged up to confront me, with his waistcoat—if I may be allowed the expression—towards me; and it was identically the waistcoat of Mr Groggles. It was the same shape, very nearly the same colour, only wanted a gold watch-chain and a bunch of seals, to *be* the waistcoat of Mr Groggles. There was what I should call a bursting expression about him in general, which was accurately the expression of Mr Groggles. I had never closely observed a Turtle's throat before. The folds of his loose cravat, I found to be precisely those of Mr Groggles's cravat. Even the intelligent eye—I mean to say, intelligent

enough for a person of correct principles, and not dangerously
so—was the eye of Mr Groggles. When the athletic young man
let him go, and, with a roll of his head, he flopped heavily down
into the tank, it was exactly the manner of Mr Groggles as I have
seen him ooze away into his seat, after opposing a sanitary motion
in the Court of Common Council!

'Snoady,' I couldn't help saying to myself, 'you have done it.
You have got an idea, Snoady, in which a great principle is involved. I congratulate you!' I followed the young man, who
dragged up several Turtle to the brinks of the various tanks. I
found them all the same—all varieties of Mr Groggles—all ex-
traordinarily like the gentlemen who usually eat them. 'Now,
Snoady,' was my next remark, 'what do you deduce from this?'

'Sir,' said I, 'what I deduce from this, is, confusion to those
Radicals and other Revolutionists who talk about improvement.
Sir,' said I, 'what I deduce from this, is, that there isn't this resemblance between the Turtles and the Groggleses for nothing. It's
meant to show mankind that the proper model for a Groggles, is
a Turtle; and that the liveliness we want in a Groggles, is the
liveliness of a Turtle, and no more.' 'Snoady,' was my reply to
this, 'you have hit it. You are right!'

I admired the idea very much, because, if I hate anything in the
world, it's change. Change has evidently no business in the world,
has nothing to do with it, and isn't intended. What we want is (as
I think I have mentioned) to be comfortable. I look at it that way.
Let us be comfortable, and leave us alone. Now, when the young
man dragged a Groggles—I mean a Turtle—out of his tank, this
was exactly what the noble animal expressed as he floundered
back again.

I have several friends besides Mr Groggles in the Common
Council, and it might be a week after this, when I said, 'Snoady,
if I was you, I would go to that court, and hear the debate today.'
I went. A good deal of it was what I call a sound, old English dis-
cussion. One eloquent speaker objected to the French as wearing
wooden shoes; and a friend of his reminded him of another objection to that foreign people, namely, that they eat frogs. I had
feared, for many years, I am sorry to say, that these wholesome

principles were gone out. How delightful to find them still remaining among the great men of the City of London, in the year one thousand eight hundred and fifty! It made me think of the Lively Turtle.

But, I soon thought more of the Lively Turtle. Some Radicals and Revolutionists have penetrated even to the Common Council —which otherwise I regard as one of the last strongholds of our afflicted constitution; and speeches were made, about removing Smithfield Market—which I consider to be a part of that Constitution—and about appointing a Medical Officer for the City, and about preserving the public health; and other treasonable practices, opposed to Church and State. These proposals Mr Groggles, as might have been expected of such a man, resisted; so warmly, that, as I afterwards understood from Mrs Groggles, he had rather a sharp attack of blood to the head that night. All the Groggles party resisted them too, and it was a fine constitutional sight to see waistcoat after waistcoat rise up in resistance of them and subside. But what struck me in the sight was this, 'Snoady,' said I, 'here is your idea carried out, sir! These Radicals and Revolutionists are the athletic young men in shirt sleeves, dragging the Lively Turtle to the edges of the tank. The Groggleses are the Turtle, looking out for a moment, and flopping down again. Honour to the Groggleses! Honour to the Court of Lively Turtle! The wisdom of the Turtle is the hope of England!'

There are three heads in the moral of what I had to say. First, Turtle and Groggles are identical; wonderfully alike externally, wonderfully alike mentally. Secondly, Turtle is a good thing every way, and the liveliness of the Turtle is intended as an example for the liveliness of man; you are not to go beyond that. Thirdly, we are all quite comfortable. Leave us alone!

Household Words, October 26th, 1850

TURNCOCK.

The City of the Absent

When I think I deserve particularly well of myself, and have
earned the right to enjoy a little treat, I stroll from Covent Garden
into the City of London, after business hours there, on a Saturday,
or—better yet—on a Sunday, and roam about its deserted nooks
and corners. It is necessary to the full enjoyment of these journeys
that they should be made in summer-time, for then the retired
spots that I love to haunt are at their idlest and dullest. A gentle
fall of rain is not objectionable, and a warm mist sets off my
favourite retreats to decided advantage.

Among these, City Churchyards hold a high place. Such strange
churchyards hide in the City of London: churchyards sometimes
so entirely detached from churches, always so pressed upon by
houses; so small, so rank, so silent, so forgotten, except by the few
people who ever look down into them from their smoky windows.
As I stand peeping in through the iron gates and rails, I can peel
the rusty metal off, like bark from an old tree. The illegible tomb-
stones are all lop-sided, the grave mounds lost their shape in the
rains of a hundred years ago, the Lombardy Poplar or Plane Tree
that was once a drysalter's daughter and several common-council-
men, has withered like those worthies, and its departed leaves are
dust beneath it. Contagion of slow ruin overhangs the place. The
discoloured tiled roofs of the environing buildings stand so awry
that they can hardly be proof against any stress of weather. Old
crazy stacks of chimneys seem to look down as they overhang,
dubiously calculating how far they will have to fall. In an angle
of the walls, what was once the toolhouse of the grave-digger rots
away, encrusted with toadstools. Pipes and spouts for carrying off
the rain from the encompassing gables, broken or feloniously cut
for old lead long ago, now let the rain drip and splash as it list

upon the weedy earth. Sometimes there is a rusty pump somewhere near, and, as I look in at the rails and meditate, I hear it
working under an unknown hand with a creaking protest: as
though the departed in the churchyard urged, 'Let us lie here in
peace; don't suck us up and drink us!'

One of my best-beloved churchyards I call the churchyard of St
Ghastly Grim; touching what men in general call it, I have no
information. It lies at the heart of the City, and the Blackwall Railway shrieks at it daily. It is a small small churchyard, with a
ferocious strong spiked iron gate, like a gaol. This gate is ornamented with skulls and cross-bones, larger than the life, wrought
in stone; but it likewise came into the mind of St Ghastly Grim
that to stick iron spikes atop of the stone skulls, as though they
were impaled, would be a pleasant device. Therefore the skulls
grin aloft horribly, thrust through and through with iron spears.
Hence, there is attraction of repulsion for me in St Ghastly Grim,
and, having often contemplated it in the daylight and the dark, I
once felt drawn towards it in a thunderstorm at midnight. 'Why
not?' I said in self-excuse. 'I have been to see the Coliseum by the
light of the moon; is it worse to go and see St Ghastly Grim by the
light of the lightning?' I repaired to the Saint in a hackney cab,
and found the skulls most effective, having the air of a public
execution, and seeming, as the lightning flashed, to wink and
grin with the pain of the spikes. Having no other person to whom
to impart my satisfaction, I communicated it to the driver. So far
from being responsive, he surveyed me—he was naturally a
bottle-nosed red-faced man—with a blanched countenance. And, as
he drove me back, he ever and again glanced in over his shoulder
through the little front window of his carriage, as mistrusting that
I was a fare originally from a grave in the churchyard of St Ghastly
Grim, who might have flitted home again without paying.

Sometimes, the queer Hall of some queer Company gives upon
a churchyard such as this, and, when the Livery dine, you may
hear them (if you are looking in through the iron rails, which
you never are when I am) toasting their own Worshipful pros-
perity. Sometimes, a wholesale house of business, requiring much
room for stowage, will occupy one or two, or even all three, sides

of the enclosing space, and the backs of bales of goods will lumber up the windows, as if they were holding some crowded trade-meeting of themselves within. Sometimes, the commanding windows are all blank, and show no more sign of life than the graves below—not so much, for *they* tell of what once upon a time was life undoubtedly. Such was the surrounding of one City churchyard that I saw last summer, on a Volunteering Saturday evening towards eight of the clock, when with astonishment I beheld an old old man and an old old woman in it, making hay. Yes, of all occupations in this world, making hay! It was a very confined patch of churchyard lying between Gracechurch Street and the Tower, capable of yielding, say, an apronful of hay. By what means the old old man and woman had got into it, with an almost toothless hay-making rake, I could not fathom. No open window was within view; no window at all was within view, sufficiently near the ground to have enabled their old legs to descend from it; the rusty churchyard gate was locked, the mouldy church was locked. Gravely among the graves they made hay, all alone by themselves. They looked like Time and his wife. There was but the one rake between them, and they both had hold of it in a pastorally loving manner, and there was hay on the old woman's black bonnet, as if the old man had recently been playful. The old man was quite an obsolete old man, in knee breeches and coarse grey stockings, and the old woman wore mittens like unto his stockings in texture and in colour. They took no heed of me as I looked on, unable to account for them. The old woman was much too bright for a pew-opener, the old man much too meek for a beadle. On an old tombstone in the foreground, between me and them were two cherubim: but for those celestial embellishments being represented as having no possible use for knee breeches, stockings, or mittens, I should have compared them with the hay-makers, and sought a likeness. I coughed and awoke the echoes, but the haymakers never looked at me. They used the rake with a measured action, drawing the scanty crop towards them; and so I was fain to leave them under three yards and a half of darkening sky, gravely making hay among the graves, all alone by themselves. Perhaps they were Spectres, and I wanted a medium.

In another City churchyard, of similar cramped dimensions, I saw, that selfsame summer, two comfortable charity children. They were making love—tremendous proof of the vigour of that immortal article, for they were in the graceful uniform under which English Charity delights to hide herself—and they were overgrown, and their legs (his legs, at least, for I am modestly incompetent to speak of hers) were as much in the wrong as mere passive weakness of character can render legs. Oh, it was a leaden churchyard, but no doubt a golden ground to those young persons! I first saw them on a Saturday evening, and, perceiving from their occupation that Saturday evening was their trysting-time, I returned that evening se'nnight, and renewed the contemplation of them. They came there to shake the bits of matting which were spread in the church aisles, and they afterwards rolled them up, he rolling his end, she rolling hers, until they met, and over the two once divided now united rolls—sweet emblem!—gave and received a chaste salute. It was so refreshing to find one of my faded churchyards blooming into flower thus that I returned a second time, and a third, and ultimately this befell: They had left the church door open in their dusting and arranging. Walking in to look at the church, I became aware, by the dim light, of him in the pulpit, of her in the reading-desk, of him looking down, of her looking up, exchanging tender discourse. Immediately both dived, and became as it were non-existent on this sphere. With an assumption of innocence I turned to leave the sacred edifice, when an obese form stood in the portal, puffily demanding Joseph, or, in default of Joseph, Celia. Taking this monster by the sleeve, and luring him forth on pretence of showing him whom he sought, I gave time for the emergence of Joseph and Celia, who presently came towards us in the churchyard, bending under dusty matting, a picture of thriving and unconscious industry. It would be superfluous to hint that I have ever since deemed this the proudest passage in my life.

But such instances, or any tokens of vitality, are rare indeed in my City churchyards. A few sparrows occasionally try to raise a lively chirrup in their solitary tree—perhaps, as taking a different view of worms from that entertained by humanity—but they are flat and hoarse of voice, like the clerk, the organ, the bell, the clergyman, and all the rest of the church-works when they are wound up for Sunday. Caged larks, thrushes, or blackbirds, hanging in neighbouring courts, pour forth their strains passionately, as scenting the tree, trying to break out, and see leaves again before they die, but their song is Willow, Willow—of a churchyard cast. So little light lives inside the churches of my churchyards, when the two are co-existent, that it is often only by an accident, and after long acquaintance, that I discover their having stained glass in some odd window. The westering sun slants into the churchyard by some unwonted entry, a few prismatic tears drop on an old tombstone, and a window that I thought was only dirty is for the moment all bejewelled. Then the light passes and the colours die. Though even then, if there be room enough for me to fall back so far as that I can gaze up to the top of the church tower, I see the rusty vane new burnished, and seeming to look out with a joyful flash over the sea of smoke at the distant shore of country.

Blinking old men, who are let out of workhouses by the hour, have a tendency to sit on bits of coping-stone in these churchyards, leaning with both hands on their sticks, and asthmatically gasping. The more depressed class of beggars, too, bring hither broken meats, and munch. I am on nodding terms with a meditative turncock who lingers in one of them, and whom I suspect of a turn for poetry; the rather as he looks out of temper when he gives the fire-plug a disparaging wrench with that large tuning-fork of his which would wear out the shoulder of his coat but for a precautionary piece of inlaid leather. Fire-ladders, which I am satisfied nobody knows anything about, and the keys of which were lost in ancient times, moulder away in the larger churchyards, under eaves like wooden eyebrows; and so removed are those corners from the haunts of men and boys that once, on a fifth of November, I found a 'Guy' trusted to take care of himself there, while his proprietors had gone to dinner. Of the expression of his face I cannot report, because it was turned to the wall; but his shrugged shoulders and his ten extended fingers appeared to denote that he had moralized, in his little straw chair, on the mystery of mortality until he gave it up as a bad job.

You do not come upon these churchyards violently; there are shades of transition in the neighbourhood. An antiquated news shop, or barber's shop, apparently bereft of customers in the earlier days of George the Third, would warn me to look out for one, if any discoveries in this respect were left for me to make. A very quiet court, in combination with an unaccountable dyer's and scourer's, would prepare me for a churchyard. An exceedingly retiring public house, with a bagatelle board shadily visible in a sawdusty parlour shaped like an omnibus, and with a shelf of punch-bowls in the bar, would apprise me that I stood near consecrated ground. A 'Dairy', exhibiting in its modest window one very little milk-can and three eggs, would suggest to me the certainty of finding the poultry hard by, pecking at my forefathers. I first inferred the vicinity of St Ghastly Grim from a certain air of extra repose and gloom pervading a vast stack of warehouses.

From the hush of these places it is congenial to pass into the hushed resorts of business. Down the lanes I like to see the carts and wagons huddled together in repose, the cranes idle, and the warehouses shut. Pausing in the alleys behind the closed banks of mighty Lombard Street, it gives one as good as a rich feeling to think of the broad counters with a rim along the edge, made for telling money out on, the scales for weighing precious metals, the ponderous ledgers, and, above all, the bright copper shovels for shovelling gold. When I draw money, it never seems so much money as when it is shovelled at me out of a bright copper shovel. I like to say, 'In gold', and to see seven pounds musically pouring out of the shovel, like seventy; the bank appearing to remark to me—I italicize *appearing*—'If you want more of this yellow earth, we keep it in barrows at your service.' To think of the banker's clerk with his deft finger turning the crisp edges of the hundred-pound notes he has taken in a fat roll out of a drawer is again to hear the rustling of that delicious south-cash wind. 'How will you have it?' I once heard this usual question asked at a bank counter of an elderly female, habited in mourning and steeped in simplicity, who answered, open-eyed, crook-fingered, laughing with expectation, 'Anyhow!' Calling these things to mind as I stroll among the banks, I wonder whether the other solitary Sunday

man I pass has designs upon the banks. For the interest and
mystery of the matter, I almost hope he may have, and that his
confederate may be at this moment taking impressions of the keys
of the iron closets in wax, and that a delightful robbery may be in
course of transaction. About College Hill, Mark Lane, and so on
towards the Tower, and Dockward, the deserted wine merchants'
cellars are fine subjects for consideration; but the deserted money
cellars of the bankers, and their plate cellars, and their jewel-
cellars, what subterranean regions of the Wonderful Lamp are
these! And again: possibly some shoeless boy in rags passed
through this street yesterday, for whom it is reserved to be a
banker in the fullness of time, and to be surpassing rich. Such reverses have been since the days of Whittington; and were long
before. I want to know whether the boy has any foreglittering of
that glittering fortune now, when he treads these stones hungry.
Much as I also want to know whether the next man to be hanged
at Newgate yonder had any suspicion upon him that he was moving
steadily towards that fate, when he talked so much about the last
man who paid the same great debt at the same small Debtors' Door.

Where are all the people who on busy working days pervade
these scenes? The locomotive banker's clerk, who carries a black
portfolio chained to him by a chain of steel, where is he? Does he
go to bed with his chain on—to church with his chain on—or does
he lay it by? And if he lays it by, what becomes of his portfolio
when he is unchained for a holiday? The wastepaper baskets of
these closed counting-houses would let me into many hints of
business matters if I had the exploration of them; and what
secrets of the heart should I discover on the 'pads' of the young
clerks—the sheets of cartridge-paper and blotting-paper inter-
posed between their writing and their desks! Pads are taken into
confidence on the tenderest occasions, and oftentimes when
I have made a business visit, and have sent in my name from
the outer office, have I had it forced on my discursive notice that
the officiating young gentleman has over and over again inscribed
AMELIA, in ink of various dates, on corners of his pad. Indeed,
the pad may be regarded as the legitimate modern successor of
the old forest tree: whereon these young knights (having no

attainable forest nearer than Epping) engrave the names of their
mistresses. After all, it is a more satisfactory process than carving,
and can be oftener repeated. So these courts in their Sunday rest
are courts of Love Omnipotent (I rejoice to bethink myself), dry
as they look. And here is Garraway's, bolted and shuttered hard
and fast! It is possible to imagine the man who cuts the sand-
wiches on his back in a hay-field; it is possible to imagine his desk,
like the desk of a clerk at church, without him; but imagination is
unable to pursue the men who wait at Garraway's all the week for
the men who never come. When they are forcibly put out of
Garraway's on Saturday night—which they must be, for they
never would go out of their own accord—where do they vanish
until Monday morning? On the first Sunday that I ever strayed
here, I expected to find them hovering about these lanes, like
restless ghosts, and trying to peep into Garraway's through
chinks in the shutters, if not endeavouring to turn the lock of the
door with false keys, picks, and screwdrivers. But the wonder is
that they go clean away! And now I think of it, the wonder is that
every working-day pervader of these scenes goes clean away. The
man who sells the dogs' collars and the little toy coal-scuttles feels
under as great an obligation to go afar off as Glyn and Co., or
Smith, Payne, and Smith. There is an old monastery crypt under
Garraway's (I have been in it among the port wine), and perhaps
Garraway's, taking pity on the mouldy men who wait in its
public room all their lives, gives them cool house room down
there over Sundays; but the catacombs of Paris would not be
large enough to hold the rest of the missing. This characteristic of
London City greatly helps its being the quaint place it is in the
weekly pause of business, and greatly helps my Sunday sensation
in it of being the Last Man. In my solitude, the ticket porters being
all gone with the rest, I venture to breathe to the quiet bricks
and stones my confidential wonderment why a ticket porter, who
never does any work with his hands, is bound to wear a white
apron, and why a great Ecclesiastical Dignitary, who never does any
work with his hands either, is equally bound to wear a black one.

All the Year Round, July 17th, 1863
The Uncommercial Traveller, Second Series, 1868

Down with the Tide

A very dark night it was, and bitter cold; the east wind blowing bleak, and bringing with it stinging particles from marsh, and moor, and fen—from the Great Desert and Old Egypt, maybe. Some of the component parts of the sharp-edged vapour that came flying up the Thames at London might be mummy-dust, dry atoms from the Temple at Jerusalem, camels' footprints, crocodiles' hatching-places, loosened grains of expression from the visages of blunt-nosed sphynxes, waifs and strays from caravans of turbaned merchants, vegetation from jungles, frozen snow from the Himalayas. Oh! It was very very dark upon the Thames, and it was bitter bitter cold.

'And yet,' said the voice within the great peacoat at my side, 'you'll have seen a good many rivers too, I dare say?'

'Truly,' said I, 'when I come to think of it, not a few. From the Niagara, downward to the mountain rivers of Italy, which are like the national spirit—very tame, or chafing suddenly and bursting bounds, only to dwindle away again. The Moselle, and the Rhine, and the Rhône; and the Seine, and the Saône; and the St Lawrence, Mississippi, and Ohio; and the Tiber, the Po, and the Arno; and the——'

Peacoat coughing as if he had had enough of that, I said no more. I could have carried the catalogue on to a teasing length, though, if I had been in the cruel mind.

'And after all,' said he, 'this looks so dismal?'

'So awful,' I returned, 'at night. The Seine at Paris is very gloomy too, at such a time, and is probably the scene of far more crime and greater wickedness; but this river looks so broad and vast, so murky and silent, seems such an image of death in the midst of the great city's life, that——'

That Peacoat coughed again. He *could not* stand my holding forth.

We were in a four-oared Thames Police galley, lying on our oars in the deep shadow of Southwark Bridge—under the corner arch on the Surrey side—having come down with the tide from Vauxhall. We were fain to hold on pretty tight, though close inshore, for the river was swollen and the tide running down very strong. We were watching certain water-rats of human growth, and lay in the deep shade as quiet as mice; our light hidden and our scraps of conversation carried on in whispers. Above us, the massive iron girders of the arch were faintly visible, and below us its ponderous shadow seemed to sink down to the bottom of the stream.

We had been lying here some half an hour. With our backs to the wind, it is true; but the wind being in a determined temper blew straight through us, and would not take the trouble to go round. I would have boarded a fireship to get into action, and mildly suggested as much to my friend Pea.

'No doubt,' says he as patiently as possible; 'but shore-going tactics wouldn't do with us. River-thieves can always get rid of stolen property in a moment by dropping it overboard. We want to take them *with* the property, so we lurk about and come out upon 'em sharp. If they see us or hear us, over it goes.'

Pea's wisdom being indisputable, there was nothing for it but to sit there and be blown through, for another half-hour. The water-rats thinking it wise to abscond at the end of that time without commission of felony, we shot out, disappointed, with the tide.

'Grim they look, don't they?' said Pea, seeing me glance over my shoulder at the lights upon the bridge, and downward at their long crooked reflections in the river.

'Very,' said I, 'and make one think with a shudder of suicides. What a night for a dreadful leap from that parapet!'

'Aye, but Waterloo's the favourite bridge for making holes in the water from,' returned Pea. 'By the by—avast pulling, lads!— would you like to speak to Waterloo on the subject?'

My face confessing a surprised desire to have some friendly

conversation with Waterloo Bridge, and my friend Pea being the most obliging of men, we put about, pulled out of the force of the stream, and in place of going at great speed with the tide, began to strive against it, close inshore again. Every colour but black seemed to have departed from the world. The air was black, the water was black, the barges and hulks were black, the piles were black, the buildings were black, the shadows were only a deeper shade of black upon a black ground. Here and there, a coal fire in an iron cresset blazed upon a wharf; but one knew that it, too, had been black a little while ago, and would be black again soon. Uncomfortable rushes of water suggestive of gurgling and drowning, ghostly rattlings of iron chains, dismal clankings of discordant engines, formed the music that accompanied the dip of our oars and their rattling in the rowlocks. Even the noises had a black sound to me—as the trumpet sounded red to the blind man.

Our dexterous boat's crew made nothing of the tide, and pulled us gallantly up to Waterloo Bridge. Here Pea and I disembarked, passed under the black stone archway, and climbed the steep stone steps. Within a few feet of their summit, Pea presented me to Waterloo (or an eminent toll-taker representing that structure), muffled up to the eyes in a thick shawl, and amply greatcoated and fur-capped.

Waterloo received us with cordiality, and observed of the night that it was 'a searcher'. He had been originally called the Strand Bridge, he informed us, but had received his present name at the suggestion of the proprietors, when Parliament had resolved to vote three hundred thousand pound for the erection of a monument in honour of the victory. Parliament took the hint (said Waterloo, with the least flavour of misanthropy) and saved the money. Of course, the late Duke of Wellington was the first passenger, and of course he paid his penny, and of course a noble lord preserved it evermore. The treadle and index at the tollhouse (a most ingenious contrivance for rendering fraud impossible), were invented by Mr Lethbridge, then property man at Drury Lane Theatre.

Was it suicide, we wanted to know about? said Waterloo. Ha! Well, he had seen a good deal of that work, he did assure us. He had prevented some. Why, one day a woman, poorish looking, came in between the hatch, slapped down a penny, and wanted to go on without the change! Waterloo suspected this, and says to his mate, "give an eye to the gate', and bolted after her. She had got to the third seat between the piers, and was on the parapet just a-going over, when he caught her and gave her in charge. At the police office next morning she said it was along of trouble and a bad husband.

'Likely enough,' observed Waterloo to Pea and myself, as he adjusted his chin in his shawl. 'There's a deal of trouble about, you see—and bad husbands, too!'

Another time, a young woman at twelve o'clock in the open day, got through, darted along; and, before Waterloo could come near her, jumped upon the parapet, and shot herself over sideways. Alarm given, watermen put off, lucky escape.—Clothes buoyed her up.

'This is where it is,' said Waterloo. 'If people jump off straight forwards from the middle of the parapet of the bays of the bridge, they are seldom killed by drowning, but are smashed, poor things; that's what *they* are; they dash themselves upon the buttress of the bridge. But you jump off,' said Waterloo to me, putting his forefinger in a buttonhole of my greatcoat; 'you jump off from the side of the bay, and you'll tumble, true, into the stream under the arch. What you have got to do is to mind how you jump in! There was poor Tom Steele from Dublin. Didn't dive! Bless you, didn't dive at all! Fell down so flat into the water that he broke his breastbone, and lived two days!'

I asked Waterloo if there were a favourite side of his bridge for this dreadful purpose? He reflected, and thought yes, there was. He should say the Surrey side.

Three decent-looking men went through one day, soberly and quietly, and went on abreast for about a dozen yards: when the middle one, he sung out, all of a sudden, 'Here goes, Jack!' and was over in a minute.

Body found? Well. Waterloo didn't rightly recollect about that. They were compositors, *they* were.

He considered it astonishing how quick people were! Why,

there was a cab came up one Boxing night, with a young woman in it, who looked, according to Waterloo's opinion of her, a little the worse for liquor; very handsome she was, too—very handsome. She stopped the cab at the gate, and said she'd pay the cabman then, which she did, though there was a little hankering about the fare, because at first she didn't seem quite to know where she wanted to be drove to. However, she paid the man, and the toll too, and looking Waterloo in the face (he thought she knew him, don't you see!) said, 'I'll finish it somehow!' Well, the cab went off, leaving Waterloo a little doubtful in his mind, and while it was going on at full speed the young woman jumped out, never fell, hardly staggered, ran along the bridge pavement a little way, passing several people, and jumped over from the second opening. At the inquest it was giv' in evidence that she had been quarrelling at the Hero of Waterloo, and it was brought in jealousy. (One of the results of Waterloo's experience was that there was a deal of jealousy about.)

'Do we ever get madmen?' said Waterloo, in answer to an inquiry of mine. 'Well we *do* get madmen. Yes, we have had one or two; escaped from 'sylums, I suppose. One hadn't a halfpenny; and because I wouldn't let him through, he went back a little way, stooped down, took a run, and butted at the hatch like a ram. He smashed his hat rarely, but his head didn't seem no worse—in my opinion on account of his being wrong in it afore. Sometimes people haven't got a halfpenny. If they are really tired and poor we give 'em one and let 'em through. Other people will leave things—pocket-handkerchiefs mostly. I *have* taken cravats and gloves, pocket-knives, tooth-picks, studs, shirt-pins, rings (generally from young gents, early in the morning), but handkerchiefs is the general thing.'

'Regular customers?' said Waterloo. 'Lord, yes! We have regular customers. One, such a worn-out used-up old file as you can scarcely picter, comes from the Surrey side as regular as ten o'clock at night comes; and goes over, *I* think, to some flash house on the Middlesex side. He comes back, he does, as reg'lar as the clock strikes three in the morning, and then can hardly drag one of his old legs after the other. He always turns down the water-stairs, comes up again, and then goes on down the Waterloo Road. He always does the same thing, and never varies a minute. Does it every night—even Sundays.'

I asked Waterloo if he had given his mind to the possibility of this particular customer going down the water-stairs at three o'clock some morning, and never coming up again? He didn't think *that* of him, he replied. In fact, it was Waterloo's opinion, founded on his observation of that file, that he know'd a trick worth two of it.

'There's another queer old customer,' said Waterloo, 'comes over, as punctual as the almanack, at eleven o'clock on the sixth of January, at eleven o'clock on the fifth of April, at eleven o'clock on the sixth of July, at eleven o'clock, on the tenth of October. Drives a shaggy little rough pony, in a sort of a rattle-trap arm-chair sort of a thing. White hair he has, and white whiskers, and muffles himself up with all manner of shawls. He comes back again the same afternoon, and we never see more of him for three months. He is a captain in the navy—retired—wery old—wery odd—and served with Lord Nelson. He is particular about drawing his pension at Somerset House afore the clock strikes twelve every quarter. I *have* heerd say that he thinks it wouldn't be according to the Act of Parliament, if he didn't draw it afore twelve.'

Having related these anecdotes in a natural manner, which was the best warranty in the world for their genuine nature, our friend Waterloo was sinking deep into his shawl again, as having exhausted his communicative powers and taken in enough east wind, when my other friend Pea in a moment brought him to the surface by asking whether he had not been occasionally the subject of assault and battery in the execution of his duty? Waterloo, recovering his spirits, instantly dashed into a new branch of his subject. We learnt how 'both these teeth'—here he pointed to the places where two front teeth were not—were knocked out by an ugly customer who one night made a dash at him (Waterloo) while his (the ugly customer's) pal and coadjutor made a dash at the toll-taking apron where the money-pockets were; how Waterloo, letting the teeth go (to Blazes, he observed indefinitely), grappled with the apron-seizer, permitting the ugly one to run away; and how he saved the bank, and captured his man, and consigned him to fine and imprisonment. Also how, on another night, 'a Cove' laid hold of Waterloo, then presiding at the horse-gate of his bridge, and threw him unceremoniously over his knee, having first cut his head open with his whip. How Waterloo 'got right', and started after the Cove all down the Waterloo Road, through Stamford Street, and round to the foot of Blackfriars Bridge, where the Cove 'cut into' a public house. How Waterloo cut in, too; but how an aider and abetter of the Cove's, who happened to be taking a promiscuous drain at the bar, stopped Waterloo; and the Cove cut out again, ran across the road down Holland Street, and where not, and into a beer-shop. How Waterloo breaking away from his detainer was close upon the Cove's heels, attended by no end of people, who, seeing him running with the blood streaming down his face, thought something worse was 'up', and roared Fire! and Murder! on the hopeful chance of the matter in hand being one or both. How the Cove was ignominiously taken, in a shed where he had run to hide, and how at the Police Court they at first wanted to make a sessions job of it; but eventually Waterloo was allowed to be 'spoke to', and the Cove made it square with Waterloo by paying his doctor's bill (W. was laid up for a week) and giving him 'Three, ten'. Likewise we learnt what we had faintly suspected before, that your sporting amateur on the Derby day, albeit a captain, can be—'if he be', as Captain Bobadil observes, 'so generously minded'—anything but a man of honour and a gentleman; not sufficiently gratifying his nice sense of humour by the witty scattering of flour and rotten eggs on obtuse civilians, but requiring the further excitement of 'bilking the toll', and 'pitching into' Waterloo, and 'cutting him about the head with his whip'; finally being, when called upon to answer for the assault, what Waterloo described as 'Minus', or, as I humbly conceived it, not to be found. Likewise did Waterloo inform us, in reply to my inquiries, admiringly and deferentially preferred through my friend Pea, that the takings at the Bridge had more than doubled in amount, since the reduction of the toll one half. And being asked if the aforesaid takings included much bad money, Waterloo responded, with a look far deeper than the deepest part of the river, *he* should think not!—and so retired into his shawl for the rest of the night.

Then did Pea and I once more embark in our four-oared galley, and glide swiftly down the river with the tide. And while the shrewd East rasped and notched us, as with jagged razors, did my friend Pea impart to me confidences of interest relating to the Thames Police; we between while finding 'duty boats' hanging in dark corners under banks, like weeds—our own was a 'supervision boat'—and they, as they reported 'All right!' flashing their hidden light on us, and we flashing ours on them. These duty boats had one sitter in each: an Inspector: and were rowed 'Ran-dan', which —for the information of those who never graduated, as I was once proud to do, under a fireman-waterman and winner of Kean's Prize Wherry: who, in the course of his tuition, took hundreds of gallons of rum and egg (at my expense) at the various houses of note above and below bridge; not by any means because he liked it, but to cure a weakness in his liver, for which the faculty had particularly recommended it—may be explained as rowed by three men, two pulling an oar each, and one a pair of skulls.

Thus, floating down our black highway, sullenly frowned upon by the knitted brows of Blackfriars, Southwark, and London, each in his lowering turn, I was shown by my friend Pea that there are, in the Thames Police Force, whose district extends from Battersea to Barking Creek, ninety-eight men, eight duty boats, and two supervision boats; and that these go about so silently, and lie in wait in such dark places, and so seem to be nowhere, and so may be anywhere, that they have gradually become a police of prevention, keeping the river almost clear of any great crimes, even while the increased vigilance on shore has made it much harder than of yore to live by 'thieving' in the streets. And as to the various kinds of water-thieves, said my friend Pea, there were the Tier-rangers, who silently dropped alongside the tiers of shipping in the Pool, by night, and who, going to the companion-head, listened for two snores—snore number one, the skipper's; snore number two, the mate's—mates and skippers always snoring great guns, and being dead sure to be hard at it if they had turned in and were asleep. Hearing the double fire, down went the

WATERMAN.

Rangers into the skipper's cabins; groped for the skipper's inexpressibles, which it was the custom of those gentlemen to shake off, watch, money, braces, boots, and all together, on the floor; and therewith made off as silently as might be. Then there were the Lumpers, or labourers employed to unload vessels. They wore loose canvas jackets with a broad hem in the bottom, turned inside, so as to form a large circular pocket in which they could conceal, like clowns in pantomimes, packages of surprising sizes. A great deal of property was stolen in this manner (Pea confided to me) from steamers; first, because steamers carry a larger number of small packages than other ships; next, because of the extreme rapidity with which they are obliged to be unladen for their return voyages. The Lumpers dispose of their booty easily to marine-store dealers, and the only remedy to be suggested is that marine store shops should be licensed, and thus brought under the eye of the police as rigidly as public houses. Lumpers also smuggle goods ashore for the crews of vessels. The smuggling of tobacco is so considerable that it is well worth the while of the sellers of smuggled tobacco to use hydraulic presses, to squeeze a single pound into a package small enough to be contained in an ordinary pocket. Next, said my friend Pea, there were the Truckers—less thieves than smugglers, whose business it was to land more considerable parcels of goods than the Lumpers could manage. They sometimes sold articles of grocery and so forth, to the crews, in order to cloak their real calling, and get aboard without suspicion. Many of them had boats of their own, and made money. Besides these, there were the Dredgermen, who, under pretence of dredging up coals and such like from the bottom of the river, hung about barges and other undecked craft, and when they saw an opportunity, threw any property they could lay their hands on overboard: in order slyly to dredge it up when the vessel was gone. Sometimes, they dexterously used their dredges to whip away anything that might lie within reach. Some of them were mighty neat at this, and the accomplishment was called dry dredging. Then, there was a vast deal of property, such as copper nails, sheathing, hardwood, etc, habitually brought away by shipwrights and other workmen from their employers' yards, and

disposed of to marine-store dealers, many of whom escaped de-
tection through hard swearing, and their extraordinary artful
ways of accounting for the possession of stolen property. Likewise, there were special-pleading practitioners, for whom barges
'drifted away of their own selves'—they having no hand in it,
except first cutting them loose, and afterwards plundering them
—innocents, meaning no harm, who had the misfortune to observe those foundlings wandering about the Thames.

We were now going in and out, with little noise and great
nicety, among the tiers of shipping, whose many hulls, lying close
together, rose out of the water like black streets. Here and there,
a Scotch, an Irish, or a foreign steamer, getting up her steam as
the tide made, looked, with her great chimney and high sides,
like a quiet factory among the common buildings. Now, the streets
opened into clearer spaces, now contracted into alleys; but the
tiers were so like houses, in the dark, that I could almost have
believed myself in the narrower byways of Venice. Everything
was wonderfully still; for it wanted full three hours of flood, and
nothing seemed awake but a dog here and there.

So we took no Tier-rangers captive, nor any Lumpers, nor
Truckers, nor Dredgermen, nor other evil-disposed person or
persons; but went ashore at Wapping, where the old Thames
Police office is now a station-house, and where the old Court, with
its cabin windows looking on the river, is a quaint charge-room:
with nothing worse in it usually than a stuffed cat in a glass case,
and a portrait, pleasant to behold, of a rare old Thames Police
officer, Mr Superintendent Evans, now succeeded by his son. We
looked over the charge books, admirably kept, and found the prevention so good that there were not five hundred entries (including drunken and disorderly) in a whole year. Then, we looked
into the store-room; where there was an oakum smell, and a
nautical seasoning of dreadnought clothing, rope yarn, boat-
hooks, sculls and oars, spare stretchers, rudders, pistols, cutlasses,
and the like. Then, into the cell, aired high up in the wooden wall
through an opening like a kitchen plate-rack: wherein there was
a drunken man, not at all warm, and very wishful to know if it
were morning yet. Then, into a better sort of watch and ward

room, where there was a squadron of stone bottles drawn up, ready to be filled with hot water and applied to any unfortunate creature who might be brought in apparently drowned. Finally, we shook hands with our worthy friend Pea, and ran all the way to Tower Hill, under strong Police suspicion occasionally, before we got warm.

Household Words, February 5th, 1853

Titbull's Almshouses

By the side of most railways out of London one may see Almshouses and Retreats (generally with a Wing or a Centre wanting,
and ambitious of being much bigger than they are), some of which
are newly founded institutions, and some old establishments
transplanted. There is a tendency in these pieces of architecture
to shoot upward unexpectedly, like Jack's bean-stalk, and to be
ornate in spires of Chapels and lanterns of Halls, which might lead
to the embellishment of the air with many castles of questionable
beauty but for the restraining consideration of expense. However,
the managers, being always of a sanguine temperament, comfort
themselves with plans and elevations of Loomings in the future,
and are influenced in the present by philanthropy towards the railway passengers. For, the question how prosperous and promising
the buildings can be made to look in their eyes usually supersedes
the lesser question how they can be turned to the best account for
the inmates.

Why none of the people who reside in these places ever look
out of window, or take an airing in the piece of ground which is
going to be a garden by and by, is one of the wonders I have added
to my always-lengthening list of the wonders of the world. I have
got it into my mind that they live in a state of chronic injury and
resentment, and, on that account, refuse to decorate the building
with a human interest. As I have known legatees deeply injured
by a bequest of five hundred pound because it was not five thousand, and as I was once acquainted with a pensioner on the Public,
to the extent of two hundred a year, who perpetually anathematized
his Country because he was not in the receipt of four, having no
claim whatever to sixpence; so perhaps it usually happens, within
certain limits, that to get a little help is to get a notion of being

defrauded of more. 'How do they pass their lives in this beautiful and peaceful place?' was the subject of my speculation with a visitor who once accompanied me to a charming rustic retreat for old men and women: a quaint ancient foundation in a pleasant English county, behind a picturesque church, and among rich old convent gardens. There were but some dozen or so of houses, and we agreed that we would talk with the inhabitants, as they sat in their groined rooms between the light of their fires and the light shining in at their latticed windows, and would find out. They passed their lives in considering themselves mulcted of certain ounces of tea by a deaf old steward who lived among them in the quadrangle. There was no reason to suppose that any such ounces of tea had ever been in existence, or that the old steward so much as knew what was the matter; he passed *his* life in considering himself periodically defrauded of a birch-broom by the beadle.

But it is neither to old Almhouses in the country, nor to new Almhouses by the railroad, that these present uncommercial notes relate. They refer back to journeys made among those common-place smoky-fronted London Almshouses, with a little paved courtyard in front enclosed by iron railings, which have got snowed up, as it were, by bricks and mortar; which were once in a suburb, but are now in the densely populated town; gaps in the busy life around them, parentheses in the close and blotted texts of the streets.

Sometimes, these Almshouses belong to a Company or Society. Sometimes, they were established by individuals, and are maintained out of private funds bequeathed in perpetuity long ago. My favourite among them is Titbull's, which establishment is a picture of many. Of Titbull I know no more than that he deceased in 1723, that his Christian name was Sampson, and his social designation Esquire, and that he founded these Almshouses as Dwellings for Nine Poor Women and Six Poor Men by his Will and Testament. I should not know even this much, but for its being inscribed on a grim stone very difficult to read, let into the front of the centre house of Titbull's Almshouses, and which stone is ornamented atop with a piece of sculptured drapery resembling the effigy of Titbull's bath-towel.

Titbull's Almshouses are in the east of London, in a great high-way, in a poor, busy, and thronged neighbourhood. Old iron and fried fish, cough drops and artificial flowers, boiled pigs' feet and household furniture that looks as if it were polished up with lip-salve, umbrellas full of vocal literature and saucers full of shell-fish in a green juice which I hope is natural to them when their health is good, garnish the paved sideways as you go to Titbull's. I take the ground to have risen in those parts since Titbull's time, and you drop into his domain by three stone steps. So did I first drop into it, very nearly striking my brows against Titbull's pump, which stands with its back to the thoroughfare just inside the gate, and has a conceited air of reviewing Titbull's pensioners.

'And a worse one,' said a virulent old man with a pitcher, 'there isn't nowhere. A harder one to work, nor grudginer one to yield, there isn't nowhere!' This old man wore a long coat, such as we see Hogarth's chairmen represented with, and it was of that peculiar green-pea hue without the green, which seems to come of poverty. It had also that peculiar smell of cupboard which seems to come of poverty.

'The pump is rusty, perhaps,' said I.

'Not *it*,' said the old man, regarding it with undiluted virulence in his watery eye. 'It never were fit to be termed a pump. That's what's the matter with *it*.'

'Whose fault is that?' said I.

The old man, who had a working mouth which seemed to be trying to masticate his anger, and to find that it was too hard and there was too much of it, replied, 'Them gentlemen.'

'What gentlemen?'

'Maybe you're one of 'em?' said the old man suspiciously.

'The trustees?'

'I wouldn't trust 'em myself,' said the virulent old man.

'If you mean the gentlemen who administer this place, no, I am not one of them; nor have I ever so much as heard of them.'

'I wish *I* never heard of them,' gasped the old man: 'at my time of life—with the rheumatics—drawing water—from that thing!' Not to be deluded into calling it a Pump, the old man gave it another virulent look, took up his pitcher, and carried it into a corner dwelling-house, shutting the door after him.

Looking around, and seeing that each little house was a house of two little rooms; and seeing that the little oblong courtyard in front was like a graveyard for the inhabitants, saving that no word was engraven on its flat dry stones; and seeing that the currents of life and noise ran to and fro outside, having no more to do with the place than if it were a sort of low-water mark on a lively beach; I say, seeing this and nothing else, I was going out at the gate when one of the doors opened.

'Was you looking for anything, sir?' asked a tiny, well-favoured woman.

Really no; I couldn't say I was.

'Not wanting anyone, sir?'

'No—at least, I—pray what is the name of the elderly gentleman who lives in the corner there?'

The tidy woman stepped out to be sure of the door I indicated, and she and the pump and I stood all three in a row, with our backs to the thoroughfare.

'Oh! *His* name is Mr Battens,' said the tidy woman, dropping her voice.

'I have just been talking with him.'

'Indeed?' said the tidy woman. 'Ho! I wonder Mr Battens talked!'

'Is he usually so silent?'

'Well, Mr Battens is the oldest here—that is to say, the oldest of the old gentlemen—in point of residence.'

She had a way of passing her hands over and under one another as she spoke, that was not only tidy, but propitiatory; so I asked her if I might look at her little sitting-room? She willingly replied Yes, and we went into it together: she leaving the door open, with an eye, as I understood, to the social proprieties. The door at once opening into the room without any intervening entry, even scandal must have been silenced by the precaution.

It was a gloomy little chamber, but clean, and with a mug of wallflower in the window. On the chimney-piece were two peacock's feathers, a carved ship, a few shells, and a black profile with one eyelash; whether this portrait purported to be male or female passed my comprehension, until my hostess informed me that it was her only son, and 'quite a speaking one'.

'He is alive, I hope?'

'No, sir,' said the widow, 'he were cast away in China.' This was said with a modest sense of its reflecting a certain geographical distinction on his mother.

'If the old gentlemen here are not given to talking,' said I, 'I hope the old ladies are?—Not that you are one.'

She shook her head. 'You see, they get so cross.'

'How is that?'

'Well, whether the gentlemen really do deprive us of any little matters which ought to be ours by rights, I cannot say for certain; but the opinion of the old ones is they do. And Mr Battens he do even go so far as to doubt whether credit is due to the Founder. For Mr Battens he do say, anyhow he got his name up by it, and he done it cheap.'

'I am afraid the pump has soured Mr Battens.'

'It may be so,' returned the tidy widow, 'but the handle does go very hard. Still, what I say to myself is, the gentlemen *may* not pocket the difference between a good pump and a bad one, and I would wish to think well of them. And the dwelling,' said my hostess, glancing round her room; 'perhaps they were convenient dwellings in the Founder's time, considered *as* his time, and therefore he should not be blamed. But Mrs Saggers is very hard upon them.'

'Mrs Saggers is the oldest here?'

'The oldest but one. Mrs Quinch being the oldest, and have totally lost her head.'

'And you?'

'I am the youngest in residence, and consequently am not looked up to. But, when Mrs Quinch makes a happy release, there will be one below me. Nor is it to be expected that Mrs Saggers will prove herself immortal.'

'True. Nor Mr Battens.'

'Regarding the old gentlemen,' said my widow slightingly, 'they count among themselves. They do not count among us. Mr

Battens is that exceptional that he have written to the gentlemen many times, and have worked the case against them. Therefore he have took a higher ground. But we do not, as a rule, greatly reckon the old gentlemen.'

Pursuing the subject, I found it to be traditionally settled among the poor ladies that the poor gentlemen, whatever their ages, were all very old indeed, and in a state of dotage. I also discovered that the juniors and new-comers preserved, for a time, a waning disposition to believe in Titbull and his trustees, but that, as they gained social standing, they lost this faith, and disparaged Titbull and all his works.

Improving my acquaintance subsequently with this respected lady, whose name was Mrs Mitts, and occasionally dropping in upon her with a little offering of sound Family Hyson in my pocket, I gradually became familiar with the inner politics and ways of Titbull's Almshouses. But I never could find out who the trustees were, or where they were: it being one of the fixed ideas of the place that those authorities must be vaguely and mysteriously mentioned as 'the gentlemen' only. The secretary of 'the gentlemen' was once pointed out to me, evidently engaged in championing the obnoxious pump against the attacks of the discontented Mr Battens; but I am not in a condition to report further of him than that he had the sprightly bearing of a lawyer's clerk. I had it from Mrs Mitts's lips, in a very confidential moment, that Mr Battens was once 'had up before the gentlemen' to stand or fall by his accusations, and that an old shoe was thrown after him on his departure from the building on this dread errand; not ineffectually, for, the interview resulting in a plumber, was considered to have encircled the temples of Mr Battens with the wreath of victory.

In Titbull's Almshouses the local society is not regarded as good society. A gentleman or lady receiving visitors from without, or going out to tea, counts, as it were, accordingly; but visitings or tea-drinkings interchanged among Titbullians do not score. Such interchanges, however, are rare, in consequence of internal dissensions occasioned by Mrs Saggers's pail: which household article has split Titbull's into almost as many parties

as there are dwellings in that precinct. The extremely complicated
nature of the conflicting articles of belief on the subject prevents
my stating them here with my usual perspicuity, but I think they
have all branched off from the root-and-trunk question, Has Mrs
Saggers any right to stand her pail outside her dwelling? The
question has been much refined upon, but, roughly stated, may be
stated in those terms.

There are two old men in Titbull's Almshouses who, I have
been given to understand, knew each other in the world beyond its
pump and iron railings, when they were both 'in trade'. They
make the best of their reverses, and are looked upon with great
contempt. They are little, stooping, blear-eyed old men of
cheerful countenance, and they hobble up and down the courtyard
wagging their chins and talking together quite gaily. This has
given offence, and has, moreover, raised the question whether
they are justified in passing any other windows than their own.
Mr Battens, however, permitting them to pass *his* windows, on
the disdainful ground that their imbecility almost amounts to
irresponsibility, they are allowed to take their walk in peace.
They live next door to one another, and take it by turns to read
the newspaper aloud (that is to say, the newest newspaper they
can get), and they play cribbage at night. On warm and sunny
days they have been known to go so far as to bring out two chairs,
and sit by the iron railings, looking forth, but this low conduct,
being much remarked upon throughout Titbull's, they were de-
terred by an outraged public opinion from repeating it. There is
a rumour—but it may be malicious—that they hold the memory
of Titbull in some weak sort of veneration, and that they once set
off together on a pilgrimage to the parish churchyard to find his
tomb. To this, perhaps, might be traced a general suspicion that
they are spies of 'the gentlemen': to which they were supposed
to have given colour, in my own presence, on the occasion of the
weak attempt at justification of the pump by the gentlemen's
clerk, when they emerged bare-headed from the doors of their
dwellings, as if their dwellings and themselves constituted an old-
fashioned weather-glass of double action with two figures of old
ladies inside, and deferentially bowed to him at intervals until he

took his departure. They are understood to be perfectly friendless and relationless. Unquestionably the two poor fellows make the very best of their lives in Titbull's Almshouses, and unquestionably they are (as before mentioned) the subjects of unmitigated contempt there.

On Saturday nights, when there is a greater stir than usual outside, and when itinerant vendors of miscellaneous wares even take their stations and light up their smoky lamps before the iron railings, Titbull's becomes flurried. Mrs Saggers has her celebrated palpitations of the heart, for the most part, on Saturday nights. But Titbull's is unfit to strive with the uproar of the streets in any of its phases. It is religiously believed at Titbull's that people push more than they used, and likewise that the foremost object of the population of England and Wales is to get you down and trample on you. Even of railroads they know, at Titbull's, little more than the shriek (which Mrs Saggers says goes through her, and ought to be taken up by Government); and the penny postage may even yet be unknown there, for I have never seen a letter delivered to any inhabitant. But there is a tall, straight, sallow lady resident in Number Seven, Titbull's, who never speaks to anybody, who is surrounded by a superstitious halo of lost wealth, who does her household work in housemaid's gloves, and who is secretly much deferred to, though openly cavilled at; and it has obscurely leaked out that this old lady has a son, grandson, nephew, or other relative, who is 'a Contractor', and who would think it nothing of a job to knock down Titbull's, pack it off into Cornwall, and knock it together again. An immense sensation was made by a gipsy party calling, in a spring van, to take this old lady up to go for a day's pleasure into Epping Forest, and notes were compared as to which of the company was the son, grandson, nephew, or other relative, the Contractor. A thick-set personage, with a white hat and a cigar in his mouth, was the favourite: though, as Titbull's had no other reason to believe that the Contractor was there at all than that this man was supposed to eye the chimney-stacks as if he would like to knock them down and cart them off, the general mind was much unsettled in arriving at a conclusion. As a way out of this difficulty, it concentrated itself on the acknowledged Beauty of the party, every stitch in whose dress was verbally unripped by the old ladies then and there, and whose 'goings-on' with another and a thinner personage in a white hat might have suffused the pump (where they were principally discussed) with blushes for months afterwards. Herein Titbull's was to Titbull's true, for it has a constitutional dislike of all strangers. As concerning innovations and improvements, it is always of opinion that what it doesn't want itself, nobody ought to want. But I think I have met with this opinion outside Titbull's.

Of the humble treasures of furniture brought into Titbull's by the inmates when they establish themselves in that place of contemplation for the rest of their days, by far the greater and more valuable part belongs to the ladies. I may claim the honour of having either crossed the threshold, or looked in at the door, of every one of the nine ladies, and I have noticed that they are all particular in the article of bedsteads, and maintain favourite and long-established bedsteads and bedding as a regular part of their rest. Generally an antiquated chest of drawers is among their cherished possessions; a tea-tray always is. I know of at least two rooms in which a little tea-kettle of genuine burnished copper vies with the cat in winking at the fire; and one old lady has a tea-urn set forth in state on the top of her chest of drawers, which urn is used as her library, and contains four duo-decimo volumes, and a black-bordered newspaper giving an account of the funeral of her Royal Highness the Princess Charlotte. Among the poor old gentlemen there are no such niceties. Their furniture has the air of being contributed, like some obsolete Literary Miscellany, 'by several hands'; their few chairs never match; old patchwork coverlets linger among them; and they have an untidy habit of keeping their wardrobes in hat-boxes. When I recall one old gentleman who is rather choice in his shoe-brushes and blacking-bottle, I have summed up the domestic elegancies of that side of the building.

On the occurrence of a death in Titbull's, it is invariably agreed among the survivors—and it is the only subject on which they do agree—that the departed did something 'to bring it on'. Judging by Titbull's, I should say the human race need never die, if they took care. But they don't take care, and they do die, and when they die in Titbull's they are buried at the cost of the Foundation. Some provision has been made for the purpose, in virtue of which (I record this on the strength of having seen the funeral of Mrs Quinch) a lively neighbouring undertaker dresses up four of the old men, and four of the old women, hustles them into a procession of four couples, and leads off with a large black bow at the back of his hat, looking over his shoulder at them airily, from time to time, to see that no member of the party has got lost, or has tumbled down; as if they were a company of dim old dolls.

Resignation of a dwelling is of very rare occurrence in Titbull's. A story does obtain there, how an old lady's son once drew a prize of thirty thousand pounds in the Lottery, and presently drove to the gate in his own carriage, with French Horns playing up behind, and whisked his mother away, and left ten guineas for a feast. But I have been unable to substantiate it by any evidence, and regard it as an Almshouse Fairy Tale. It is curious that the only proved case of resignation happened within my knowledge.

It happened on this wise. There is a sharp competition among the ladies respecting the gentility of their visitors, and I have so often observed visitors to be dressed as for a holiday occasion that I suppose the ladies to have besought them to make all possible display when they come. In these circumstances much excitement was one day occasioned by Mrs Mitts receiving a visit from a Greenwich Pensioner. He was a Pensioner of a bluff and warlike appearance, with an empty coat-sleeve, and he was got up with unusual care; his coat buttons were extremely bright, he wore his empty coat-sleeve in a graceful festoon, and he had a walking-stick in his hand that must have cost money. When, with the head of his walking-stick, he knocked at Mrs Mitts's door—there are no knockers in Titbull's—Mrs Mitts was overheard by a next-door neighbour to utter a cry of surprise expressing much agitation; and the same neighbour did afterwards solemnly affirm that, when he was admitted into Mrs Mitts's room, she heard a smack. Heard a smack which was not a blow.

There was an air about this Greenwich Pensioner, when he took his departure, which imbued all Titbull's with the conviction that he was coming again. He was eagerly looked for, and Mrs Mitts was closely watched. In the meantime, if anything could have placed the unfortunate six old gentlemen at a greater disadvantage than that at which they chronically stood, it would have been the apparition of this Greenwich Pensioner. They were well shrunken already, but they shrunk to nothing in comparison with the Pensioner. Even the poor old gentlemen themselves seemed conscious of their inferiority, and to know submissively that they could never hope to hold their own against the Pensioner, with his warlike and maritime experience in the past, and his tobacco money in the present: his chequered career of blue water, black gunpowder, and red bloodshed for England, home, and beauty.

Before three weeks were out, the Pensioner reappeared. Again he knocked at Mrs Mitts's door with the handle of his stick, and again was he admitted. But not again did he depart alone; for Mrs Mitts, in a bonnet identified as having been re-embellished, went out walking with him, and stayed out till the ten-o'clock beer, Greenwich time.

There was now a truce even as to the troubled waters of Mrs Saggers's pail; nothing was spoken of among the ladies but the conduct of Mrs Mitts, and its blighting influence on the reputation of Titbull's. It was agreed that Mr Battens 'ought to take it up', and Mr Battens was communicated with on the subject. That unsatisfactory individual replied 'that he didn't see his way yet', and it was unanimously voted by the ladies that aggravation was in his nature.

How it came to pass, with some appearance of inconsistency, that Mrs Mitts was cut by all the ladies and the Pensioner admired by all the ladies, matters not. Before another week was out, Titbull's was startled by another phenomenon. At ten o'clock in the forenoon appeared a cab, containing not only the Greenwich Pensioner with one arm, but, to boot, a Chelsea Pensioner with one leg. Both dismounting to assist Mrs Mitts into the cab, the Greenwich Pensioner bore her company inside, and the Chelsea Pensioner mounted the box by the driver: his wooden leg sticking out after the manner of a bowsprit, as if in jocular homage to his

friend's sea-going career. Thus the equipage drove away. No Mrs
Mitts returned that night.

What Mr Battens might have done in the matter of taking it
up, goaded by the infuriated state of public feeling next morning,
was anticipated by another phenomenon. A truck, propelled by
the Greenwich Pensioner and the Chelsea Pensioner, each placidly
smoking a pipe, and pushing his warrior breast against the handle.

The display on the part of the Greenwich Pensioner of his
'marriage lines', and his announcement that himself and friend
had looked in for the furniture of Mrs G. Pensioner, late Mitts,
by no means reconciled the ladies to the conduct of their sister; on
the contrary, it is said that they appeared more than ever exasperated. Nevertheless, my stray visits to Titbull's, since the date
of this occurrence, have confirmed me in an impression that it was
a wholesome fillip. The nine ladies are smarter, both in mind and
dress, than they used to be, though it must be admitted that they
despise the six gentlemen to the last extent. They have a much
greater interest in the external thoroughfare, too, than they had
when I first knew Titbull's. And whenever I chance to be leaning
my back against the pump or the iron railings, and to be talking
to one of the junior ladies, and to see that a flush has passed over
her face, I immediately know, without looking round, that a
Greenwich Pensioner has gone past.

All the Year Round, October 24th, 1862
The Uncommercial Traveller, Second Series, 1868

Some Recollections
Of Mortality

————⊃∘◉∘⊂————

I had parted from the small bird at somewhere about four o'clock in the morning, when he had got out at Arras, and had been received by two shovel hats in waiting at the station, who presented an appropriately ornithological and crow-like appearance. My compatriot and I had gone on to Paris; my compatriot enlightening me occasionally with a long list of the enormous grievances of French railway travelling: every one of which, as I am a sinner, was perfectly new to me, though I have as much experience of French railways as most uncommercials. I had left him at the terminus (through his conviction, against all explanation and remonstrance, that his baggage ticket was his passenger ticket), insisting in a very high temper, to the functionary on duty, that in his own personal identity he was four packages weighing so many kilogrammes—as if he had been Cassim Baba! I had bathed and breakfasted, and was strolling on the bright quays. The subject of my meditations was the question whether it is positively in the essence and nature of things, as a certain school of Britons would seem to think it, that a Capital must be ensnared and enslaved before it can be made beautiful: when I lifted up my eyes, and found that my feet, straying like my mind, had brought me to Notre-Dame.

That is to say, Notre-Dame was before me, but there was a large open space between us. A very little while gone, I had left that space covered with buildings densely crowded; and now it was cleared for some new wonder in the way of public Street, Place, Garden, Fountain, or all four. Only the obscene little Morgue, slinking on the brink of the river, and soon to come down, was left there, looking mortally ashamed of itself, and

George Cruikshank

PARISH BEADLE.

supremely wicked. I had but glanced at this acquaintance, when I beheld an airy procession coming round in front of Notre-Dame, past the great hospital. It had something of a Masaniello look, with fluttering striped curtains in the midst of it, and it came dancing round the cathedral in the liveliest manner.

I was speculating on a marriage in Blouse-life, or a Christening, or some other domestic festivity which I would see out, when I found, from the talk of a quick rush of Blouses past me, that it was a Body coming to the Morgue. Having never before chanced upon this initiation, I constituted myself a Blouse likewise, and ran into the Morgue with the rest. It was a very muddy day, and we took in a quantity of mire with us, and the procession, coming in upon our heels, brought a quantity more. The procession was in the highest spirits, and consisted of idlers who had come with the curtained litter from its starting-place, and of all the reinforcements it had picked up by the way. It set the litter down in the midst of the Morgue, and then two Custodians proclaimed aloud that we were all 'invited' to go out. This invitation was rendered the more pressing, if not the more flattering, by our being shoved out, and the folding gates being barred upon us.

Those who have never seen the Morgue may see it perfectly, by presenting to themselves an indifferently paved coach-house, accessible from the street by a pair of folding gates; on the left of the coach-house, occupying its width, any large London tailor's or linendraper's plate-glass window reaching to the ground; within the window, on two rows of inclined planes, what the coach-house has to show; hanging above, like irregular stalactites from the roof of a cave, a quantity of clothes—the clothes of the dead-and-buried shows of the coach-house.

We had been excited in the highest degree by seeing the Custodians pull off their coats and tuck up their shirt-sleeves as the procession came along. It looked so interestingly like business. Shut out in the muddy street, we now became quite ravenous to know all about it. Was it river, pistol, knife, love, gambling, robbery, hatred, how many stabs, how many bullets, fresh or decomposed, suicide or murder? All wedged together, and all staring at one another with our heads thrust forward, we propounded these inquiries, and a hundred more such. Imperceptibly it came to be known that Monsieur the tall and sallow mason yonder was acquainted with the facts. Would Monsieur the tall and sallow mason, surged at by a new wave of us, have the goodness to impart? It was but a poor old man, passing along the street under one of the new buildings, on whom a stone had fallen, and who had tumbled dead. His age? Another wave surged up against the tall and sallow mason, and our wave swept on and broke, and he was any age from sixty-five to ninety.

An old man was not much: moreover, we could have wished he had been killed by human agency—his own, or somebody else's: the latter preferable—but our comfort was that he had nothing about him to lead to his identification, and that his people must seek him here. Perhaps they were waiting dinner for him even now? We liked that. Such of us as had pocket-handkerchiefs took a slow, intense, protracted wipe at our noses, and then crammed our handkerchiefs into the breast of our blouses. Others of us who had no handkerchiefs administered a similar relief to our overwrought minds, by means of prolonged smears or wipes of our mouths on our sleeves. One man with a gloomy malformation of brow—a homicidal worker in white-lead, to judge from his blue tone of colour, and a certain flavour of paralysis pervading him—got his coat collar between his teeth, and bit at it with an appetite. Several decent women arrived upon the outskirts of the crowd, and prepared to launch themselves into the dismal coach-house when opportunity should come; among them, a pretty young mother, pretending to bite the forefinger of her baby boy, kept it between her rosy lips that it might be handy for guiding to point at the show. Meantime, all faces were turned towards the building, and we men waited with a fixed and stern resolution: for the most part with folded arms. Surely, it was the only public French sight these uncommercial eyes had seen, at which the expectant people did not form *en queue*. But there was no such order of arrangement here; nothing but a general determination to make a rush for it, and a disposition to object to some boys who had mounted on the two stone posts by the hinges of the gates, with the design of swooping in when the hinges should turn. Now they turned, and we rushed! Great pressure, and a scream or two from the front. Then a laugh or two, some expressions of disappointment, and a slackening of the pressure and subsidence of the struggle.—Old man not there.

'But what would you have?' the Custodian reasonably argues as he looks out at his little door. 'Patience, patience! We make his toilet, gentlemen. He will be exposed presently. It is necessary to proceed according to rule. His toilet is not made all at a blow. He will be exposed in good time, gentlemen, in good time.' And so retires, smoking, with a wave of his sleeveless arm towards the window, importing, 'Entertain yourselves meanwhile with the other curiosities. Fortunately the Museum is not empty today.'

Who would have thought of public fickleness even at the Morgue? But there it was on that occasion. Three lately popular articles, that had been attracting greatly when the litter was first descried, coming dancing round the corner by the great cathedral, were so completely deposed now, that nobody save two little girls (one showing them to a doll) would look at them. Yet the chief of the three, the article in the front row, had received jagged injury of the left temple; and the other two in the back row, the drowned two lying side by side with their heads very slightly turned towards each other, seemed to be comparing notes about it. Indeed, those two of the back row were so furtive of appearance, and so (in their puffed way) assassinatingly knowing as to the one of the front, that it was hard to think the three had never come together in their lives, and were only chance companions after death. Whether or no this was the general, as it was the uncommercial, fancy, it is not to be disputed that the group had drawn exceedingly within ten minutes. Yet now the inconstant public turned its back upon them, and even leaned its elbows carelessly against the bar outside the window, and shook off the mud from its shoes, and also lent and borrowed fire for pipes.

Custodian re-enters from his door. 'Again once, gentlemen, you are invited——' No further invitation necessary. Ready dash into the street. Toilet finished. Old man coming out.

This time, the interest was grown too hot to admit of toleration of the boys on the stone posts. The homicidal white-lead worker made a pounce upon one boy who was hoisting himself up, and brought him to earth amidst general commendation. Closely stowed as we were, we yet formed into groups—groups of conversation, without separation from the mass—to discuss the old man. Rivals of the tall and sallow mason sprang into being, and here, again, was popular inconstanty. These rivals attracted audiences, and were greedily listened to; and whereas they had derived their information solely from the tall and sallow one, officious members of the crowd now sought to enlighten *him* on their authority. Changed by this social experience into an ironvisaged and inveterate misanthrope, the mason glared at mankind, and evidently cherished in his breast the wish that the whole of the present company could change places with the deceased old man. And now listeners became inattentive, and people made a start forward at a slight sound, and an unholy fire kindled in the public eye, and those next the gate beat at them impatiently, as if they were of the cannibal species and hungry.

Again the hinges creaked, and we rushed. Disorderly pressure for some time ensued before the uncommercial unit got figured into the front row of the sum. It was strange to see so much heat and uproar seething about one poor spare white-haired old man, quiet for evermore. He was calm of feature and undisfigured, as he lay on his back—having been struck upon the hinder part of the head, and thrown forward—and something like a tear or two had started from the closed eyes, and lay wet upon the face. The uncommercial interest, sated at a glance, directed itself upon the striving crowd on either side and behind: wondering whether one might have guessed, from the expression of those faces merely, what kind of sight they were looking at. The differences of expression were not many. There was a little pity, but not much, and that mostly with a selfish touch in it—as who would say, 'Shall I, poor I, look like that when the time comes?' There was more of a secretly brooding contemplation and curiosity, as, 'That man I don't like, and have the grudge against; would such be his appearance, if some one—not to mention names—by any

chance gave him an ugly knock?' There was a wolfish stare at the
object, in which the homicidal white-lead worker shone conspicuous. And there was a much more general, purposeless, vacant
staring at it—like looking at wax-work without a catalogue, and
not knowing what to make of it. But all these expressions con-
curred in possessing the one underlying expression of *looking at
something that could not return a look*. The uncommercial notice
had established this as very remarkable, when a new pressure all
at once coming up from the street pinioned him ignominiously,
and hurried him into the arms (now sleeved again) of the Custodian smoking at his door, and answering questions, between
puffs, with a certain placid meritorious air of not being proud,
though high in office. And, mentioning pride, it may be observed,
by the way, that one could not well help investing the original
sole occupant of the front row with an air depreciatory of the
legitimate attraction of the poor old man: while the two in the
second row seemed to exult at his superseded popularity.

Pacing presently round the garden of the Tower of St Jacques
de la Boucherie, and presently again in front of the Hôtel de Ville,
I called to mind a certain desolate open-air Morgue that I happened to light upon in London, one day in the hard winter of 1861,
and which seemed as strange to me, at the time of seeing it, as if
I had found it in China. Towards that hour of a winter's afternoon
when the lamplighters are beginning to light the lamps in the
streets a little before they are wanted, because the darkness
thickens fast and soon, I was walking in from the country on the
northern side of the Regent's Park—hard frozen and deserted—
when I saw an empty hansom cab drive up to the lodge at Glou-
cester Gate, and the driver with great agitation call to the man
there: who quickly reached a long pole from a tree, and, deftly
collared by the driver, jumped to the step of his little seat, and so
the hansom rattled out at the gate, galloping over the iron-bound
road. I followed running, though not so fast but that when I came
to the right-hand Canal Bridge, near the cross-path to Chalk
Farm, the hansom was stationary, the horse was smoking hot, the
long pole was idle on the ground, and the driver and the park-
keeper were looking over the bridge parapet. Looking over too,

I saw, lying on the towing-path, with her face turned up towards us, a woman, dead a day or two, and under thirty, as I guessed, poorly dressed in black. The feet were lightly crossed at the ankles, and the dark hair, all pushed back from the face, as though that had been the last action of her desperate hands, streamed over the ground. Dabbled all about her were the water and the broken ice that had dropped from her dress, and had splashed as she was got out. The policeman who had just got her out, and the passing costermonger who had helped him, were standing near the body; the latter with that stare at it which I have likened to being at a wax-work exhibition without a catalogue; the former looking over his stock, with professional stiffness and coolness, in the direction in which the bearers he had sent for were expected. So dreadfully forlorn, so dreadfully sad, so dreadfully mysterious, the spectacle of our dear sister here departed! A barge came up, breaking the floating ice and the silence, and a woman steered it. The man with the horse that towed it cared so little for the body, that the stumbling hoofs had been among the hair, and the tow-rope had caught and turned the head, before our cry of horror took him to the bridle. At which sound the steering woman looked up at us on the bridge with contempt unutterable, and then looking down at the body with a similar expression—as if it were made in another likeness from herself, had been informed with other passions, had been lost by other chances, had had another nature dragged down to perdition—steered a spurning streak of mud at it, and passed on.

A better experience, but also of the Morgue kind, in which chance happily made me useful in a slight degree, arose to my remembrance as I took my way by the Boulevard de Sebastopol to the brighter scenes of Paris.

The thing happened, say, five-and-twenty years ago. I was a modest young uncommercial then, and timid and inexperienced. Many suns and winds have browned me in the line, but those were my pale days. Having newly taken the lease of a house in a certain distinguished metropolitan parish—a house which then appeared to me to be a frightfully first-class Family Mansion, involving awful responsibilities—I became the prey of a Beadle. I think the

Beadle must have seen me going in or coming out, and must have observed that I tottered under the weight of my grandeur. Or he may have been hiding under straw when I bought my first horse (in the desirable stable-yard attached to the first-class Family Mansion), and when the vendor remarked to me, in an original manner, on bringing him for approval, taking his cloth off and smacking him, 'There, sir! *There's* a Orse!' And when I said gallantly, 'How much do you want for him?' and when the vendor said, 'No more than sixty guineas from you'; and when I said smartly, 'Why not more than sixty from *me*?' And when he said crushingly, 'Because, upon my soul and body, he'd be considered cheap at seventy by one who understood the subject—but you don't.'—I say, the Beadle may have been in hiding under straw when this disgrace befell me, or he may have noted that I was too raw and young an Atlas to carry the first-class Family Mansion in a knowing manner. Be this as it may, the Beadle did what Melancholy did to the youth in Gray's Elegy—he marked me for his own. And the way in which the Beadle did it was this: he summoned me as a Juryman on his Coroner's Inquests.

In my first feverish alarm I repaired 'for safety and for succour' —like those sagacious Northern shepherds who, having had no previous reason whatever to believe in young Norval, very prudently did not originate the hazardous idea of believing in him— to a deep householder. This profound man informed me that the Beadle counted on my buying him off; on my bribing him not to summon me; and that if I would attend an Inquest with a cheerful countenance, and profess alacrity in that branch of my country's service, the Beadle would be disheartened, and would give up the game.

I roused my energies, and, the next time the wily Beadle summoned me, I went. The Beadle was the blankest Beadle I have ever looked on when I answered to my name, and his discomfiture gave me courage to go through with it.

We were empanelled to inquire concerning the death of a very little mite of a child. It was the old miserable story. Whether the mother had committed the minor offence of concealing the birth, or whether she had committed the major offence of killing the child, was the question on which we were wanted. We must commit her on one of the two issues.

The Inquest came off in the parish workhouse, and I have yet a lively impression that I was unanimously received by my brother Jurymen as a brother of the utmost conceivable insignificance. Also that, before we began, a broker who had lately cheated me fearfully in the matter of a pair of card-tables, was for the utmost rigour of the law. I remember that we sat in a sort of card-room, on such very large square horsehair chairs that I wondered what race of Patagonians they were made for; and further, that an undertaker gave me his card when we were in the full moral freshness of having just been sworn, as 'an inhabitant that was newly come into the parish, and was likely to have a young family'. The case was then stated to us by the Coroner, and then we went downstairs—led by the plotting Beadle—to view the body. From that day to this, the poor little figure, on which that sounding legal appellation was bestowed, has lain in the same place, and with the same surroundings, to my thinking. In a kind of crypt devoted to the warehousing of the parochial coffins, and in the midst of a perfect Panorama of coffins of all sizes, it was stretched on a box; the mother had put it in her box—this box—almost as soon as it was born, and it had been presently found there. It had been opened, and neatly sewn up, and, regarded from that point of view, it looked like a stuffed creature. It rested on a clean white cloth, with a a surgical instrument or so at hand, and, regarded from that point of view, it looked as if the cloth were 'laid', and the Giant were coming to dinner. There was nothing repellent about the poor piece of innocence, and it demanded a mere form of looking at. So, we looked at an old pauper who was going about among the coffins with a foot-rule, as if he were a case of Self-Measurement; and we looked at one another; and we said the place was well whitewashed anyhow; and then our conversational powers as a British Jury flagged, and the foreman said, 'All right, gentlemen? Back again, Mr Beadle!'

The miserable young creature who had given birth to this child within a very few days, and who had cleaned the cold wet doorsteps immediately afterwards, was brought before us when we resumed our horsehair chairs, and was present during the proceedings. She had a horsehair chair herself, being very weak and ill; and I remember how she turned to the unsympathetic nurse who attended her, and who might have been the figure-head of a pauper ship, and how she hid her face and sobs and tears upon that wooden shoulder. I remember, too, how hard her mistress was upon her (she was a servant-of-all-work), and with what a cruel pertinacity that piece of Virtue spun her thread of evidence double, by intertwisting it with the sternest thread of construction. Smitten hard by the terrible low wail from the utterly friendless orphan girl, which never ceased during the whole inquiry, I took heart to ask this witness a question or two, which hopefully admitted of an answer that might give a favourable turn to the case. She made the turn as little favourable as it could be, but it did some good, and the Coroner, who was nobly patient and humane (he was the late Mr Wakley), cast a look of strong encouragement in my direction. Then we had the doctor who had made the examination, and the usual tests as to whether the child was born alive; but he was a timid muddle-headed doctor, and got confused and contradictory, and wouldn't say this, and couldn't answer for that, and the immaculate broker was too much for him, and our side slid back again. However, I tried again, and the Coroner backed me again, for which I ever afterwards felt grateful to him, as I do now to his memory; and we got another favourable turn out of some other witness, some member of the family with a strong prepossession against the sinner; and I think we had the doctor back again; and I know that the Coroner summed up for our side, and that I and my British brothers turned round to discuss our verdict, and get ourselves into great difficulties with our large chairs and the broker. At that stage of the case I tried hard again, being convinced that I had cause for it; and at last we found for the minor offence of only concealing the birth; and the poor desolate creature, who had been taken out during our deliberation, being brought in again to be told of the verdict, then dropped upon her knees before us, with protestations that we were right—protestations among the most affecting that I have ever heard in my life—and was carried away insensible.

(In private conversation after this was all over, the Coroner showed me his reasons, as a trained surgeon, for perceiving it to be impossible that the child could, under the most favourable circumstances, have drawn many breaths, in the very doubtful case of its having ever breathed at all; this, owing to the discovery of some foreign matter in the windpipe, quite irreconcilable with many moments of life.)

When the agonized girl had made those final protestations, I had seen her face, and it was in unison with her distracted heartbroken voice, and it was very moving. It certainly did not impress me by any beauty that it had, and if I ever see it again in another world I shall only know it by the help of some new sense or intelligence. But it came to me in my sleep that night, and I selfishly dismissed it in the most efficient way I could think of. I caused some extra care to be taken of her in the prison, and counsel to be retained for her defence when she was tried at the Old Bailey; and her sentence was lenient, and her history and conduct proved that it was right. In doing the little I did for her, I remember to have had the kind help of some gentle-hearted functionary to whom I addressed myself—but what functionary I have long forgotten—who I suppose was officially present at the Inquest.

I regard this as a very notable uncommercial experience, because this good came of a Beadle. And, to the best of my knowledge, information, and belief, it is the only good that ever did come of a Beadle since the first Beadle put on his cocked hat.

All the Year Round, May 16th, 1863
The Uncommercial Traveller, Second Series, 1868

Shy Neighbourhoods

So much of my travelling is done on foot that if I cherished betting propensities I should probably be found registered in sporting newspapers under some such title as the Elastic Novice, challenging all eleven-stone mankind to competition in walking. My last special feat was turning out of bed at two, after a hard day, pedestrian and otherwise, and walking thirty miles into the country to breakfast. The road was so lonely in the night that I fell asleep to the monotonous sound of my own feet doing their regular four miles an hour. Mile after mile I walked without the slightest sense of exertion, dozing heavily and dreaming constantly. It was only when I made a stumble like a drunken man, or struck out into the road to avoid a horseman close upon me on the path—who had no existence—that I came to myself and looked about. The day broke mistily (it was autumn-time), and I could not disembarrass myself of the idea that I had to climb those heights and banks of clouds, and that there was an Alpine Convent somewhere behind the sun, where I was going to breakfast. This sleepy notion was so much stronger than such substantial objects as villages and haystacks that, after the sun was up and bright, and when I was sufficiently awake to have a sense of pleasure in the prospect, I still occasionally caught myself looking about for wooden arms to point the right track up the mountain, and wondering there was no snow yet. It is a curiosity of broken sleep that I made immense quantities of verses on that pedestrian occasion (of course, I never make any when I am in my right senses), and that I spoke a certain language once pretty familiar to me, but which I have nearly forgotten from disuse, with fluency. Of both these phenomena I have such frequent experience in the state between sleeping and waking that I sometimes argue with myself that I know

I cannot be awake, for, if I were, I should not be half so ready. The readiness is not imaginary, because I often recall long strings of the verses, and many turns of the fluent speech, after I am broad awake.

My walking is of two kinds: one, straight on end to a definite goal at a round pace; one, objectless, loitering, and purely vagabond. In the latter state no gipsy on earth is a greater vagabond than myself; it is so natural to me, and strong with me, that I think I must be the descendant, at no great distance, of some irreclaimable tramp.

One of the pleasantest things I have lately met with, in a vagabond course of shy metropolitan neighbourhoods and small shops, is the fancy of a humble artist, as exemplified in two portraits representing Mr Thomas Sayers, of Great Britain, and Mr John Heenan, of the United States of America. These illustrious men are highly coloured in fighting trim, and a fighting attitude. To suggest the pastoral and meditative nature of their peaceful calling, Mr Heenan is represented on emerald sward, with primroses and other modest flowers springing up under the heels of his half-boots; while Mr Sayers is impelled to the administration of his favourite blow, the Auctioneer, by the silent eloquence of a village church. The humble homes of England, with their domestic virtues and honeysuckle porches, urge both heroes to go in and win; and the lark and other singing birds are observable in the upper air, ecstatically carolling their thanks to Heaven for a fight. On the whole, the associations entwined with the pugilistic art by this artist are much in the manner of Izaak Walton.

But, it is with the lower animals of backstreets and by-ways that my present purpose rests. For human notes we may return to such neighbourhoods when leisure and opportunity serve.

Nothing in shy neighbourhoods perplexes my mind more than the bad company birds keep. Foreign birds often get into good society, but British birds are inseparable from low associates. There is a whole street of them in St Giles's; and I always find them in poor and immoral neighbourhoods, convenient to the public house and the pawnbroker's. They seem to lead people into drinking, and even the man who makes their cages usually gets into a chronic state of black eye. Why is this? Also, they will do things for people in short-skirted velveteen coats with bone buttons, or in sleeved waistcoats and fur caps, which they cannot be persuaded by the respectable orders of society to undertake. In a dirty court in Spitalfields, once, I found a goldfinch drawing his own water, and drawing as much of it as if he were in a consuming fever. That goldfinch lived at a bird shop, and offered, in writing, to barter himself against old clothes, empty bottles, or even kitchen-stuff. Surely a low thing and a depraved taste in any finch! I bought that goldfinch for money. He was sent home, and hung upon a nail over against my table. He lived outside a counterfeit dwelling-house, supposed (as I argued) to be a dyer's; otherwise it would have been impossible to account for his perch sticking out of the garret window. From the time of his appearance in my room, either he left off being thirsty—which was not in the bond—or he could not make up his mind to hear his little bucket drop back into his well when he let it go: a shock which in the best of times had made him tremble. He drew no water but by stealth, and under the cloak of night. After an interval of futile and at length hopeless expectation, the merchant who had educated him was appealed to. The merchant was a bow-legged character, with a flat and cushiony nose, like the last new strawberry. He wore a fur cap, and shorts, and was of the velveteen race, velveteeny. He sent word that he would 'look round'. He looked round, appeared in the doorway of the room, and slightly cocked up his evil eye at the goldfinch. Instantly a raging thirst beset that bird; when it was appeased, he still drew several unnecessary buckets of water; and finally leaped about his perch and sharpened his bill, as if he had been to the nearest wine vaults and got drunk.

Donkeys, again. I know shy neighbourhoods where the donkey goes in at the street door, and appears to live upstairs, for I have examined the backyard from over the palings, and have been unable to make him out. Gentility, nobility, Royalty, would appeal to that donkey in vain to do what he does for the costermonger. Feed him with oats at the highest price, put an infant prince and princess in a pair of panniers on his back, adjust his delicate trappings to a nicety, take him to the softest slopes at Windsor, and try what pace you can get out of him. Then, starve him, harness him anyhow to a truck with a flat tray on it, and see him bowl from Whitechapel to Bayswater. There appears to be no particular private understanding between birds and donkeys in a state of nature; but, in the shy neighbourhood state, you shall see them always in the same hands, and always developing their very best energies for the very worst company. I have known a donkey—by sight; we were not on speaking terms—who lived over on the Surrey side of London Bridge, among the fastnesses of Jacob's Island and Dockhead. It was the habit of that animal, when his services were not in immediate requisition, to go out alone, idling. I have met him a mile from his place of residence, loitering about the streets; and the expression of his countenance at such times was most degraded. He was attached to the establishment of an elderly lady who sold periwinkles, and he used to stand on Saturday nights with a cartful of those delicacies outside a gin-shop, pricking up his ears when a customer came to the cart, and too evidently deriving satisfaction from the knowledge that they got bad measure. His mistress was sometimes overtaken by inebriety. The last time I ever saw him (about five years ago) he was in circumstances of difficulty, caused by this failing. Having been left alone with the cart of periwinkles, and forgotten, he went off idling. He prowled among his usual low haunts for some time, gratifying his depraved tastes, until, not taking the cart into his calculations, he endeavoured to turn up a narrow alley, and became greatly involved. He was taken into custody by the police, and the Green Yard of the district being near at hand, was backed into that place of durance. At that crisis I encountered him; the stubborn sense he evinced of being—not to compromise the expression—a blackguard, I never saw exceeded in the human subject. A flaring candle in a paper shade, stuck in among his periwinkles, showed him, with his ragged harness broken and his cart extensively shattered, twitching his mouth and shaking his hanging head, a picture of disgrace and obduracy. I have seen boys being taken to station-houses, who were as like him as his own brother.

The dogs of shy neighbourhoods I observe to avoid play, and

to be conscious of poverty. They avoid work too, if they can, of course; that is in the nature of all animals. I have the pleasure to know a dog in a back-street in the neighbourhood of Walworth, who has greatly distinguished himself in the minor drama, and who takes his portrait with him when he makes an engagement, for the illustration of the playbill. His portrait (which is not at all like him) represents him in the act of dragging to the earth a recreant Indian, who is supposed to have tomahawked, or essayed to tomahawk, a British officer. The design is pure poetry, for there is no such Indian in the piece, and no such incident. He is a dog of the Newfoundland breed, for whose honesty I would be bail to any amount; but whose intellectual qualities in association with dramatic fiction I cannot rate high. Indeed, he is too honest for the profession he has entered. Being at a town in Yorkshire last summer, and seeing him posted in the bill of the night, I attended the performance. His first scene was eminently success-ful; but, as it occupied a second in its representation (and five lines in the bill), it scarcely afforded ground for a cool and de-liberate judgment of his powers. He had merely to bark, run on, and jump through an inn window after a comic fugitive. The next scene of importance to the fable was a little marred in its interest by his overanxiety; forasmuch as while his master (a belated soldier in a den of robbers on a tempestuous night) was feelingly lamenting the absence of his faithful dog, and laying great stress on the fact that he was thirty leagues away, the faithful dog was barking furiously in the prompter's box, and clearly choking him-self against his collar. But it was in his greatest scene of all that his honesty got the better of him. He had to enter a dense and trackless forest, on the trail of the murderer, and there to fly at the murderer when he found him resting at the foot of a tree, with his victim bound ready for slaughter. It was a hot night, and he came into the forest from an altogether unexpected direction, in the sweetest temper, at a very deliberate trot, not in the least ex-cited; trotted to the footlights with his tongue out; and there sat down, panting, and amiably surveying the audience, with his tail beating on the boards like a Dutch clock. Meanwhile, the mur-derer, impatient to receive his doom, was audibly calling to him 'co-o-ome here!' while the victim, struggling with his bonds, assailed him with the most injurious expressions. It happened, through these means, that when he was in course of time persuaded to trot up and rend the murderer limb from limb, he made it (for dramatic purposes) a little too obvious that he worked out that awful retribution by licking butter off his blood-stained hands.

In a shy street, behind Long Acre, two honest dogs live, who perform in Punch's shows. I may venture to say that I am on terms of intimacy with both, and that I never saw either guilty of the falsehood of failing to look down at the man inside the show during the whole performance. The difficulty other dogs have in satisfying their minds about these dogs appears to be never overcome by time. The same dogs must encounter them over and over again, as they trudge along in their off-minutes behind the legs of the show and beside the drum; but all dogs seem to suspect their frills and jackets, and to sniff at them as if they thought those articles of personal adornment an eruption— a something in the nature of mange, perhaps. From this Covent Garden of mine I noticed a country dog, only the other day, who had come up to Covent Garden Market under a cart, and had broken his cord, an end of which he still trailed along with him. He loitered about the corners of the four streets commanded by my window; and bad London dogs came up, and told him lies that he didn't believe; and worse London dogs came up, and made proposals to him to go and steal in the market, which his principles rejected; and the ways of the town confused him, and he crept aside and lay down in a doorway. He had scarcely got a wink of sleep, when up comes Punch with Toby. He was darting to Toby for consolation and advice, when he saw the frill, and stopped, in the middle of the street, appalled. The show was pitched, Toby retired behind the drapery, the audience formed, the drum and pipes struck up. My country dog remained immovable, intently staring at these strange appearances, until Toby opened the drama by appearing on his ledge, and to him entered Punch, who put a tobacco-pipe into Toby's mouth. At this spectacle the country dog threw up his head, gave one terrible howl, and fled due west.

We talk of men keeping dogs, but we might often talk more expressively of dogs keeping men. I know a bulldog in a shy corner of Hammersmith who keeps a man. He keeps him up a yard, and makes him go to public houses and lay wagers on him, and obliges him to lean against posts and look at him, and forces him to neglect work for him, and keeps him under rigid coercion. I once knew a fancy terrier who kept a gentleman—a gentleman who had been brought up at Oxford, too. The dog kept the gentleman entirely for his glorification, and the gentleman never talked about anything but the terrier. This, however, was not in a shy neighbourhood, and is a digression consequently.

There are a great many dogs in shy neighbourhoods who keep boys. I have my eye on a mongrel in Somers Town who keeps three boys. He feigns that he can bring down sparrows, and unburrow rats (he can do neither), and he takes the boys out on sporting pretences into all sorts of suburban fields. He has likewise made them believe that he possesses some mysterious knowledge of the art of fishing, and they consider themselves incompletely equipped for the Hampstead ponds, with a pickle-jar and a wide-mouthed bottle, unless he is with them, and barking tremendously. There is a dog residing in the Borough of Southwark who keeps a blind man. He may be seen, most days, in Oxford Street, haling the blind man away on expeditions wholly uncontemplated by, and unintelligible to, the man: wholly of the dog's conception and execution. Contrariwise, when the man has projects, the dog will sit down in a crowded thoroughfare and meditate. I saw him yesterday wearing the money-tray like an easy collar, instead of offering it to the public, taking the man against his will, on the invitation of a disreputable cur, apparently to visit a dog at Harrow—he was so intent on that direction. The north wall of Burlington House Gardens, between the Arcade and the Albany, offers a shy spot for appointment among blind men at about two or three o'clock in the afternoon. They sit (very uncomfortably) on a sloping stone there, and compare notes. Their dogs may always be observed, at the same time, openly disparaging the men they keep to one another, and settling where they shall respectively take their men when they begin to move again.

At a small butcher's, in the shy neighbourhood (there is no reason
for suppressing the name; it is by Notting Hill, and gives upon the
district called the Potteries), I know a shaggy black and white dog
who keeps a drover. He is a dog of an easy disposition, and too
frequently allows this drover to get drunk. On these occasions, it
is the dog's custom to sit outside the public house, keeping his eye
on a few sheep, and thinking. I have seen him with six sheep,
plainly casting up in his mind how many he began with when he
left the market, and at what places he has left the rest. I have seen
him perplexed by not being able to account to himself for certain
particular sheep. A light has gradually broken on him, he has
remembered at what butcher's he left them, and in a burst of grave
satisfaction has caught a fly off his nose, and shown himself much
relieved. If I could at any time have doubted the fact that it was
he who kept the drover, and not the drover who kept him, it
would have been abundantly proved by his way of taking un-
divided charge of the six sheep, when the drover came out besmeared with red ochre and beer, and gave him wrong directions,
which he calmly disregarded. He has taken the sheep entirely into
his own hands, has merely remarked, with respectful firmness,
'That instruction would place them under an omnibus; you had
better confine your attention to yourself—you will want it all';
and has driven his charge away, with an intelligence of ears and
tail, and a knowledge of business, that has left his lout of a man
very, very far behind.

As the dogs of shy neighbourhoods usually betray a slinking
consciousness of being in poor circumstances—for the most part
manifested in an aspect of anxiety, an awkwardness in their play,
and a misgiving that somebody is going to harness them to something, to pick up a living—so the cats of shy neighbourhoods
exhibit a strong tendency to relapse into barbarism. Not only are
they made selfishly ferocious by ruminating on the surplus population around them, and on the densely crowded state of all the
avenues to cat's-meat; not only is there a moral and politico-
economical haggardness in them, traceable to these reflections;
but they evince a physical deterioration. Their linen is not clean,
and is wretchedly got up; their black turns rusty, like old mourning;

they wear very indifferent fur; and take to the shabbiest cotton velvet, instead of silk velvet. I am on terms of recognition with several small streets of cats about the Obelisk in St George's Fields, and also in the vicinity of Clerkenwell Green, and also in the back-settlements of Drury Lane. In appearance they are very like the women among whom they live. They seem to turn out of their unwholesome beds into the street without any preparation. They leave their young families to stagger about the gutters un-assisted, while they frowzily quarrel and swear and scratch and spit at street corners. In particular, I remark that when they are about to increase their families (an event of frequent occurrence), the resemblance is strongly expressed in a certain dusty dowdi-ness, down-at-heel self-neglect, and general giving up of things. I cannot honestly report that I have ever seen a feline matron of this class washing her face when in an interesting condition.

Not to prolong these notes of uncommercial travel among the lower animals of shy neighbourhoods by dwelling at length upon the exasperated moodiness of the tom-cats, and their resemblance in many respects to a man and a brother, I will come to a close with a word on the fowls of the same localities.

That anything born of an egg, and invested with wings, should have got to the pass that it hops contentedly down a ladder into a cellar, and calls *that* going home, is a circumstance so amazing as to leave one nothing more in this connection to wonder at. Other-wise I might wonder at the completeness with which these fowls have become separated from all the birds of the air—have taken to grovelling in bricks and mortar and mud—have forgotten all about live trees, and make roosting-places of shopboards, barrows, oyster tubs, bulk-heads, and door-scrapers. I wonder at nothing concerning them, and take them as they are. I accept as products of Nature and things of course a reduced Bantam family of my acquaintance in the Hackney Road, who are incessantly at the pawnbroker's. I cannot say that they enjoy themselves, for they are of a melancholy temperament; but what enjoy-ment they are capable of, they derive from crowding together in the pawnbroker's side-entry. Here they are always to be found in a feeble flutter, as if they were newly come down in the world, and were afraid of being identified. I know a low fellow, originally of a good family from Dorking, who takes his whole establishment of wives, in single file, in at the door of the Jug Department of a disorderly tavern near the Haymarket, manoeuvres them among the company's legs, emerges with them at the Bottle Entrance, and so passes his life; seldom, in the season, going to bed before two in the morning. Over Waterloo Bridge there is a shabby old speckled couple (they belong to the wooden French-bedstead, washing-stand, and towel-horse making trade), who are always trying to get in at the door of a chapel. Whether the old lady, under a delusion reminding one of Mrs Southcott, has an idea of entrusting an egg to that particular denomination, or merely understands that she has no business in the building, and is consequently frantic to enter it, I cannot determine; but she is constantly endeavouring to undermine the principal door; while her partner, who is infirm upon his legs, walks up and down, encouraging her, and defying the Universe. But, the family I have been best acquainted with, since the removal from this trying sphere of a Chinese circle at Brentford, reside in the densest part of Bethnal Green. Their abstraction from the objects among which they live, or rather, their conviction that those objects have all come into existence in express subservience to fowls, has so enchanted me that I have made them the subject of many journeys at divers hours. After careful observation of the two lords and the ten ladies of whom this family consists, I have come to the conclusion that their opinions are represented by the leading lord and leading lady: the latter, as I judge, an aged personage, afflicted with a paucity of feather and visibility of quill that gives her the appearance of a bundle of office pens. When a railway goods van that would crush an elephant comes round the corner, tearing over these fowls, they emerge unharmed from under the horses, perfectly satisfied that the whole rush was a passing property in the air, which may have left something to eat behind it. They look upon old shoes, wrecks of kettles and saucepans, and fragments of bonnets as a kind of meteoric discharge for fowls to peck at. Peg-tops and hoops they account, I think, as a sort of hail; shuttle-cocks, as rain, or dew. Gaslight comes quite as natural to them as

BUTCHER'S BOY.

any other light; and I have more than a suspicion that in the minds of the two lords, the early public house at the corner has superseded the sun. I have established it as a certain fact that they always begin to crow when the public-house shutters begin to be taken down, and that they salute the potboy, the instant he appears to perform that duty, as if he were Phœbus in person.

All the Year Round, May 26th, 1860
The Uncommercial Traveller, Second Series, 1868

Night Walks

Some years ago, a temporary inability to sleep, referable to a distressing impression, caused me to walk about the streets all night for a series of several nights. The disorder might have taken a long time to conquer, if it had been faintly experimented on in bed; but, it was soon defeated by the brisk treatment of getting up directly after lying down, and going out, and coming home tired at sunrise.

In the course of those nights I finished my education in a fair amateur experience of Houselessness. My principal object being to get through the night, the pursuit of it brought me into sympathetic relations with people who have no other object every night in the year.

The month was March, and the weather damp, cloudy, and cold. The sun not rising before half-past five, the night perspective looked sufficiently long at half-past twelve: which was about my time for confronting it.

The restlessness of a great city, and the way in which it tumbles and tosses before it can get to sleep, formed one of the first entertainments offered to the contemplation of us houseless people. It lasted about two hours. We lost a great deal of companionship when the late public houses turned their lamps out, and when the potmen thrust the last brawling drunkards into the street; but stray vehicles and stray people were left us after that. If we were very lucky, a policeman's rattle sprang, and a fray turned up; but, in general, surprisingly little of this diversion was provided. Except in the Haymarket, which is the worst-kept part of London, and about Kent Street in the Borough, and along a portion of the line of the Old Kent Road, the peace was seldom violently broken. But, it was always the case that London, as if in imitation of individual citizens belonging to it, had expiring fits and starts of restlessness. After all seemed quiet, if one cab rattled by, half a dozen would surely follow; and Houselessness even observed that intoxicated people appeared to be magnetically attracted towards each other; so that we knew, when we saw one drunken object staggering against the shutters of a shop, that another drunken object would stagger up before five minutes were out, to fraternize or fight with it. When we made a divergence from the regular species of drunkard, the thin-armed, puff-faced, leaden-lipped gin-drinker, and encountered a rarer specimen of a more decent appearance, fifty to one but that specimen was dressed in soiled mourning. As the street experience in the night, so the street experience in the day; the common folk who come unexpectedly into a little property, come unexpectedly into a deal of liquor.

At length these flickering sparks would die away, worn out— the last veritable sparks of waking life trailed from some late pie-man or hot-potato man—and London would sink to rest. And then the yearning of the houseless mind would be for any sign of company, any lighted place, any movement, anything suggestive of any one being up—nay, even so much as awake, for the house-less eye looked out for lights in windows.

Walking the streets under the pattering rain, Houselessness would walk and walk and walk, seeing nothing but the interminable tangle of streets, save at a corner, here and there, two policemen in conversation, or the sergeant or inspector looking after his men. Now and then in the night—but rarely—Houselessness would become aware of a furtive head peering out of a doorway a few yards before him, and, coming up with the head, would find a man standing bolt upright to keep within the doorway's shadow, and evidently intent upon no particular service to society. Under a kind of fascination, and in a ghostly silence suitable to the time, Houselessness and this gentleman would eye one another from head to foot, and so, without exchange of speech, part, mutually suspicious. Drip, drip, drip, from ledge and coping, splash from pipes and water-spouts, and by and by the houseless shadow would fall upon the stones that pave the way to Waterloo Bridge; it

being in the houseless mind to have a halfpennyworth of excuse
for saying 'Good night' to the tollkeeper, and catching a glimpse
of his fire. A good fire, and a good greatcoat and a good woollen
neck-shawl, were comfortable things to see in conjunction with
the tollkeeper; also his brisk wakefulness was excellent company
when he rattled the change of halfpence down upon that metal
table of his, like a man who defied the night, with all its sorrowful thoughts, and didn't care for the coming of dawn. There was
need of encouragement on the threshold of the bridge, for the
bridge was dreary. The chopped-up murdered man had not been
lowered with a rope over the parapet when those nights were; he
was alive, and slept then quietly enough most likely, and undis-
turbed by any dream of where he was to come. But the river had
an awful look, the buildings on the banks were muffled in black
shrouds, and the reflected lights seemed to originate deep in the
water, as if the spectres of suicides were holding them to show
where they went down. The wild moon and clouds were as restless
as an evil conscience in a tumbled bed, and the very shadow of the
immensity of London seemed to lie oppressively upon the river.

Between the bridge and the two great theatres there was but
the distance of a few hundred paces, so the theatres came next.
Grim and black within, at night, those great dry Wells, and lone-
some to imagine, with the rows of faces faded out, the lights extinguished, and the seats all empty. One would think that nothing
in them knew itself at such a time but Yorick's skull. In one of my
night walks, as the church steeples were shaking the March winds
and rain with the strokes of four, I passed the outer boundary of
one of these great deserts, and entered it. With a dim lantern in
my hand, I groped my well-known way to the stage, and looked
over the orchestra—which was like a great grave dug for a time
of pestilence—into the void beyond. A dismal cavern of an immense aspect, with the chandelier gone dead like everything else,
and nothing visible, through mist and fog and space, but tiers of
winding-sheets. The ground at my feet, where, when last there,
I had seen the peasantry of Naples dancing among the vines, reck-
less of the burning mountain which threatened to overwhelm
them, was now in possession of a strong serpent of engine-hose,

watchfully lying in wait for the serpent Fire, and ready to fly at it
if it showed its forked tongue. A ghost of a watchman, carrying a
faint corpse-candle, haunted the distant upper gallery and flitted
away. Retiring within the proscenium, and holding my light above
my head towards the rolled-up curtain—green no more, but black
as ebony—my sight lost itself in a gloomy vault, showing faint
indications in it of a shipwreck of canvas and cordage. Methought
I felt much as a diver might at the bottom of the sea.

In those small hours when there was no movement in the
streets, it afforded matter for reflection to take Newgate in the
way, and, touching its rough stone, to think of the prisoners in
their sleep, and then to glance in at the lodge over the spiked
wicket, and see the fire and light of the watching turnkeys on the
white wall. Not an inappropriate time, either, to linger by that
wicked little Debtors' Door—shutting tighter than any other
door one ever saw—which has been Death's Door to so many.
In the days of the uttering of forged one-pound notes by people
tempted up from the country, how many hundreds of wretched
creatures of both sexes—many quite innocent—swung out of a
pitiless and inconsistent world, with the tower of yonder Christian church of St Sepulchre monstrously before their eyes! Is there
any haunting of the Bank Parlour, by the remorseful souls of old
directors, in the nights of these later days, I wonder, or is it as
quiet as this degenerate Aceldama of an Old Bailey?

To walk on to the Bank, lamenting the good old times and be-
moaning the present evil period, would be an easy next step, so
I would take it, and would make my houseless circuit of the
Bank, and give a thought to the treasure within; likewise to the
guard of soldiers passing the night there, and nodding over the
fire. Next, I went to Billingsgate, in some hope of market-people,
but it proving as yet too early, crossed London Bridge, and got
down by the water-side on the Surrey shore, among the buildings
of the great brewery. There was plenty going on at the brewery;
and the reek, and the smell of grains, and the rattling of the plump
dray horses at their mangers, were capital company. Quite re-
freshed by having mingled with this good society, I made a new
start with a new heart, setting the old King's Bench Prison before

me for my next object, and resolving, when I should come to the wall, to think of poor Horace Kinch, and the Dry Rot in men.

A very curious disease the Dry Rot in men, and difficult to detect the beginning of. It had carried Horace Kinch inside the wall of the old King's Bench Prison, and it had carried him out with his feet foremost. He was a likely man to look at, in the prime of life, well to do, as clever as he needed to be, and popular among many friends. He was suitably married, and had healthy and pretty children. But, like some fair-looking houses or fair-looking ships, he took the Dry Rot. The first strong external revelation of the Dry Rot in men is a tendency to lurk and lounge; to be at street corners without intelligible reason; to be going anywhere when met; to be about many places rather than at any; to do nothing tangible, but to have an intention of performing a variety of intangible duties tomorrow, or the day after. When this manifestation of the disease is observed, the observer will usually connect it with a vague impression once formed or received, that the patient was living a little too hard. He will scarcely have had leisure to turn it over in his mind, and form the terrible suspicion 'Dry Rot', when he will notice a change for the worse in the patient's appearance: a certain slovenliness and deterioration which is not poverty, nor dirt, nor intoxication, nor ill-health, but simply Dry Rot. To this succeeds a smell as of strong waters in the morning; to that, a looseness respecting money; to that, a stronger smell as of strong waters at all times; to that, a looseness respecting everything; to that, a trembling of the limbs, somnolency, misery, and crumbling to pieces. As it is in wood, so it is in men. Dry Rot advances at a compound usury quite incalculable. A plank is found infected with it, and the whole structure is devoted. Thus it had been with the unhappy Horace Kinch, lately buried by a small subscription. Those who knew him had not nigh done saying, 'So well off, so comfortably established, with such hope before him—and yet, it is feared, with a slight touch of Dry Rot!' when lo! the man was all Dry Rot and dust.

From the dead wall associated on those houseless nights with this too common story, I chose next to wander by Bethlehem Hospital; partly because it lay on my road round to Westminster;

partly because I had a night fancy in my head which could be best pursued within sight of its walls and dome. And the fancy was this: Are not the sane and insane equal at night as the sane lie a-dreaming? Are not all of us outside this hospital, who dream, more or less in the condition of those inside it, every night of our lives? Are we not nightly persuaded, as they daily are, that we associate preposterously with kings and queens, emperors and empresses, and notabilities of all sorts? Do we not nightly jumble events and personages, and times and places, as these do daily? Are we not sometimes troubled by our own sleeping inconsistencies, and do we not vexedly try to account for them or excuse them, just as these do sometimes in respect of their waking delusions? Said an afflicted man to me, when I was last in a hospital like this, 'Sir, I can frequently fly'. I was half ashamed to reflect that so could I—by night. Said a woman to me on the same occasion, 'Queen Victoria frequently comes to dine with me, and Her Majesty and I dine off peaches and macaroni in our nightgowns, and His Royal Highness the Prince Consort does us the honour to make a third on horseback in a Field-Marshal's uniform.' Could I refrain from reddening with consciousness when I remembered the amazing royal parties I myself had given (at night), the unaccountable viands I had put on table, and my extraordinary manner of conducting myself on those distinguished occasions? I wonder that the great master who knew everything, when he called Sleep the death of each day's life, did not call Dreams the insanity of each day's sanity.

By this time I had left the hospital behind me, and was again setting towards the river; and in a short breathing-space I was on Westminster Bridge, regaling my houseless eyes with the external walls of the British Parliament—the perfection of a stupendous institution, I know, and the admiration of all surrounding nations and succeeding ages, I do not doubt, but perhaps a little the better, now and then, for being pricked up to its work. Turning off into Old Palace Yard, the Courts of Law kept me company for a quarter of an hour; hinting in low whispers what numbers of people they were keeping awake, and how intensely wretched and horrible they were rendering the small hours to unfortunate suitors. Westminster Abbey was fine gloomy society for another quarter of an hour; suggesting a wonderful procession of its dead among the dark arches and pillars, each century more amazed by the century following it than by all the centuries going before. And, indeed, in those houseless night walks—which even included cemeteries where watchmen went round among the graves at stated times, and moved the tell-tale handle of an index which recorded that they had touched it at such an hour—it was a solemn consideration what enormous hosts of dead belong to one old great city, and how, if they were raised while the living slept, there would not be the space of a pin's point in all the streets and ways for the living to come out into. Not only that, but the vast armies of dead would overflow the hills and valleys beyond the city, and would stretch away all round it, God knows how far.

When a church clock strikes on houseless ears in the dead of the night, it may be at first mistaken for company, and hailed as such. But, as the spreading circles of vibration, which you may perceive at such time with great clearness, go opening out, for ever and ever afterwards widening, perhaps (as the philosopher has suggested) in external space, the mistake is rectified, and the sense of loneliness is profounder. Once—it was after leaving the Abbey, and turning my face north—I came to the great steps of St Martin's Church as the clock was striking three. Suddenly, a thing that in a moment more I should have trodden upon without seeing, rose up at my feet with a cry of loneliness and houselessness, struck out of it by the bell, the like of which I never heard. We then stood face to face looking at one another, frightened by one another. The creature was like a beetle-browed hare-lipped youth of twenty, and it had a loose bundle of rags on, which it held together with one of its hands. It shivered from head to foot, and its teeth chattered, and as it stared at me—persecutor, devil, ghost, whatever it thought me—it made with its whining mouth as if it were snapping at me, like a worried dog. Intending to give this ugly object money, I put out my hand to stay it—for it recoiled as it whined and snapped—and laid my hand upon its shoulder. Instantly, it twisted out of its garment, like the young

WATCHMAN.

man in the New Testament, and left me standing alone with its rags in my hand.

Covent Garden Market, when it was market morning, was wonderful company. The great wagons of cabbages, with growers' men and boys lying asleep under them, and with sharp dogs from market-garden neighbourhoods looking after the whole, were as good as a party. But one of the worst night sights I know in London is to be found in the children who prowl about this place; who sleep in the baskets, fight for the offal, dart at any object they think they can lay their thieving hands on, dive under the carts and barrows, dodge the constables, and are perpetually making a blunt pattering on the pavement of the Piazza with the rain of their naked feet. A painful and unnatural result comes of the comparison one is forced to institute between the growth of corruption as displayed in the so much improved and cared-for fruits of the earth, and the growth of corruption as displayed in these all-uncared-for (except inasmuch as ever-hunted) savages.

There was early coffee to be got about Covent Garden Market, and that was more company—warm company, too, which was better. Toast of a very substantial quality was likewise procurable: though the tousled-headed man who made it, in an inner chamber within the coffee-room, hadn't got his coat on yet, and was so heavy with sleep that in every interval of toast and coffee he went off anew behind the partition into complicated crossroads of choke and snore, and lost his way directly. Into one of these establishments (among the earliest) near Bow Street there came one morning, as I sat over my houseless cup, pondering where to go next, a man in a high and long snuff-coloured coat, and shoes, and, to the best of my belief, nothing else but a hat, who took out of his hat a large cold meat-pudding; a meat-pudding so large that it was a very tight fit, and brought the lining of the hat out with it. This mysterious man was known by his pudding, for, on his entering, the man of sleep brought him a pint of hot tea, a small loaf, and a large knife and fork and plate. Left to himself in his box, he stood the pudding on the bare table, and, instead of cutting it, stabbed it, overhand, with the knife, like a mortal enemy; then took the knife out, wiped it on his sleeve, tore the pudding asunder with his fingers, and ate it all up. The remembrance of this man with the pudding remains with me as the remembrance of the most spectral person my houselessness encountered. Twice only was I in that establishment, and twice I saw him stalk in (as I should say, just out of bed, and presently going back to bed), take out his pudding, stab his pudding, wipe the dagger, and eat his pudding all up. He was a man whose figure promised cadaverousness, but who had an excessively red face, though shaped like a horse's. On the second occasion of my seeing him, he said huskily to the man of sleep, 'Am I red tonight?' 'You are,' he uncompromisingly answered. 'My mother,' said the spectre, 'was a red-faced woman that liked drink, and I looked at her hard when she laid in her coffin, and I took the complexion.' Somehow, the pudding seemed an unwholesome pudding after that, and I put myself in its way no more.

When there was no market, or when I wanted variety, a railway terminus, with the morning mails coming in, was remunerative company. But, like most of the company to be had in this world, it lasted only a very short time. The station lamps would burst out ablaze, the porters would emerge from places of concealment, the cabs and trucks would rattle to their places (the Post Office carts were already in theirs), and finally, the bell would strike up, and the train would come banging in. But there were few passengers and little luggage, and everything scuttled away with the greatest expedition. The locomotive post offices, with their great nets—as if they had been dragging the country for bodies—would fly open as to their doors, and would disgorge a smell of lamp, an exhausted clerk, a guard in a red coat, and their bags of letters; the engine would blow and heave and perspire, like an engine wiping its forehead, and saying what a run it had had; and within ten minutes the lamps were out, and I was houseless and alone again.

But now there were driven cattle on the highroad near, wanting (as cattle always do) to turn into the midst of stone walls, and squeeze themselves through six inches' width of iron railing, and getting their heads down (also as cattle always do) for

tossing-purchase at quite imaginary dogs, and giving themselves
and every devoted creature associated with them a most extraordinary amount of unnecessary trouble. Now, too, the conscious gas
began to grow pale with the knowledge that daylight was coming, and straggling workpeople were already in the streets, and,
as waking life had become extinguished with the last pieman's
sparks, so it began to be rekindled with the fires of the first street-
corner breakfast-sellers. And so by faster and faster degrees,
until the last degrees were very fast, the day came, and I was tired
and could sleep. And it is not, as I used to think, going home at
such times, the least wonderful thing in London, that, in the real
desert region of the night, the houseless wanderer is alone there.
I knew well enough where to find Vice and Misfortune of all
kinds, if I had chosen; but they were put out of sight, and my
houselessness had many miles upon miles of streets in which it
could, and did, have its own solitary way.

All the Year Round, July 21st, 1860
The Uncommercial Traveller, First Series, 1861